CURRICULUM
COMPACTING

*The Complete Guide to Modifying the Regular Curriculum
for High Ability Students*

**Sally M. Reis
Deborah E. Burns
Joseph S. Renzulli**

Creative Learning Press, Inc.
P.O. Box 320, Mansfield Center, Connecticut 06250

STREAM OF CONSCIOUSNESS
LIGHTBULB POLITICS

"Gains in (technology) are never registered automatically in society; they require equally adroit inventions and adaptations in politics… Lacking a cooperative social intelligence and good-will, our most refined technics promises no more for society's improvement than an electric bulb would promise to a monkey in the midst of a jungle."

—Lewis Mumford
Technics and Civilization
(1934)

"Education is the acquisition of the art of the utilization of knowledge. This is an art very difficult to impart. Whenever a textbook is written of real educational worth, you may be quite certain that some reviewer will say that it will be difficult to teach from it. Of course it will be difficult to teach from it. If it were easy, the book ought to be burned; for it cannot be educational. In education, as elsewhere, the broad primrose path leads to a nasty place."

—Alfred North Whitehead
Aims of Education and Other Essays
(1929)

CONTENTS

CURRICULUM
COMPACTING

INTRODUCTION ■ COMPACTED VERSION

All chapters in this book begin with a "Compacted Version" in a shaded box as you see here. In it, the material from each chapter is compacted or condensed to give you a simple overview of its contents. You may choose to read just the Compacted Version throughout and turn to additional information and expanded explanations within the chapters only as needed or read the Compacted Version to review the chapter.

"All students, including those who are exceptional, are entitled to a public-supported education in which instruction is geared to their needs, interests and developmental levels."

School districts nationwide indicate in policy statements such as the one above a commitment to serve students' individual needs. Yet many districts lack the capacity to put such policy into practice. The sad result is that our brightest students are often left repeating lessons they already know, which can lead to frustration, boredom and, ultimately, underachievement.

Many educators would like to help by adapting the regular curriculum for students with above-average ability. But accomplishing this is no small task. Too little time, too many curricular objectives and poor organizational structures can all take their toll on even the most dedicated professionals.

This book is designed to help teachers overcome those obstacles. It explains how to streamline or "compact" curriculum through a practical, step-by-step approach. Teachers will learn the skills required to modify curriculum and the techniques for pretesting students and preparing enrichment options. Practical issues such as recordkeeping and administrative support are also included. Both efficient and complete, these guidelines will save valuable classroom time for both teachers and students.

Curriculum compacting, as presented in this book, has been field tested since 1975. It can be used with individuals and groups of students with above-average ability in any academic, artistic or vocational area. Most important, it has proven beneficial. Current research demonstrates that compacting the curriculum can dramatically reduce redundancy and challenge students to new heights of excellence.

INTRODUCTION

"All students, including those who are exceptional, are entitled to a public-supported education in which instruction is geared to their needs, interests and developmental levels."

A statement similar to the one printed above is likely contained in the first four or five pages of your school district's policy manual. This provision for meeting the individual needs of all students is commonly cited in the policy statements of school districts throughout the United States. What is less common is a school district's ability to *implement* such a policy statement. Many of our brightest youngsters are frequently forced to participate in practice exercises or instructional groups that deal with skills or content that they have previously mastered. These same students also suggest that school is "too easy" and that they spend far too much time during the school day doing assignments that they already know how to do.

The parents of these youngsters may also be less than satisfied with the way schools are meeting the needs of their children. Many bright students are bored and disinterested in school, and their parents frequently wonder when or if their children's academic needs will be met by their local school district. Unfortunately, even with the creation of a gifted program or the implementation of enrichment options, these students still may not have a challenging program available to them in their regular classroom.

Many educators would like to develop curriculum that is adapted to the learning needs, rates and interests of their students of abov- average ability. Yet, these same educators frequently find that there are many obstacles that make it difficult to accomplish such a goal. Too little planning time, a need for a better organizational structure, and unclear curricular objectives often make the task even more challenging. This book has been developed in order to provide the interested teacher with the knowledge and techniques that might be used to overcome such obstacles. The book's major purpose is to help teachers learn how to modify or "streamline" the grade-level curriculum in order to eliminate repetition of previously mastered material. In doing so, these same teachers will be able to better challenge their above-average-ability learners and provide them with time for appropriate enrichment or acceleration activities while ensuring mastery of the basic skills curriculum.

Frequent examples are located throughout the text providing the reader with an opportunity to examine the skills that will be needed in the classroom when making such curricular modifications for their high ability students. A rationale for curricular modification is also included, as well as detailed instructions for systematically planning for student pretesting, instruction, enrichment and acceleration options. Practical issues such as record keeping, commercial materials, and administrative support are also covered.

It is our intent that this book be used as an "inservice experience" for concerned teachers who are tired of the frustration that comes from assigning work that is too easy for some of the bright students in their classes. We have tried to make our suggestions for curricular change systematic, realistic and practical. These suggestions are presented in a step-by-step fashion and should provide sufficient training to implement such curricular change without the need for additional workshops or training sessions. It is our hope that this sequential and easy-to-follow approach will save time for *both* the teacher and the student.

Our work in the area of curriculum modification is a part of a system that has been field tested for the last fifteen years in various school districts throughout the country and has proven to be effective in reducing boredom for bright students as well as providing more challenging alternatives to the regular curriculum (Renzulli, 1977; Renzulli, Reis & Smith, 1981; Renzulli & Reis, 1985). Curriculum compacting involves a few relatively easy steps: determining the goals and objectives of the regular curriculum, assessing whether or not students have previous mastery of those goals, and substituting more challenging and appropriate work for students. Curriculum compacting can be done with individual students or with groups of students who demonstrate above-average ability in any academic, artistic, or vocational area. In addition, it can benefit any students who demonstrate strength or expertise in a specific content area.

In this book, Chapter 1 provides a history of and rationale for curriculum compacting. Chapter 2 includes a thorough explanation of curriculum compacting including steps for completing the process. Chapter 3 gives practical help for keeping records of the compacting process including examples of completed Compactors (a record-keeping form). It also includes numerous examples of alternatives for enrichment and acceleration. Chapter 4 addresses the challenges that are frequently encountered in implementing compacting and answers the most frequently asked questions.

CHAPTER 1 ■ COMPACTED VERSION

A Definition Of Curriculum Compacting

Curriculum compacting is a procedure used to streamline the regular curriculum for students who are capable of mastering it at a faster pace.

The compacting process has three basic phases:

• Determine the goals and objectives of the regular curriculum
• Assess students for previous mastery of these objectives
• Substitute more appropriate (challenging) options

These components can be broken down into eight steps:

1. Identify the objectives
2. Find appropriate pretests
3. Identify students who should be pretested
4. Pretest students
5. Eliminate instructional time for students who show mastery of the objectives
6. Streamline instruction of those objectives students have not mastered but are capable of mastering more quickly than their classmates
7. Offer challenging alternatives for time provided by compacting
8. Keep records

Although enrichment and acceleration may be part of the process, compacting encompasses much more. It is, in fact, more closely associated with diagnosis and prescription: a method used in remedial education to point out learning objectives students have not yet mastered. Instruction is intended to help them "catch up" with the rest of the class. With compacting, pretesting identifies learning objectives already mastered, and students are allowed to "test out" of certain academic exercises and move on to new material.

Brief History of Compacting in American Schools

While the term *compacting* is relatively new, a similar technique was introduced in the 1860s. High school students in St. Louis, Missouri were permitted to "compress" their academic requirements through accelerated courses and thus graduate a semester ahead of their peers.

Compression, enrichment, acceleration and *ability grouping* are referenced repeatedly in the early literature on gifted education. Acceleration is often used interchangeably with compression and includes grade skipping, early entrance into college, high school or elementary school, the opportunity to complete two semesters of work in one; and the option of taking part in independent study or small group training. Acceleration may begin with or result from the compacting process.

Rationale for Curriculum Compacting

In initiating the compacting process, teachers may need the following rationale:

1. Students already know much of their text's content before "learning it."

In recent studies, 78–88% of fifth- and sixth-grade average and above-average readers could pass pretests on basal comprehension skills before these were covered in the basal. The average readers were performing at approximately 92% accuracy, and the better readers at 93% on the pretests of comprehension skills.

Field tests indicate that most elementary teachers can eliminate as much as 40–50% of the basal regular curriculum for approximately 10–15% of all students. In basal language arts and mathematics programs, extremely bright youngsters can often have 70-80% of the curriculum eliminated. Field tests of compacting at the middle school level show that grouping students by their prior knowledge *of* and interest *in* the subject can eliminate approximately 50% of the regular curriculum.

2. Textbooks have been "dumbed down."

One reason so many students can show mastery of the regular curriculum is that contemporary textbooks have dropped two grade levels in difficulty over the past ten to fifteen years. Former Secretary of Education Terrel Bell has labeled this practice the "dumbing down" of textbooks.

The prevailing belief is that students will be able to read and understand only if they are given textbooks written at their grade level, and publishers respond to this concern with readability formulas. A pattern of underachievement may result that frequently causes many bright students to falter when they reach secondary school or college, simply because for the first time they are enrolled in classes with many students who are just as bright as they are, and their instructors expect much more from them. They find themselves lacking the study habits and perseverance that are essential to academic success.

3. The quality of textbooks has failed to improve.

The recommendations of the National Commission on Excellence in Education in *A Nation at Risk*—that textbooks become more rigorous and demanding—seem not to have been followed. Readability levels did not change in any appreciable way between the 1979 and 1989 versions; where changes were made, they were toward greater ease, not greater difficulty.

Although some well-designed, challenging textbooks are available, educators may have inadvertently contributed to the decline of textbook content by attempting to align the curriculum with standardized tests in order to produce higher scores on the tests.

4. The needs of high-ability students often are not met in classrooms.

To meet the learning needs of high-ability students, we must provide an appropriate content curriculum and opportunities for students to explore interests and develop self-directed learning habits. Two recent studies conducted by The National Research Center on the Gifted and Talented indicate that many elementary classroom teachers are not providing major modifications in their classrooms to meet the needs of high-ability students. The major finding of this study is that classroom teachers make only minor modifications in the regular curriculum.

Many students respond negatively to what they perceive to be a boring and repetitive environment. Students may become behavior problems or drop-outs because our schools have failed to provide them with a challenging curriculum. At the very least, the lack of curriculum compacting can promote "game playing" by bright students who have come to believe that the best way to succeed in school is to do exactly what the teacher asks: nothing less, and nothing more, simply marking time in the classroom. In order to promote the love of learning and the independent study habits that we want to foster, a drastic change in the academic preparation of higher ability students is required.

5. Compacting provides time for more challenging learning experiences.

One of the greatest benefits of curriculum compacting is the time saved. Students whose curriculum is compacted may participate in the gifted program, pursue independent studies, read self-selected materials, or one of many other options.

6. The pace of instruction and practice time can be modified.

Because repetition is built into all curricular approaches to reinforce learning, many gifted students spend much of their time in school practicing skills and reading content they already know. In an attempt to provide equal educational opportunities to all students, officials have, in some cases, mandated an end to any form of grouping or acceleration for fear of damaging the achievement or self-esteem of the students in the lower ability groups. This approach contradicts the available research on grouping and impedes the achievement potential of above-average students. The only way to change this situation is to develop a program that uses an appropriate curriculum in the resource room *and* in the regular classroom.

7. Compacting guarantees educational accountability.

In this age of educational accountability, the use of compacting procedures can guarantee that students who are allowed to skip assignments or to be excused from participation in lessons are doing so because the teacher can document the professional appropriateness of this decision.

1 HISTORY AND RATIONALE OF CURRICULUM COMPACTING

Many of us remember Mark Twain's stinging commentary on his time in school, "My education was only interrupted by the twelve years I spent in school." On a more contemporary note, Woody Allen provides a similar epilogue to his years of public education. "My teachers loathed me. I never did homework. I'm amazed they expected me to work on those sleazy projects. To this day I wake up in the morning, clutch on to the bed and thank God I don't have to go to school."

Why do so many adults remember their school experiences in this way? Perhaps some of it has to do with the boredom faced by many bright youngsters in many traditional classrooms. It would be flattering to our current educational system if we could say that the situation has improved or even changed; however, that is simply not the case. The thousands of letters and phone calls we receive from parents of above-average students every year clearly indicate that school remains unchallenging for many of our most able students. Curriculum compacting addresses this problem.

THE DEFINITION AND HISTORY OF COMPACTING

The term *curriculum compacting* refers to a process in which a teacher preassesses above-average-ability students' skills or knowledge about content prior to instruction and uses this information to modify curriculum. As we have defined it, compacting is an eight-part process in which a teacher will do the following:

1. Identify the relevant learning objectives in a subject area or grade level.

2. Find or develop a means of pretesting students on one or more of these objectives prior to instruction.

3. Identify students who may benefit from curriculum compacting and should be pretested.

4. Pretest students to determine mastery levels of the chosen objectives.

5. Eliminate practice, drill or instructional time for students who have demonstrated prior mastery of these objectives.

6. Streamline instruction of those objectives students have not yet mastered but are capable of mastering more quickly than their classmates.

7. Offer enrichment or acceleration options for students whose curriculum has been compacted.

8. Keep records of this process and the instructional options available to "compacted" students.

Compacting is not synonymous with enrichment, nor is it synonymous with acceleration. Either of these two academic options may be available to students who receive curriculum compacting, but the decision to enrich or to accelerate is one that is made jointly with the student, the teacher, and in some cases, the parents. Compacting *is* closely associated with *diagnosis and prescription*, an educational technique that has been used for students in remedial education for several decades; however, some subtle differences exist between them. When a teacher is using diagnosis and prescription in remedial education, the intent is to identify those learning objectives that the student has not yet mastered but were taught at an earlier grade level. The intent of the remedial instruction is to help the student "catch up" with the rest of the class by providing remedial instruction as needed. Curriculum compacting involves pretesting, or diagnosis, but when it is used with the above-average population, the intent is to identify those grade-level learning objectives that have been previously mastered so that students do not have to repeat those exercises, lectures or small-group training experiences. This provides time for accelerated instruction of content or interest-based enrichment. While the prescription of remedial education usually involves a basic set of skills or concepts appropriate for all students, compacting prescribes expanded learning experiences beyond the confines of the grade-level curriculum.

A BRIEF HISTORY OF COMPACTING IN AMERICAN SCHOOLS

Although the term *compacting* may be relatively new to some educators, the purpose for it is not. As early as the 1860s, St. Louis, Missouri schools were offering above-average-ability students the opportunity to "compress" their academic requirements by participating in an accelerated track of courses that would allow them to graduate at least one semester earlier than their peers. The terms *enrichment, acceleration, ability grouping* and *compression* have been found repeatedly in the early literature on gifted education. These terms were used to describe a variety of options that allowed bright students to participate in advanced level learning options or to progress through the academic curriculum at an appropriate pace. Many researchers who have conducted reviews of the literature have found that early educators and practitioners defined the term *acceleration* or *compression* in a variety of ways. In some cases, acceleration was used interchangeably with compression and included grade skipping and early entrance into college, high school, or elementary school (Clark, 1985; Rogers, 1989; Tannenbaum, 1983).

Rogers (1989) also notes that *compression* allowed students to work in out-of-level texts while enrolling in a grade level that was closely correlated with their chronological age. Historically, bright students have also had the option of participating in independent study, small-group training, programmed instruction, cross-grade groups for math or reading instruction or credit by examination. These provisions were made in order to better provide them with a course of study that was suited to the rapid pace with which many were capable of learning new skills or new concepts. Dual enrollment in high school and local college courses, honors courses, tracking in the secondary schools, or compressing four years of high school into three years with flexible schedules and calendars, have all been cited as examples of compression or acceleration.

As has been mentioned, confusion exists concerning the meanings of the terms *compacting, compression* or *acceleration*. As Kulik and Kulik (1984) have stated, acceleration or compression was often "what educational evaluators and reviewers said it was." What, then, is the relationship between these curricular options for compression or acceleration, and "curriculum compacting"? For the purposes of this text, we have defined curriculum compacting as the process of identifying learning objectives, pretesting students for prior mastery of these objectives, and eliminating needless teaching or practice if mastery can be documented. The time saved through this process may be used to provide either acceleration or enrichment for students. Viewed this way, acceleration, compression, or the use of ability groups may begin with, or result from, the use of the compacting process with above-average-ability learners. Acceleration can be defined several ways, including grade skipping (either one or several years), early admission to elementary school or to college, and content acceleration (for example, having a second grader do fifth-grade math in his/her classroom).

Curriculum compacting is the process of identifying learning objectives, pretesting students for prior mastery of these objectives, and eliminating needless teaching or practice if mastery can be documented. The time saved through this process may be used to provide either acceleration or enrichment for students.

Regardless how acceleration is defined, it is interesting to note that educators, parents and community members have had widely differing opinions about the effects of acceleration and ability grouping on students and their peers. In 1983, the Commission on Excellence in Education recommended that placement and grouping of gifted students be guided by their academic progress and instructional needs, rather than by a rigid adherence to their chronological age. Supporters of gifted education have suggested that acceleration options help students develop better study habits by providing them with a more challenging curriculum. These same students are able to finish school faster because they were provided with acceleration (defined in this case as grade skipping) and therefore will have more productive adult careers and less expense attached to their schooling. Proponents also suggest that students are less likely to be bored or frustrated with the curriculum and should maintain more positive attitudes towards school and learning in general as a result.

Critics of acceleration worry that identifying students who could benefit from acceleration might be difficult. They also question the assumption that an academically able student can, or should be automatically accelerated in all content areas. Fears concerning student self-esteem, socialization, peer relations, elitism and inferiority are also prevalent. In order to answer these questions and to sort out prejudice from fact, several research studies have been conducted during the last sixty years. These studies vary in quality, but most claim to have examined one or more of the acceleration or compression options described above in order to measure the effects on student achievement, aptitude, self-concept or socialization. Most of the reviewers who have analyzed the better-designed studies have concluded that acceleration and ability grouping have had a generally positive effect on gifted students. In fact, in a 1958 review, Goldberg stated that it was difficult to find a single research study showing acceleration to be harmful to students. A subsequent review by Gowan and Demos (1964) revealed similar findings for students who participated in accelerated options. Kulik and Kulik (1982) found that honors classes for gifted students were also effective in raising student achievement. Subsequent meta-analyses of research studies involving accelerated instruction (Kulik & Kulik, 1984; Rogers, 1990) suggested positive gains for gifted students. Yet these researchers also found that it is *how* ability grouping or acceleration was approached that often accounted for the difference between the gains made by the gifted students in the experimental groups. In other words, merely reducing class size or changing an organizational pattern is insufficient: teaching style, pacing and the instructional materials themselves must also be revised. The most recent analyses of grouping patterns for gifted students have been completed by Rogers (1991) and Kulik (1992) and are available from the National Research Center on the Gifted and Talented at The University of Connecticut. As a sample, Kulik's recommendations are included in Appendix C. Recommendations of an additional study of the impact of the use of cooperative learning (Robinson, 1992) is also included in Appendix C.

A more thorough understanding of the optimal conditions for success with ability grouping, acceleration or compression is vital if we are to better serve the needs of our high-ability youngsters. Kulik and Kulik (1984) have suggested that homogeneously grouped, accelerated, gifted students appear to make greater achievement gains than students who receive acceleration through independent study, programmed instruction or small group training in a heterogeneous classroom.

The notion of homogeneously grouping students according to academic ability is not a popular option for schools at the present time. A report issued by the Carnegie Council (1989), which called tracking a destructive practice has had a major impact on grouping practices across the country. At a National Governors' Conference, the governors in our nation called for the end of ability grouping and tracking by insisting that ability grouping causes low expectations that may become self-fulfilling prophecies. A great deal of discussion about the benefits of heterogeneous grouping for lower ability students has prompted many administrators to disregard the research concerning acceleration and homogeneous grouping for gifted students, and instead, disband honors classes and discourage grouping in their elementary and secondary schools. Despite research to the contrary "no paradox is more striking than the inconsistency between research findings on acceleration and the failure of our society to reduce the time spent by superior students in formal education" (Gold, 1965, p.238).

FOR MORE INFORMATION...

...on the subjects of tracking, acceleration, ability grouping or compacting, check your local college library for the following articles. See Appendices A and C also.

- ✓ Feldhusen, J.F. & Moon, S.M. (1992). Grouping gifted students: Issues and concerns. *Gifted Child Quarterly, 36* (2), 63–67.

- ✓ Kulik, J. A. & Kulik, C. C. (1992). Meta-Analytic Findings on grouping programs. *Gifted Child Quarterly, 36* (2), 73–77.

- ✓ Feldhusen, J. F. (March/April, 1989). Why the public schools will continue to neglect the gifted. *GCT*, 55-59.

- ✓ Feldhusen, J. F. (March, 1989). Synthesis of research on gifted youth. *Educational Leadership*, 6-11.

- ✓ Slavin, R. E. (1987). Ability grouping and student achievement in elementary schools: A best evidence synthesis. *Review of Educational Research*, 57(3), 293-336.

RATIONALE FOR CURRICULUM COMPACTING

Before initiating the compacting process, it is important to be able to explain and provide a rationale for our use of this instructional practice. Teachers who need supporting information about the rationale for compacting can use the following reasons to demonstrate why this procedure should be implemented in most classrooms:

1. Students already know most of their text's content before "learning it"
2. Textbooks have been "dumbed down"
3. The quality of textbooks has failed to improve
4. The needs of high-ability students are not often met in classrooms
5. Compacting frees time for more challenging learning experiences
6. The pace of instruction and practice time can be modified
7. Compacting guarantees educational accountability

REASON ONE: STUDENTS ALREADY KNOW MOST OF THEIR TEXT'S CONTENT BEFORE "LEARNING IT"

Many parents and educators believe a major problem facing gifted and talented students is the lack of challenge in the work they are assigned in regular classroom settings. One need only enter an American classroom to realize that the work assigned to gifted students is often too easy. Research also supports this claim (see excerpt below). In a more recent study dealing with average and above-average readers, Taylor and Frye (1988) found that seventy-eight to eighty-eight percent of fifth- and sixth-grade average readers could pass pretests on basal comprehension skills *before* they were covered by the basal reader (see excerpt on page 13).

Perhaps the repetition of content has been most reported in mathematics textbooks. Since the publication of *A Nation at Risk* (which promulgated the idea that the declining difficulty of textbooks may have had negative effects on students' learning) one visible theme of complaints about American education is that students fail to demonstrate adequate achievement in problem solving and higher order thinking. For example, the

Consumer Group Finds Students Knew Most Of Their Texts' Content Before They Spent a Year "Learning It"

SOURCE: *EDUCATIONAL R & D REPORT*, 3(4), 1980-81.

FOR THE LAST two years, EPIE Institute, a nonprofit educational consumer agency, has been testing fourth and tenth graders on the content of their textbooks before and after year-long use.

Sixty percent of the fourth graders in the wealthier communities were able to score over 80% on a test of the content of their math text *before* they had used it for the school year. Seven percent of "disadvantaged" fourth graders tested in poor communities scored 38% or less at the start of the year, and showed little or no gain after a year.

Similar findings were reported on tests of textbook content with students in fourth- and tenth-grade science and in tenth-grade social studies. The two-year study, conducted in schools on Long Island, NY, by James R. George, EPIE's Research Director, was funded by the National Institute of Education.

FOR MORE INFORMATION ON THIS AND OTHER EPIE PROGRAMS, WRITE:
P. KENNETH KOMOSKI
EPIE INSTITUTE
P.O. BOX 620
STONY BROOK, NY 11790

second International Association for the Evaluation of Educational Achievement (IEA) study on mathematics, which assessed mathematics achievement for eighth-grade students at the end of the 1981-82 school year, found that U.S. students were slightly above the international average in computational arithmetic but well below the international average in problem solving (McKnight, 1987). U.S. eighth-graders' achievement in geometry placed in the bottom 25% of participating countries in a sample of which nearly 20% were third-world nations. One possible explanation for these disappointing international comparisons may lie in what U.S. elementary school teachers emphasize in their instruction (Porter, 1989).

The content of mathematics textbooks is troubling. McGinty, Van Beynen and Zalewski (1986) found that we have actually regressed in the expectations of our students. Their study revealed that the number of word problems found in 1984 textbooks was only one-third the number found in textbooks from 1924, in which the number of drill problems increased by almost 57%. In two studies of Michigan teachers, 70% to 75% of mathematics instruction was spent teaching skills—essentially how to add, subtract, multiply and divide—and occasionally how to read a graph. The emphasis on skill development found among teachers was mirrored by the textbooks they used. In content analyses of fourth-grade textbooks, 65% to 80% of the exercises were on skill practice, while 10% to 24% were on conceptual understanding and 6% to 13% on problem solving (Porter, 1989).

Another distinctive feature of elementary school mathematics is the slowness with which content changes as students progress through the grades. Content overlaps across grades because topics begun at the end of one grade are continued into the beginning of the next grade. To some extent, topics are returned to again and again, each time seeking a greater depth of understanding (Porter, 1989). Flanders (1987) investigated three separate mathematics textbook series to examine just how much new content is presented each year. His primary finding was that a relatively steady decrease occurs in the amount of new content over the years up through eighth grade, where less than

Pretesting: Minimize Time Spent on Skill Work for Intermediate Readers

BY BARBARA M. TAYLOR AND
BARBARA J. FRYE

PRETESTING CAN HELP teachers eliminate unnecessary basal skill instruction and use the time for other activities.

In both studies, seventy-eight to eighty-eight percent of fifth- and sixth-grade average and above-average readers could pass pretests on basal comprehension skills before these were covered in the basal. The average readers were performing at approximately ninety-two percent accuracy, and the better readers at ninety-three percent on the pretests of comprehension skills.

These students did not complete skill sheets or workbook pages on those skills. Instead, they did independent reading when the other students in their reading group, who had not passed skills pretests, were receiving instruction and completing skills sheets and workbook pages.

In the follow-up to Study I, only twenty-seven percent of the fifth- and sixth grade teachers in the district were using skills pretests after being encouraged to do so. Only one out of thirty-one teachers in grades four, five, and six in the two schools in which Study II occurred was using skills pretests even though use had been encouraged by the district's elementary supervisor.

THE READING TEACHER
NOVEMBER, 1988

one-third of the material taught is new to students. Overall, students in grades two to five encounter approximately 40% to 65% new content, an equivalent of new material just two or three days per week. By eighth grade, this amount has dropped to 30%, just one and one-half days per week. Flanders found that most of the new content in any text is found in the second half of the book. In grades seven to eight, where the total new content is lowest, new material occurs in less than 28% of the first half of the books. Flanders' study shows that the mathematical content of some textbooks is mostly review of previous topics. Flanders states, "The result is that earlier in the year, when students are likely to be more eager to study, they repeat what they have seen before. Later on, whey they are sufficiently bored, they see new material—if they get to the end of the book (p.22)." He elaborates, "There should be little wonder why good students get bored: they do the same thing year after year. Average or slower-than-average students get the same message, and who could blame them for becoming complacent about their mathematics studies? They know that if they don't learn it now, it will be retaught next year (p.23)."

Usiskin (1987) indicates that not only have textbooks decreased in difficulty, but also they incorporate a large percentage of repetition to facilitate learning. Usiskin argues that even average eighth-grade students should study algebra since only 25% of the pages in typical seventh- and eighth-grade mathematics texts contain new content. Usiskin points out that the current practice of spending a great deal of time reviewing work of earlier grades in the same context as the earlier grades is counterproductive. He states, "For the student who does not know the material, the review is simply repeating what they are bad at. We find out what some students do not know and give them little else. It is not the spiral approach winding its way up to the helix of understanding; it is the circular approach going round and round and back to the same place (p.432)."

REASON TWO: TEXTBOOKS HAVE BEEN "DUMBED DOWN"

Another reason that so many average and above-average students can demonstrate mastery of the regular curriculum is that contemporary textbooks are so much easier than they were only two or three decades ago. The term *dumbed down* was coined by Terrel Bell to describe this phenomenon of decreasing difficulty in texts. (See excerpt below). Related research has concluded that textbooks have dropped two grade levels in difficulty over the past ten to fifteen years. (See excerpt on page 15).

Do Adoption Committees Perpetuate Mediocre Textbooks?

BY ROGER FARR AND MICHAEL TULLY

ONE OF THE MOST outspoken critics of textbooks is former Secretary of Education Terrel Bell. In a speech before the American Association of School Administrators in February, 1984, Bell criticized the publishing industry, textbook content, and the policies and procedures of textbook adoption committees. Bell used *A Nation At Risk* as the basis for his attacks, saying that schools were not spending enough for textbooks, that a disproportionate concern with readability levels had brought about a "dumbing down" of textbooks, and that current methods of selection should be replaced by cooperative efforts that would give educators greater influence in shaping textbook content.

PHI DELTA KAPPAN
MARCH, 1985

Chall and Conrad (1991) also cite that above-average students are not satisfied with easy textbooks.

> Another group not adequately served was those who read about two grades or more above the norm. Their reading textbooks, especially, provided little or no challenge since they were matched to students' grade placement, not their reading levels. Many students were aware of this and said in their interviews that they preferred harder books because they learned harder words and ideas from them. Since harder reading textbooks are readily available, one may ask why they were not used with the more able readers, as were the easier reading textbooks for the less able readers. This practice of using grade-level reading textbooks for those who read two or more grades above the norms has changed little through the years, although it has been repeatedly questioned (See Chall, 1967, 1983). It would appear that, for various administrative reasons, teachers do not use a reading textbook above the student's grade placement. The reason most often mentioned is really a question: If the third-grade teacher uses fourth grade books, what is the fourth-grade teacher going to do? (p.111).

Further, Chall and Conard stress the importance of the match between a learner's abilities and the difficulty of the instructional task, stating that the optimal match should be slightly above the learner's current level of functioning. When the match is optimal, learning is enhanced. However, "if the match is not optimal [i.e. the match is below or above the child's level of understanding/knowledge], learning is less efficient and development may be halted" (p.19). It is clear that the current trend of selecting textbooks that the majority of students can read is a problem for high-ability students.

Researchers trace the beginning of the dumbing down of textbooks to the late 1920's, when the vocabulary load of reading textbooks decreased with each subsequent edition. Comparative studies document the introduction of fewer and fewer new words and more repetition of them (Chall, 1967). Within a period of ten years, the average number of different words in second-grade readers decreased from 1,147 to 913 (Hockett, 1938). During this same period new words introduced in first-grade readers decreased from 644 to 462 and within the following ten years to 338. This simplification of vocabulary in reading textbooks continued through the 1950's and into the 1960's, during which new words in first-grade readers were repeated on an average of six to ten times immediately following their introduction (Willows, Borwick and Hayvren, 1981). Reading textbooks for the upper elementary textbooks also became much easier. The vocabulary in sixth-grade basals decreased consistently from 1947 to 1967, and Gates (1961) described the vocabularies of fourth-grade basals published in the early 1960's as limited enough to be appropriate for average third-grade students.

"How to Improve Schools Without Spending More Money"

BY MICHAEL W. KIRST

MEANWHILE, with regard to content and materials, a sample of U.S. publishers agreed that their textbooks had dropped two grade levels in difficulty over the last ten to fifteen years, according to *The Los Angeles Times*.

When Californians tried to reserve two slots on the statewide adoption list for textbooks that would challenge the top one-third of students, no publisher had a book to present. They could only suggest reissuing textbooks from the late sixties (now unacceptable because of their inaccurate portrayals of women and minorities) or writing new ones, a three- to five-year project.

PHI DELTA KAPPAN, SEPTEMBER, 1982

Changes in the difficulty of content in textbooks beginning in the late 1920's were similar to those found in reading books. Horn (1937) identified this downward trend in difficulty in social studies textbooks as early as the 1930's, and Chall, Conrad and Harris (1961) documented a continuation of this trend almost thirty years later. It was not until the 1960's when national concern that the American educational system might be lagging behind the Soviet Union gained momentum that educational views on textbook difficulty seemed to change (Elliott and Woodward, 1990). Publishers reacted, and by the middle 1960's, evidence of a reversal of the trend toward ease began to appear. Willows, Borwick and Hayvren (1981) noted a fivefold increase in the rate of vocabulary introduction in first-grade readers from 1962 to 1972, and increasing difficulty in sixth-grade readers from 1967 to 1975 was reported by Chall, Conrad and Harris (1981). Yet by the late 1970's, this trend of increasing challenge subsided, and concern for the overall quality of education had reached national proportions. Journalists as well as educators described textbooks as being "dumbed down," a slogan that caught the public's imagination and united various textbooks critics. Publishers were accused of lowering academic requirements by oversimplifying or watering down their textbooks (Chall and Conrad, 1991).

Chall's and Conrad's (1991) research indicates the subject-matter textbooks published in the United States represents a rather narrow range of difficulty for each grade level analyzed—more narrow than the range of reading ability found among students. Chall and Conrad indicate that this range is also narrower than the range found on standardized tests. "Although the publishers described their textbooks as being developed for "wide use" or for "more able" or "less able" readers, our analysis found them suitable mainly for the middle range of achievement within each grade. Practically none of the content textbooks seemed to be written for the students in the lowest quartile in reading. Further, the books that publishers labeled for less able readers were often more difficult than those labeled for a wide audience or for more able readers (p.111)."

The lack of challenge in textbooks has been cited by every major content group in our country. In a national report to our nation on the future of mathematics, Lynn Arthur Steen, a professor of mathematics at St. Olaf College, aptly summarizes the problems associated with the lack of challenge in mathematics: "In practice, although not in law, we have a national curriculum in mathematics education. It is an 'underachieving' curriculum that follows a spiral of almost constant radius, reviewing each year so much of the past that little new learning takes place" (1989, p.45).

The dumbing down of the curriculum in elementary mathematics has been eloquently summarized by parents in numerous letters that we have received. Consider the editorial by Kie Ho that recently appeared in *Education Week* (See article on page 17). In it, excellent examples are provided of the need to deal with the problems caused by selecting textbooks that do not challenge the above-average students in our classrooms.

Another example of the dumbing down of the regular curriculum provided by Gilbert Sewall (1988) may make the problems facing bright students even more apparent. The first example below contains a 1950 fifth-grade history textbook excerpt about the battle of John Paul Jones:

> After a time Captain Jones had command of another ship, the "Bonhomme Richard." It was an old vessel and not very strong. But in it the brave captain began a battle with one of England's fine ships. The cannons on the two ships kept up a steady roar. The masts were

broken, and the sails hung in rags above the decks. Many of the men on the "Bonhomme Richard" lay about the deck dead or dying. The two vessels crashed together, and with his own hands the American captain lashed them together. By this time the American ship had so many cannon-ball holes in its side that it was beginning to sink. The English captain shouted:

"Do you surrender?"

"Surrender? I've just begun to fight," John Paul Jones roared back at him.

It was true. The Americans shot so straight and fast that the English sailors dared not stay on the deck of their ship.

Their cannons were silent. At last the English captain surrendered.

Compare the above excerpt with a description of the same battle from a popular fifth-grade social-studies textbook entitled *The United States and Its Neighbors*:

The greatest American naval officer was John Paul Jones. He was daring. He attacked ships off the British coast. In a famous battle, Jones' ship, the "Bonhomme Richard," fought the British ship "Serapis." At one point in the battle Jones' ship was sinking. When asked to give up, Jones answered, "I have not yet begun to fight." He went on to win.

The comparison of these two excerpts is shocking and somewhat dramatically illustrates the "dumbing down" of the curriculum described by Terrel Bell and others. The sentences are short and choppy, and adjectives and other descriptors are eliminated.

Ohanian (1987) refers to the basal readers in American classrooms as "homogenized and bowdlerized grade-school texts, edited according to elaborate readability formulas

Parents Must Act to Change Schools

"Five girls and three boys reached the top of Hurricane Mountain. How many children reached the top together?"
"Mark, Theo, and Jake are brothers. Theo was born second. Mark is the youngest. Who is the oldest?"

BY KIE HO

IN AN UNSCIENTIFIC survey, I passed the above problems to fifteen children, all under eight years old; two were kindergartners. To no one's surprise, they solved them handily. **These problems,** however, did not come from first- or second-grade textbooks; they appear in a mathematics textbook for fifth graders in one of the most prestigious public schools in California.

I have lived in different cities from coast to coast, and I have noticed that everywhere, instruction in addition and subtraction is repeated religiously from first to seventh grade. As a frustrated parent, I once stormed into a high-school principal's office to protest—futilely—the repetition of division and multiplication in my son's tenth-grade class. At another time, I was saddened to discover that what was taught to fourteen-year-olds in the Netherlands and Indonesia—the solution of quadratic equations—was given at the college level here.

My anguish is shared by many immigrant parents. In Taiwan, a fifth grader has already started studying motion problems ("At what time will the two cars meet?"). In the Dutch system, multiplication and division are considered finished by the third-grade level.

Our ten-year-olds, however, are still in the crawling stage with the most basic of fractions (one-third equals two-sixths). When I took a peek at a Japanese fifth-grade-level math book in a bookstore in Los Angeles, I felt sad, embarrassed, and outraged. Who made the decision that our fifth graders, even in classes for the gifted, are not qualified to learn elementary algebra (negative numbers and first-degree equations) and geometry (Pythagorean theorem) like their counterparts in Asia?

I shudder to think that if this is happening in schools that are nationally ranked in the ninetieth percentile, what is being taught to our children in the inner cities?

EDUCATION WEEK
1990

and syllable schemes" (p.20). Ohanian points out another example of "dumbing down" by illustrating how children's literature is altered by textbooks companies using the story of *Flat Stanley* by Jeff Brown. Stanley has gotten himself flattened, and the story describes the very special things that a flat boy can do, including travel across the country by mail. Brown describes Stanley's experience below:

> The envelope fit Stanley very well. There was even room left over, Mrs. Lamchop discovered, for an egg-salad sandwich made with thin bread, and a flat cigarette case filled with milk.

> They had to put a great many stamps on the envelope to pay for both airmail and insurance, but it was still much less expensive than a train or airplane ticket to California would have been.

Here is how the description appears in a basal reader:

> The envelope fit Stanley very well. There was even room left over for a sandwich (p.20)."

Harriet Tyson-Bernstein (1985), who has written extensively on the politics of textbook adoption and the mandated use of readability formulas, believes that publishers have been impelled to change textbooks to meet state or local readability formulas. She believes that these formulas have resulted in textbooks that skip from topic to topic and result in what textbook researchers call "mentioning" (See excerpt below). Tyson-Bernstein (1988) further examined the mentioning problem in social studies textbooks and reported, "The Thirty Years' War will be 'covered' in a paragraph; the Nixon presidency in two sentences... All of the small facts and terms that can be tested on a multiple-choice test will appear in the index, because that is where adoption committees usually check on curricular and test 'congruence' if they check at all (p.30)." Gagnon (1988) also refers to this problem. Following an extensive content analysis of the five leading American-history textbooks, he found the texts "omit or dumb down the Old World background, as though it were of little importance... The Middle Ages, when

The New Politics of Textbook Adoption

BY HARRIET TYSON-BERNSTEIN

RESEARCHERS have also found that textbooks in nearly every category tackle too many subjects and cover them so superficially that students have difficulty understanding what is being said. Books flit from topic to topic; chapters wander between the truly important and the trivial; even paragraphs can be jumbled and lacking in evident focus. Researchers call this phenomenon "*mentioning*," and the primary cause of the problem seems to be educators themselves. In most jurisdictions, adoption authorities have required textbooks to cover all the topics in a course.

Publishers have tried to accommodate the list of required topics from several major adoption states in order to sell to as large a market as possible. The result is a magazine-style book—filled with tidbits but lacking context, adequate explanation, or clarifying examples.

PHI DELTA KAPPAN
MARCH, 1985

they are mentioned at all, are dark and stagnant, their people without ideas or curiosity and interested only in life after the grave... Then, suddenly, the Renaissance springs forth, as "Europe Awakens." People begin to think for themselves and seek "new horizons." Hence, the explorers, and the discovery of America (p.49)." Sewall (1988) provides further insight in his analysis of one leading elementary level history textbook as an example of the problem. He states, "Abraham Lincoln warrants two paragraphs, slightly more than Molly Pitcher... Valley Forge goes unmentioned, and World War Two receives about two pages of text, a little more than the Dawes Act and the production of maple syrup. Explanations may simply be absent: "In 1816, James Monroe was elected President. Things went so smoothly that this time is called the Era of Good Feelings (p.555)."

Sewall (1988) criticizes the readability formulas that plague the textbook industry. He concludes:

> These entrenched, mechanistic, absurd systems claim to measure the readability of a text. Instead, they homogenize and dull down. All good writing has a human voice and makes strong use of verbs, vivid anecdotes, lively quotations, and other literary devices. Textbook buyers should welcome complex sentences and challenging vocabulary, where appropriate, if such writing has style and drama that students can appreciate and remember. Clear expository writing can spur interest, help comprehension, and add to the appreciation of literature, even for less-able students (p.557)."

Bernstein aptly summarizes the problem that current textbooks pose for gifted and talented students: "Even if there were good rules of thumb about the touchy subject of the difficulty of textbooks, the issue becomes moot when a school district buys only one textbook, usually at 'grade level,' for all students in a subject or grade. Such a purchasing policy pressures adoption committees to buy books that the least able students can read. As a result, the needs of more advanced students are sacrificed" (p.465).

Imagine, for example, the frustration faced by a precocious reader entering kindergarten or first grade. When a six-year-old student who loves to read and is accustomed to reading several books a day encounters the typical basal reading system, the beginning of the end of a love affair with reading may result. As Brown and Rogan (1983) have stated, "For primary level gifted children who have already begun to read, modification toward the mean represents a serious regression" (p.6). Experts in reading also caution us against the exclusive use of basals in teaching the gifted (Labuda, 1985). Savage (1983) believes that basals may not be the best way to promote reading interest and ability. "Very capable readers often find the story content uninteresting, the reading level unchallenging, and the tedious inevitability of the follow-up workbook pages an anathema. Children with considerable reading ability can be held back by rigidly marching page by page through a basal program" (p.9). Brown and Rogan (1983) stress that since basal reading programs are designed with pacing needed by average-ability students, these basals can become boring and sterile for gifted students. "Keeping the gifted children plugged into the regular reading program frustrates their belief that their schools and all the wonderful books found there were going to be exciting and joyful" (p.6). How much better for these students if curriculum compacting had allowed them to demonstrate mastery of the skills taught by the basal series and move on to the more challenging trade books available to students of all ages.

Many bright students are using textbooks at least one or two years below their ability level. This situation is likely to promote apathy, poor attitudes toward learning, and a habit of doing only what is necessary to survive in the school setting. Students who are not provided with a challenging learning environment that meets their ability level often find school too easy and are therefore unlikely to learn how to deal with the frustration that is frequently experienced when learning new and difficult skills or concepts.

A pattern of underachievement may result that frequently causes many bright students to falter when they reach secondary school or college, simply because they are enrolled in classes for the first time in their lives with many students who are just as bright as they are. Their instructors expect much more from them, and the students find themselves lacking the study habits and perseverance that are essential to academic success.

REASON THREE: THE QUALITY OF TEXTBOOKS HAS FAILED TO IMPROVE

Since the publication of *A Nation at Risk,* the focus of reports on American education and of school reform efforts has been on the poor performance of students, the low expectations of student achievement, and the school curricula and not on textbook quality (Tyson-Bernstein & Woodward, 1989). Still missing from the reform debate is the acknowledgment that in many cases the textbook defines curriculum and the scope, sequence, and method of instruction.

At both the elementary and secondary levels, textbooks have been harshly criticized. In 1983, the National Commission on Excellence in Education (NCEE) concluded that textbooks had been "written down" and recommended in its widely disseminated report *A Nation at Risk* that (these) and other tools of learning and teaching be upgraded to assure more rigorous content" and that states and school districts should evaluate texts and other materials on their ability to present rigorous and challenging material (p.28)."

The recommendations of the NCEE in *A Nation at Risk*—that textbooks become more rigorous and demanding—seem not to have been followed. A thorough examination by Chall and Conrad (1991) does not support the suggestions made following the NCEE report that publishers should develop more difficult books. Readability levels did not change in any appreciable way between the 1979 and 1989 versions. The qualitative analysis done by Chall and Conrad indicates that where changes were made, they were toward greater ease, not greater difficulty (1991, p.2).

Earlier studies by Kantor, Anderson and Armbruster (1983) and by Armbruster and Anderson (1984) found texts to be "badly written, rambling, inconsistent, disconnected and inconsiderate (p.61)." They concluded that students would have difficulty making sense out of the text prose. Armbruster (1984) completed a study in which adults were asked to read twenty paragraphs from several sixth grade texts, and underline or state the main idea. Adults were unable to state the main idea because of disjointed writing and dumbed down content. Today's textbooks are written by committees and designed to be simplistic and to offend no one, making them incredibly dull. Downey (1980) suggests that one reason for the poor quality of textbooks is that true scholars have little or no role or interest in the writing of textbooks any longer.

Tyson-Bernstein and Woodward (1989) found that in the last decade, educators themselves have made the greatest contribution to the decline of textbook content. They describe the problem by stating, "As the public began demanding evidence that schools were making good use of their money, educators tried to produce higher student performance on standardized tests. That effort, in turn, has led them to attempt aligning the curriculum, the textbooks and the tests. This self-defeating congruence between the elements of the instructional program rests on the unassailable logic that students will achieve higher scores if they are tested on what they have studied. Following that logic, adoption-state authorities have increasingly begun to specify, in excruciating detail, all the facts, terms and topics that must be included in the textbooks they are willing to buy (p.6)."

Tyson-Bernstein (1988) points out that publishers of elementary reading books have become concerned with test improvement because their principal customers—teachers—are becoming increasingly nervous about their students' test performance. She states, "Instead of designing a book from the standpoint of its subject or its capacity to capture the children's imagination, editors are increasingly organizing elementary reading series around the content and timing of standardized tests (p.26)." Mehlinger (1989) reinforces this further stating, "Teachers want textbooks to be at or below the reading level of every student in their classes... teachers want textbooks to provide the factual information that will be assessed on standardized tests. Since most such tests are multiple choice or short answer, teachers who want their students to look good on tests make sure that all topics likely to be covered on the test are covered in the textbook.

This concern for coverage contributes to the 'mentioning' problem that textbook critics frequently cite (p.34)." Books accused of mentioning are usually filled with the facts and terms, but they are short on ideas and explanations. Without the necessary context, readers often fail to see the significance of the connections between statements (Tyson-Bernstein and Woodward, 1989).

Some well-designed and challenging textbooks are available. They are usually written by a single author who has reasonable control over the editorial treatment of the manuscripts. Usually these textbooks have small, specific markets and do not attempt to copy the production quality of mass-market textbooks. Few of these exceptional textbooks are among the best-sellers because they generally fail to pass adoption criteria. Tradebooks are also available that treat a subject in depth. Other less known offerings can be found from small publishers who do not compete in the state adoption markets, but few teachers have access to these alternative materials. In many cases, they are either officially prohibited from buying them, or they lack the funds to do so (Tyson-Bernstein and Woodward, 1989).

REASON FOUR: THE NEEDS OF HIGH-ABILITY STUDENTS ARE NOT OFTEN MET IN CLASSROOMS

Two recent studies conducted by The National Research Center on the Gifted and Talented indicate that elementary teachers are not providing major modifications in their classrooms to meet the needs of high-ability students. The first study, entitled "The Classroom Practices Survey" (Archambault, et al, 1992) was conducted to determine the extent to which gifted and talented students receive differentiated education in regular classrooms. Approximately 7,300 third- and fourth-grade teachers in public schools, private schools and schools with high concentrations of four types of ethnic minorities were randomly selected to participate in this research. The major finding of this study is that classroom teachers make only minor modifications in the curriculum to meet the needs of gifted and talented students in various parts of the country and for various types of communities.

The second study, "The Classroom Practices Observational Study" (Westberg, et al., 1992), was conducted to corroborate the findings of the survey. Systematic observations in forty-six third- and fourth-grade classrooms were conducted throughout the United States to determine if and how classroom teachers meet the needs of gifted and talented students in the regular classroom. Two students, one high-ability student and one average-ability student, were selected as target students for each observation day. The *Classroom Practices Record (CPR)* was developed to document the types and frequencies of differentiated instruction that gifted students receive through modification in curricular activities, materials, and teacher-student verbal interactions. Descriptive statistics and chi-square procedures were used to analyze the *CPR* data. The results indicated little differentiation in the instructional and curricular practices, including grouping arrangements and verbal interactions, for gifted and talented students in the regular classroom. Across five subject areas and ninety-two observation days, gifted students received instruction in homogenous groups only twenty-one percent of the time and more alarmingly, the target gifted and talented or high-ability students experienced no instructional or curricular differentiation in eighty-four percent of the instructional activities in which they participated.

These findings may account for the fact that many students "turn off" long before secondary school, responding negatively to what they perceive to be a boring and repetitive environment. Students may become behavior problems, drop-outs, or, as John Feldhusen suggests, become "systematically demotivated" (1989, p.58) because our schools have failed to provide them with a challenging curriculum. These students may grow to dislike learning simply because their academic curriculum did not meet their ability level. At the very least, the lack of curriculum compacting can promote "game playing" by bright students who have come to believe that the best way to succeed in school is to do exactly what the teacher asks: nothing less, and nothing more. Educators must insure that our high-ability students do more than simply mark time in the classroom. In order to promote love of learning and independent study habits, a drastic change in the academic preparation of higher ability students is required.

The education of high-ability students means more than providing minicourses, speakers or individual research opportunities. A simple tally of the phone calls to our office suggests that problems associated with the regular curriculum are parents' greatest concerns. In order to meet all of the learning needs of our high-ability students, we must provide an appropriate content curriculum as well as an opportunity for a student to explore interests and develop self-directed learning habits. If being above average means that a child either knows more or learns faster than peers, it is apparent that procedures for implementing curriculum compacting are vital to insure a challenging curriculum for our brightest students.

REASON FIVE: COMPACTING PROVIDES TIME FOR MORE CHALLENGING LEARNING EXPERIENCES

One of the greatest benefits of curriculum compacting is the time saved for alternate learning experiences for students who do not need to do all of the work being assigned in a classroom setting. Students may participate in the gifted program, pursue independent studies, read self-selected materials or pursue one of many other options. Many suggestions for replacing work that has already been mastered or work that can be mastered in much less time are provided in later chapters. It is essential to note that whatever is replaced should provide adequate challenge for these students because, as noted earlier, many bright students do not learn how to tackle difficult assignments. However, if only difficult assignments are used to replace what students have already mastered, they may quickly learn not to demonstrate mastery in order to avoid harder work. In later chapters, many alternatives are discussed for providing a variety of options, including those based on students' interests.

REASON SIX: THE PACE OF INSTRUCTION AND PRACTICE TIME CAN BE MODIFIED

Because of the change in textbooks and because repetition is built into all curricular approaches to reinforce learning, many gifted students spend much of their time in school practicing skills and reading content they already know. This is documented by the widespread dissatisfaction expressed by so many school personnel about the use of basal textbooks for high-ability students.

Parents of bright youngsters are also disturbed about the amount of whole-class instruction that they find in their children's classrooms. Seatwork assignments and homework papers frequently confirm the parents' fear that this kind of instruction is forcing their child to practice repeatedly skills and concepts that had initially been mastered two or three years earlier. Imagine the surprise of a father (whose first-grade child is already reading a complete Nancy Drew novel in three hours) when he finds that his daughter is still being asked to complete phonics worksheets that practice the sound of the short vowels! Because the recent elimination of any ability grouping in our classrooms has been widespread, more frustrations may result for high-ability students.

Consider the added frustration of parents when they witness countless school officials ignoring—or worse yet, misrepresenting—the research of the effects of grouping on student's abilities and self-esteem. In a misguided attempt to provide equal educational opportunities to all students, these officials have, in some cases, mandated an end to any form of grouping or acceleration for fear of damaging the achievement or self-esteem of the students in the lower ability groups. We believe that this approach directly contradicts the available research on the subject. (See Appendix C.) It also impedes the achievement potential of the students in the above-average-ability groups. The only way to change this situation is through the development of a program that addresses the concept of an appropriate curriculum in the resource room *and* in the regular classroom. The only way to change this situation is to develop a program that uses an appropriate curriculum in the resource room *and* in the regular classroom. In addition, research concerning the effects of ability-grouping (Slavin, 1987; Kulik and Kulik, 1982) suggest that grouping, without an accompanying change in instructional strategies, produces little positive change in student achievement.

Is it any wonder that these same parents are so interested in the development of a gifted program in their district? Often, however, parents who support new gifted programs may be disappointed to find that it provides limited enrichment services in a resource setting for a few hours a week or in a limited number of grades or classrooms. Consider the problems encountered by parents in the Centennial School District in Pennsylvania when they asked for curricular revisions to meet the learning needs of their bright son (see Appendix B). They met resistance from several school representatives, none of whom appeared to take accountability for the learning needs of their son.

In our field tests of curriculum modification through curriculum compacting during the last decade, we have found that most elementary classroom teachers can eliminate as much as forty to fifty percent of the basal regular curriculum for high-ability students. In basal language arts and mathematics programs, it is not unusual for extremely bright youngsters to have seventy to eighty percent of their regular curriculum eliminated. Our field tests of compacting at the middle school level have demonstrated that in classes where students can be grouped by their prior knowledge of and interest in the subject, approximately fifty percent of the regular curriculum can be eliminated. In fact, many content area teachers who have worked with bright students in self-contained classes indicate that they cover the regular curriculum in two days a week, leaving the majority of time for alternate work.

REASON SEVEN: COMPACTING GUARANTEES EDUCATIONAL ACCOUNTABILITY

It is obvious that many bright students should not have to participate in curricular activities that they have previously mastered, but it cannot be automatically assumed that all high-ability students can be excused from all assignments in all content areas. This "batch" approach to acceleration or compacting can produce gaps in students' education just as the practice of grade skipping often does. When students were allowed to skip an entire grade level, the new teacher assumed, often erroneously, that all material covered in the skipped grade was mastered by the accelerated student. Yet the student may not have a good grasp of some material, such as of the rules of punctuation or multiplication tables, because those were taught in the grade skipped and no effort was made to assess gaps or skills.

In this age of educational accountability, the use of compacting procedures can guarantee that students who are allowed to skip assignments or be excused from participation in lessons or lectures are doing so because the teacher can document the professional appropriateness of this decision. Teachers who use the compacting techniques described in this book will undoubtedly find that some of their above-average-ability students perform well in one subject area and not another, while others demonstrate advanced abilities in several content areas.

SUMMARY

Research suggests that the challenge level of textbooks is declining and that the prevailing instructional strategy in American schools is whole-class instruction. For these reasons, curriculum modification is necessary to meet the needs of gifted and talented students in regular classroom settings. One technique that has been designed to accomplish this goal is *curriculum compacting*. Curriculum compacting is a part of a total educational program for gifted and talented students developed and field-tested over the past fifteen years. It can be used as a part of any educational program for gifted and talented students and has been mentioned by several other developers of programming models as a method for modifying curriculum for gifted students (Betts, 1986; Clifford, Runions & Smith, 1986; Feldhusen & Kolloff, 1986; & Treffinger, 1986). Tannenbaum has advocated a similar process called telescoping in which students "...complete the basics in the least amount of time, thereby sparing themselves the tedium of dwelling on content that they either know already or can absorb in short order" (1986, p.409).

Because of the changes in textbooks and the repetition required to master basic skills in many whole group instructional settings, we have tried to point out that many bright students spend most of their time in school doing things they already know. Imagine what it must be like to spend hour after hour completing exercises and activities that you have known for years! Adults would never tolerate the type of repetitiveness that many of our brightest students face every day in their school. Quite often, our very brightest youngsters find everything they encounter in their first few years of school so easy that they never really learn how to work. Unfortunately, unless the regular curricular work assigned to these students is significantly altered, what many of them will learn about going to school is how to expend *minimum* effort.

If students are consistently bringing home papers with perfect scores, this may indicate that work being assigned is too easy. If this happens in the primary grade level, it often becomes the standard way that many of our brightest students go to school. By initiating the curriculum compacting process, we can remedy this situation by increasing the challenge level of the work that students are expected to complete while also providing enrichment experiences and other types of opportunities including independent and small group work that is commensurate with their abilities. Chapter Two will describe curriculum compacting in detail and discuss how to carry out this procedure.

The Eight Steps for Implementing Curriculum Compacting

| Step One | Identify the objectives in a given subject area.

An objective is the *outcome* or the behavior that we help students to attain by having them participate in learning activities. Any experienced teacher is aware that most curriculum guides and textbooks contain far more suggested activities than can be taught in the allotted time. Teachers must be able to decide which activities are appropriate and which are irrelevant or redundant in terms of the objectives. Teachers may refer to the formal curriculum guides issued by school districts or states or the informal guides provided by textbook publishers to identify learning objectives. After locating the objectives, teachers must focus on those that are appropriate for their students. Often there is a discrepancy between the objectives noted in the curriculum guides and those actually tested by the school districts. Other objectives may be redundant or overly ambitious.

To assist in the task of narrowing down the field of alternatives, teachers may consider the following criteria:

1. Do these objectives represent *new* learning?
2. Which objectives will equip students to use this content area?
3. Which objectives can be applied to the workplace?
4. Which objectives develop skills or concepts—not just present facts?
5. Which objectives do high-ability students need to understand?
6. Which objectives cannot be learned without formal or sustained instruction?
7. Which objectives reflect the priorities of the school district or state department of education?

Prioritizing Objectives

After the objectives are selected, they should be listed by priority. Because of their importance, the higher-ranked items are the ones teachers will stress with the entire class, while the less relevant objectives become prime candidates for compacting.

Simply having a set of learning objectives doesn't tell a teacher how or if these objectives meet students' individual needs. Teachers must know the subject matter, as well as their students' learning styles to determine their relevance. Step two in the compacting process can help teachers make these evaluations.

Step Two | Find appropriate pretests.

Pretesting, as its name implies, is intended to measure students' skills and strengths before instruction begins. Pretesting provides teachers with precise information:

1. Which objectives have already been mastered by the student
2. Which objectives have not already been mastered by the student
3. The problems that might be causing students to fall short of reaching any of the objectives.

Objective-Referenced Tests

Ideally a pretest should determine whether a student has full, partial or little mastery of an objective. Objective-referenced tests can do that effectively, as they usually assess one objective at a time through short answer or multiple choice responses. On a practical level, these "paper and pencil" tests appeal to teachers because they can be administered in large group settings, require little time to oversee or correct, and are readily available from textbook publishers or testing companies.

The Scholastic Research Associates, The Psychological Corporation, and several other publishers of test instruments can be consulted for valid and reliable objective-referenced or diagnostic tests. The Stanford Diagnostic Reading Test and the Stanford Diagnostic Math Test can be used in grades one to twelve.

Performance-Based Assessment

Performance-based assessment is a popular alternative to criterion-referenced tests. By asking students to do oral, written or manipulative work, teachers can observe and evaluate the process students use to reach an answer. This procedure is especially successful with younger children who are not ready for paper and pencil tests.

Students may be evaluated individually or in small groups, through conferences, interviews or portfolios of completed work. As with objective-referenced tests, this requires preplanning. Teachers must take the time to locate or create the performance tests, making sure that they're aligned with the desired learning objectives.

Step Three | Identify students who should be pretested.

In step three, teachers identify students who should be pretested prior to instruction. To do this, teachers must first discern students' specific strengths.

Students normally have peaks and valleys with respect to their academic performance in various content areas. Rather than assuming that all bright students are above average in all content areas, this step can be used to identify particular content area strengths. This ensures that students who are excused from class for enrichment activities will be absent only during their curricular strength times. Second, it eliminates the need to assign make-up work when the students return to the classroom.

Academic records, standardized tests, class performance and evaluations from former teachers are all effective means of pinpointing candidates for pretesting. Teachers should also watch for students who complete tasks quickly and accurately, finish reading assignments ahead of their peers, seem bored or lost in daydreams, or bring extra reading from home.

Using Test Scores

Achievement and aptitude tests can be a valuable gauge of academic ability. By comparing students' subset scores with local or national norms, educators can easily identify the students who score within the above-average ranges. Since these students usually know more or learn faster than their peers, it's safe to assume that they may benefit from compacting.

All test instruments are flawed to some degree. The debate still rages over "how high is high?" Overall, students who score at the 85th percentile and above on subtests of norm-referenced achievement tests may be considered viable candidates for compacting.

Step Four **Pretest students to determine their mastery level of the chosen objectives.**

Pretests, both formal and informal, help teachers determine student mastery of course material. But what constitutes mastery? Most educators set the criterion for regular curriculum at 80–85% proficiency; however, because definitions vary so, teachers within the same school should strive to reach a consensus. At the same time, factors such as being educationally deprived or having culturally different backgrounds and learning disabilities must be taken into consideration apart from rigid "cut-off" scores.

Administering Formal Pretests

Pretesting students can be a time-intensive exercise. One shortcut is to increase the number of students or objectives examined at one time; for example, if a chapter in a math text covers ten objectives, a small group of students could be tested on the entire chapter.

Before starting the testing process, teachers should

1. Point out that some students will already be familiar with the material
2. Ask if any students would like to "test out" of the unit by demonstrating that they already know the objectives being taught
3. Assure the students that they're not expected to be competent in all the objectives being tested
4. Tell the students that their curriculum may be streamlined if they can exhibit partial mastery of the objectives
5. Help the students understand that they will not be labeled "poor learners" if they can't pass one or more sections of the test

Parts of the examination may be taken independently, reducing the amount of time teachers must serve as monitors. If small group testing is not feasible, teachers can follow the same procedures with individual students. A permanent "testing table" can be installed for this purpose; or students can score and record their own test results to save time. Another option is to pretest the entire class. Involving everyone in the process can boost individual confidence and build a stronger sense of community in the classroom. A matrix used to record the results will make it easy to form flexible skill groups.

Performance-Based Testing

Some teachers may want to use performance-based tests. If so, they should observe students closely by taking notes, tracing thought patterns, and posing open-ended questions to assess proficiency of the objectives. For example, the student could be instructed to write and submit a persuasive essay which teachers would read and analyze for content. Teachers could then ask students how they went about organizing their thoughts to see if they truly understand the assignment.

Similar sessions can be held to assess other abilities such as decoding skills, problem solving or science process skills. Student portfolios and work samples provide valuable assessment tools also. Through these evaluations, many teachers will discover the value of performance-based testing as an alternative to paper and pencil pretests.

Teachers can secure help in administering pretests:
- Parent volunteers, aides and tutors to administer tests
- Reading, math and other curriculum specialists to help identify learning objectives and student strengths
- District consultants and teachers of gifted children may be available to help with pretests and other aspects of compacting.
- New computer technology to pretest and provide individual instruction.

| Step Five | **Eliminate instructional time for students who show mastery of the objectives.** |

Students who have a thorough grasp of the learning objectives should be allowed to take part in enrichment or acceleration activities. This exposes them, during class time, to material that is not only new and stimulating, but more closely aligned to their learning rates and abilities.

If a student has mastered three out of five objectives in a unit, that student should not take part in the classroom instruction of those three objectives. Students may be excused from specific class sessions (for example, the Monday and Wednesday portions of vocabulary building), while others may skip certain chapters or pages in the text or specific learning activities.

| Step Six | **Streamline instruction of those objectives students have not yet mastered but are capable of mastering more quickly than classmates.** |

If students demonstrate mastery of some, but not all of the objectives, the teacher may decide to allow these students to progress at a faster pace than their peers by minimizing repetitive practice exercise. Bright students frequently need less practice to master new objectives than their peers.

Content compacting differs from skills compacting. Skills compacting eliminates specific skills that students have already acquired. Content compacting is designed for general knowledge subjects—social studies, science and literature—whereas skills compacting is intended for mathematics, spelling, grammar and language mechanics.

Skills compacting is easier to accomplish. Pretesting is a simpler process, and mastery can be documented more efficiently. Content compacting is more flexible in that students can absorb the material at their own speed. In content compacting, the means of evaluation are also less formal; teachers may require an essay, an interview or an open-ended, short-answer test.

Individualized instruction, as with any kind of instruction, needs four conditions to be satisfied in order to be effective: (1) it must be high quality, (2) it must be appropriate to the students' levels, (3) students must be motivated to work on the tasks, and (4) they must have adequate time to learn.

Providing a streamlined curriculum can require a great deal of preparation time for the teacher who must be creative in finding alternative instruction for those students who have demonstrated partial mastery. Some of these options for instruction, enrichment, grouping and pacing may be available in teachers' manuals.

Step Seven Offer challenging alternatives for time provided by compacting.

This step is the most challenging and creative for teachers. The possibilities for replacement activities include the following:

- Accelerated curriculum based on advanced concepts
- More challenging content (alternate texts, fiction or non-fiction works)
- Classwork adapted to individual curricular needs or learning styles
- Individual or small group projects using contracts or management plans
- Interest or learning centers
- Opportunities for self-directed learning or decision making
- Mini-courses on research topics or other high interest areas
- Small seminar groups for advanced studies
- Mentors to guide in learning advanced content or pursuing independent studies
- Units or assignments that are self-directed, such as creative writing, game creation, creative and critical thinking training.

Teachers will have to decide which replacement activities to use and base their decisions on factors such as time, space, resources, school policy and help from other faculty (such as a gifted program teacher or a library media-specialist). But ultimately, the decision should depend on the need for academic challenge and students' interests. If students understand that by demonstrating proficiency they will earn some time to pursue their own interests, they will often work to earn this opportunity. Our role as teachers is to provide adequate academic challenges.

Step Eight Keep records of this process and the instructional options available to "compacted" students.

Any differentiated program requires added record keeping. Unlike large-group teaching where all students are on the same page or exercise, teachers who provide a compacted curriculum have students doing different assignments at different levels and different times. Keeping concise records is essential and can be time consuming without proper planning. Teachers, faculty and administors should collectively decide how the compacting process should be documented. Regardless of form, all written documentation should contain these basics:

1. Student strength areas, as verified by test scores or performance
2. The pretests used to determine mastery and the learning objectives that were eliminated
3. Recommended enrichment and acceleration activities.

2 AN OVERVIEW OF CURRICULUM COMPACTING

Curriculum compacting is a system designed to adapt the regular curriculum to meet the needs of above-average students by either eliminating work that has been previously mastered or streamlining work that can be mastered at a pace commensurate with the student's ability. In addition to creating a more challenging learning environment, compacting helps teachers to guarantee proficiency in the basic curriculum and to provide time for more appropriate enrichment or acceleration activities. The time provided by compacting is referred to as "compacted time."

Many good classroom teachers already compact the curriculum as part of their daily tasks. For a skill which most students require one or more review worksheets to understand, a teacher may substitute more challenging work for a student who has mastered the skill. This procedure is "compacting" in its simplest form.

Another example might involve the way grammar is taught in an upper-elementary-grade classroom. By dividing the students into two or three groups, the teacher can better meet individual needs. Some of the bright students may have previously mastered all of the grammar that is to be covered in the regular curriculum that year and can be provided with advanced reading materials and challenging language arts enrichment activities, or they can become involved in creative or expository writing in one section of the room. Or they might receive a library pass on the days that grammar is taught to work on an advanced, independent study project. Those students who know very little of the grammar that had been covered in previous years, and need the grammar review, can work with the teacher in another section of the classroom. All students in the classroom should take the pretests to determine either their proficiency for the advanced group or their need for all or part of the grammar review.

Spelling can easily be compacted. Many above-average children are excellent spellers and consistently achieve top scores on spelling tests, yet they are expected to do the routine review tasks assigned to average spellers. They may have to write the spelling words five times each, use the words in sentences, spell them phonetically, look up definitions, create a word search or crossword puzzle, or do the twelve or fifteen exercises provided in the book. If the excellent spellers were allowed to take a pre-test on Monday, and did well on it, they could work in other areas during the spelling time: perhaps research a topic or begin reading a challenging fiction or non-fiction book.

Another easy way to explain the compacting system is through the method devised by an efficient and creative math teacher who simply let his more able middle-school students attempt to do the hardest of their assigned twenty-five math problems first. If they were successful at the five most difficult problems (usually found at the end of the worksheet), he excused them from the easier twenty problems and, instead, provided time for a variety of math enrichment options.

Compacting can involve the entire classroom. In this case, a classroom teacher can pretest the whole class in certain content area for specified objectives, then set up *ad hoc* small groups for instruction based on need. As students fulfill requirements, they may pursue various opportunities for enrichment when they are not in an instructional group or doing practice work.

This chapter will explain the eight steps for implementing curriculum compacting. Each step includes several examples.

EIGHT STEPS FOR IMPLEMENTING CURRICULUM COMPACTING

IDENTIFY NEED FOR COMPACTING	**Step One**	Identify the relevant learning objectives in a given subject area or grade level.
	Step Two	Find or develop some means of pretesting students on one or more of these objectives prior to instruction.
	Step Three	Identify students who may benefit from curriculum compacting and should be pretested.
	Step Four	Pretest students to determine their mastery levels of the chosen objectives.
COMPACT REGULAR CURRICULUM	**Step Five**	Eliminate practice, drill or instructional time for students who have demonstrated prior mastery of these objectives.
	Step Six	Streamline instruction of those objectives students have not yet mastered but are capable of mastering more quickly than their classmates.
PROVIDE ALTERNATIVES	**Step Seven**	Offer enrichment or acceleration options for students whose curriculum has been compacted.
KEEP RECORDS	**Step Eight**	Keep records of this process and the instructional options available to "compacted" students.

STEP ONE: IDENTIFY THE OBJECTIVES IN A GIVEN SUBJECT AREA

In order to begin the process of curriculum compacting effectively, teachers must examine a curricular area and ask themselves:

- *Why am I teaching this? What are my goals?*
- *Do any of my students already know this material?*
- *How will I evaluate whether my students have mastered this material?*
- *What can be done to modify the material and to make available alternative opportunities for learning?*

Teachers must be able to determine their overall objectives for teaching a topic, a unit or a certain section of a textbook. The following questions should be asked:

> • *What are the major themes that students should learn?*
> • *What are the teacher's goals for the particular unit in terms of what students should know at the conclusion of the unit?*

By determining the major goals *before* beginning the unit, teachers are not only providing outstanding examples of the ways in which instruction should be organized, but are also establishing a means to evaluate students' mastery of these instructional goals.

The first requirement for initiating the compacting process is a thorough knowledge of the content and objectives of a unit of instruction or a grade level curriculum. These learning objectives usually involve the teaching of skills, concepts or knowledge related to a particular academic discipline. The teacher should generate or locate a list of these objectives before beginning the compacting process. Without such information, the teacher will be unable to document the reasons that a student is receiving special options that depart from the regular curriculum.

LOCATING YOUR CURRICULUM GUIDE

Most school districts have developed curriculum guides that contain a list of these objectives. In these districts, the curriculum guides are updated every three to five years by a committee of representative teachers. In some states (like New York and Texas) the department of education issues a mandated curriculum that teachers are expected to follow for their grade level or content areas. In other states (like Michigan or California) the department of education provides curriculum documents, but they are published as *guides,* rather than a mandated set of curriculum objectives (see page 35).

In other districts, a formal curriculum guide is not available. In these instances, teachers have indicated that the objectives developed by the publisher of the adopted textbook series suffice as the formal curriculum guide for the district. In yet other settings, teachers may find themselves in a school district that encourages individual teachers to create their own instructional units and curriculum guides.

CLARIFYING THE DIFFERENCE BETWEEN AN OBJECTIVE AND AN ACTIVITY

The objectives for instruction must be identified before the compacting process begins. At this point, special attention should be paid to the difference between an objective and a learning activity. A learning activity, whether it is a lecture, a simulation, a seatwork assignment or assigned reading in a textbook, is a *means* to an end. The objective itself is the end goal. An objective is the *outcome* or the behavior that students are to attain as the result of their participation in the learning activities. It is important to distinguish between objectives and activities in order to identify which aspects of the curriculum can be streamlined or compacted for an able student.

The purpose behind a *learning activity* is varied: activities can be used in the classroom to introduce, teach, guide, practice, reinforce, transfer, or test. Some learning activities require a passive role for the student, others involve hands-on experiences, and others use paper and pencil exercises. Activities can vary in the amount of time required for completion, the grouping structure, or the modality used. Students' learning styles, adult teaching styles, and prior mastery of prerequisite objectives also play a vital role in identifying which learning activities are appropriate for a given set of students.

STATE DEPARTMENT OF EDUCATION OBJECTIVES

Writing

As a result of education in grades K—12, each student should be able to

- write standard English sentences with correct sentence structure, verb form, punctuation, capitalization, possessives, plural forms, word choice and spelling;

- select, organize and relate ideas and develop them in coherent paragraphs;

- organize sentences and paragraphs into a variety of forms and produce writing of an appropriate length using a variety of composition types;

- use varying language, information, style and format appropriate to the purpose and the selected audience;

- conceive ideas and select and use detailed examples, illustrations, evidence and logic to develop the topic;

- gather information from primary and secondary sources; write a report using that information; quote, paraphrase and summarize accurately; and cite sources properly;

- improve his or her own writing by restructuring, correcting errors and rewriting.

Speaking, Listening and Viewing

As a result of education in grades K—12, each student should be able to

- engage critically and constructively in an oral exchange of ideas;

- ask and answer questions correctly and concisely;

- understand spoken instructions and give spoken instructions to others;

- distinguish relevant from irrelevant information and the intent from the details of an oral message;

- identify and comprehend the main and subordinate ideas in speeches, discussions, audio and video presentations, and report accurately what has been presented;

- comprehend verbal and nonverbal presentations at the literal, inferential and evaluative levels;

- deliver oral presentations using a coherent sequence of thought, clarity of presentation, suitable vocabulary and length, and nonverbal communication appropriate for the purpose and audience.

A *learning objective,* on the other hand, is a statement or a description of the desired behavior that is to be learned as a result of participating in these activities. Comprehensive curriculum guides usually contain both learning objectives and learning activities. The activities are the suggested techniques for helping students master the objective or learn the required behavior. When comparing a set of objectives with the learned behaviors of your brightest students, you will find that some of these students already demonstrate at least partial mastery of the objectives and do not need to participate in all of the learning activities that accompany these objectives because of the very traits that caused these students to be labeled "able," "bright" or gifted" (advanced vocabulary, rapid learning rate, independent learning, ability for abstract thought, etc.) in the first place.

An activity can be confused with an objective. If a language arts program, for instance, suggests that students read *Tom Sawyer,* the teacher must determine whether this is a suggested learning activity or a curriculum objective. If it is an objective, then all students who have not read the book, but are capable of doing so, should read the book, regardless of their prior experience with American literature in the nineteenth century or other works of Mark Twain. If, on the other hand, the reading of *Tom Sawyer* is an activity that is suggested by the curriculum guide to introduce students to life in middle America during the nineteenth century, then numerous ways of achieving this objective besides reading this novel can be found. Teachers who believe that *participation* in a learning activity is equivalent to *mastery* of a learning objective will have a difficult time implementing curriculum compacting—participation does not guarantee mastery or even give us a tool to measure the degree of learning.

A thorough knowledge of the curricular objectives also allows a teacher to change the time necessary to complete the suggested learning activities by modifying the activities themselves. If, for example, a student is reading *Tom Sawyer* to gain an understanding of life in the nineteenth century, the class reading and discussion of the novel can be substituted with independent reading and discussion of a briefer text describing life in the nineteenth century or *Tom Sawyer* could be read independently and the student excused from class discussion.

Students may be excused from related activities because pretesting has indicated that they have sufficient understanding of the curricular objective. Any teacher with more than two or three years of teaching experience is aware that most curriculum guides and textbooks contain far more suggested activities than can be taught in the allotted time. Teachers must be able to decide which activities are appropriate and which are irrelevant or redundant if the compacting process is to succeed. One of the biggest differences between a teacher who "teaches by the book" and one who can adapt the rate, quantity and quality of various learning activities to meet students' needs, is the latter's ability to make professional judgments. Teachers must also be able to decide which learning objectives are relevant and which are superfluous.

SELECTING RELEVANT OBJECTIVES

Once the curriculum guide or the learning objectives have been located, the next step is to identify relevant objectives for the students who are eligible for compacting. To do this, the teacher must be aware that not all objectives in a subject or grade level curriculum are necessarily relevant for those students who have above-average ability.

Many curriculum guides or scope and sequence documents use the spiral approach to curriculum development that was explained in Chapter One. When this happens, the curriculum contains several skill or knowledge objectives that were previously introduced, taught or practiced at one or more of the earlier grade levels. If this is the case, many of the more able students in the classroom may have mastered the objective the first time it was taught, and subsequent instruction or practice may not be necessary. In other situations, teachers may find dozens of objectives described in their subject area curriculum, all of which could not possibly be taught in one school year. Some of these objectives tend to be less important than others and are often unnecessary for a student's understanding of the content area being addressed.

Teachers may also find that a conflict exists between the objectives that the curriculum guide lists for their grade level, the objectives tested by the district's achievement tests, and the objectives covered in the adopted textbook series. The illustration on page 38 demonstrates this problem well. In analyzing the school district's curriculum, the researcher found major incongruences between objectives listed in the scope and sequence document, those listed in the test's administration manual, and those taught by the textbook series. The poor alignment of objectives, the irrelevance of some objectives, and the redundancy of others, results in confusion for the teacher who is trying to provide instruction. In these situations, teachers who wish to pursue compacting must make responsible decisions concerning which objectives are most relevant for their most able students. One way to do this is to view the listed objectives as instructional alternatives or choices, then using a teacher-developed set of criteria to choose the most relevant objectives from the list of alternatives. The teacher can thus narrow the set of objectives to a more manageable size for instruction and pretesting.

Examples of these criteria might include the following questions:

1. To what extent do these objectives represent *new* learning?

2. Which of the objectives in this curriculum will best equip students to use these skills in other content areas?

3. Which of the objectives have relevance to the world of work?

4. Which of the objectives deal with the development of skills or concepts rather than merely the memorization of facts or knowledge?

5. Which of the objectives are important for high-ability students to understand?

6. Which of the objectives are unlikely to be learned by even the most able of students without formal, sustained or direct instruction?

7. Which objectives reflect the priorities of the school district or state department of education?

Whenever alternatives are prioritized, some subjective judgement is used. The choice of our criteria reflects this subjectivity, and for that reason, the criteria listed above may not be relevant for all teachers, but the use of some set of criteria is an extremely efficient way to choose relevant objectives for instruction.

The objectives that tend to be ranked lower, or are less relevant are the ones that are most likely to be compacted during Steps Three and Four of the compacting process. In other words, the less relevant objectives should become the ones that are pretested first in order to document mastery by the above-average students in that content area. Objectives with a higher ranking are likely to be those that will be taught in the classroom because of their relative importance to the teacher or the student. Some of the more important objectives may require several years to teach, regardless of student ability, while others can be learned with a minimal amount of repetition.

Simply having a set of learning objectives does not tell a teacher how or *if* these learning objectives can be modified to meet the individual needs of students. The teacher's knowledge of the subject matter, students' learning styles and learning characteristics are vital in determining the relevance of various learning objectives for all of the students in the classroom. The second step in the compacting process can help teachers make these evaluations.

A POORLY ALIGNED (TYPICAL) CURRICULUM

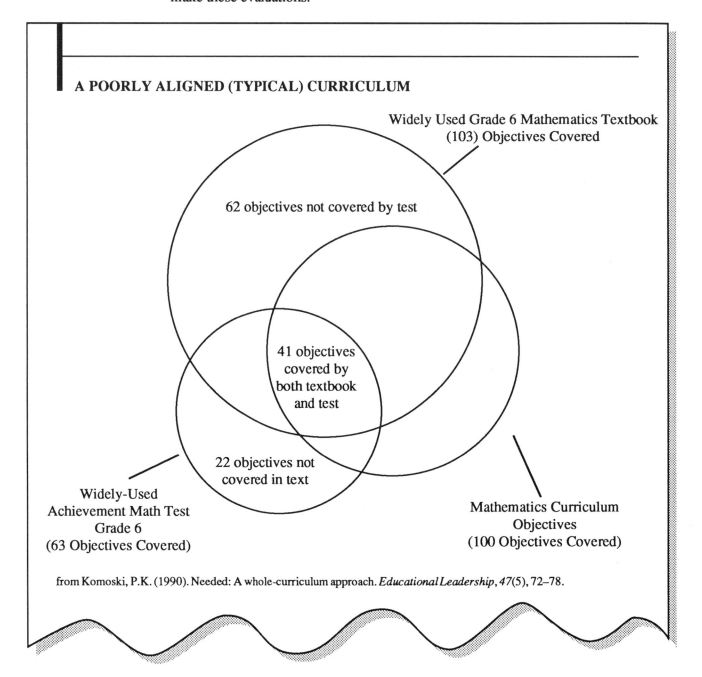

Widely Used Grade 6 Mathematics Textbook
(103) Objectives Covered

62 objectives not covered by test

41 objectives covered by both textbook and test

22 objectives not covered in text

Widely-Used
Achievement Math Test
Grade 6
(63 Objectives Covered)

Mathematics Curriculum
Objectives
(100 Objectives Covered)

from Komoski, P.K. (1990). Needed: A whole-curriculum approach. *Educational Leadership*, 47(5), 72–78.

STEP TWO: FIND APPROPRIATE PRETESTS

After the objectives for learning have been identified and prioritized, a means of measuring student competency on those objectives is needed. In most cases this means that the teacher must locate or create formal or informal pretests for these objectives. The purpose for pretesting should be to provide teachers with information about students' skills and abilities *prior* to instruction.

Pretesting is a teacher's way of diagnosing or identifying students' needs based on their ability to perform relevant learning objectives. The teacher should use pretesting to determine which objectives have already been achieved. After this has been accomplished, the results of pretesting are used to determine more appropriate learning objectives for the student. As a result of pretesting, teachers should be able to identify the following:

1. Which objectives have already been mastered by the student

2. Which objectives have not already been mastered by the student

3. The problems that might be causing students to fall short of reaching any of the objectives.

Knowing the answers to these questions helps a teacher decide how capable a student is with respect to the objective being assessed. No student should be asked to study something that he or she already knows. If pretesting reveals that a student already possesses many of the learning behaviors that a teacher has designated for instruction, the original objectives must be revised accordingly or new objectives selected. This approach can save hundreds of hours that can be used for the interest-based enrichment, research or investigation that is a part of many gifted programs. This information can also be used to decide how much guidance is required for the student who demonstrates partial mastery of the objective being analyzed. For this reason, some form of curriculum modification usually follows pretesting.

OBJECTIVE-REFERENCED ASSESSMENT

Ideally, a good pretest should provide enough information for a teacher to be able to decide whether the student exhibits full, partial or little mastery of the skill or content objective being measured. An objective-referenced assessment is the most frequently used format for pretesting students and allows a teacher to measure student proficiency with specific skills or knowledge objectives. Each assessment instrument is usually designed to measure only one learning objective. Most objective-referenced assessments are tests that allow students to provide short answers or multiple choice responses. Sufficient practice items or examples are necessary to assure teachers that the student does or does not possess mastery of the objective being measured. Teachers often find these paper and pencil pretests appealing because they can be administered to a large group, require little time to administer or correct, and are readily available from textbook publishers or testing companies.

Diagnostic pretests in the basic skill areas (language arts and mathematics) are usually available in the form of pretests, end-of-unit tests, or summary exercises that contain a sampling of the major concepts presented in a designated unit of instruction. In the

Houghton Mifflin Reading Program, for instance, the teacher is provided with several valuable diagnostic tools. An informal reading inventory, included in each teacher's resource file, is designed to assess the instructional reading level, comprehension and decoding skills (see page 41). The excerpts in the inventory are graded for readability, and specific instructions are provided to help the teacher determine the child's appropriate reading level. The inventory also provides information that can be used to identify weaknesses in areas such as word attack skills or background information that could lead to reading difficulties. The inventory is designed to be administered to individual students and takes approximately thirty minutes to complete.

In addition to the informal reading inventories, teachers may also use the pretests provided by their math or language arts series. These instruments are correlated with specific objectives listed at the beginning of each unit and covered by a set of lessons. By locating and filing these pretests according to the objective being tested, the teacher can create a bank of pretests that are correlated to the objectives that have been selected for grade level instruction. These tests can be administered to large groups, small groups or to individuals who may require curriculum compacting.

Houghton Mifflin and many of the other major publishers usually provide these pretests for teachers who are using their series. It is amazing to find that many teachers are not aware of their existence. In some cases, these pretests are never purchased by the school districts. In other cases, they are available in the building or the school district, but the teacher has no knowledge of their availability. Sometimes it is simply a case of limited planning time that prevents a teacher from finding or using the available pretests. We recommend that teachers locate these pretests as soon as they have identified the learning objectives for their grade level and content area. A workshop can be offered by the textbook publisher's representative if teachers need additional help, or other educators in the district can be asked to share information about how they have organized and used pretests with their students.

The publishers' pretests are usually referenced to the typical language arts and mathematics skills taught in most elementary schools. The Dictionary Guide Words Test on page 42 is an example of one of these tests from the Houghton Mifflin Company. This particular test was designed to measure students' ability to use guide words in a dictionary. By offering the teacher and the student five response items, rather than the typical one or two that you might find in a norm-referenced achievement test, the teacher can identify skill weaknesses and strengths with greater reliability. Most major publishers also have objective-referenced tests available in a computer format that enable teachers to type in the name or code of the appropriate test and watch as a single copy automatically appears on the printer. The computer format includes a data base to record all students' progress.

ADDITIONAL SOURCES OF DIAGNOSTIC TESTS

The Scholastic Research Associates, The Psychological Corporation, and several other publishers of test instruments also can be consulted for valid and reliable objective-referenced or diagnostic tests. Like other objective-referenced tests, these can be administered in a large group or a small group situation and have the added benefit of research to support their reliability and validity.

HOUGHTON MIFFLIN INFORMATION READING INVENTORY

You will be reading part of a story about a boy named Vicente, who is a computer whiz. What do you think a computer whiz is? Read this part of the story and find out some things about Vicente.

Until I invented Try-Athlon, the most popular video game ever to hit our school, nobody took much notice of me. I didn't mind much. I worked at not being noticed. The truth was, I spent most of fourth grade trying to be invisible.

To do that, I stayed away from all sports. Sports had always made me look silly. Not only did I have legs like sticks, but I ducked any ball that came to me. I hated to jump over things. Put all this together and you don't get Mr. Sports.

The Mr. Sports in our class was Ramos Alonzo. He was so good at everything that no one cared if he acted like king of the class.

In what grade was Vicente? (*fourth*)

What did Vicente mean when he said he spent most of his time trying to be invisible? (*He didn't want people to notice him.*)

What made people notice Vicente? (*He invented the most popular video game at school.*)

What was the name of Vicente's video game? (*Try-Athlon*)

How did Vicente feel about sports? (*He didn't like to play sports.*)

What about Vicente would make him a bad baseball player? (*He ducked the ball that came to him.*)

Why might you think Vicente did not have strong legs? (*He said he had legs like sticks; he implied he didn't get much exercise.*)

Who was Ramos Alonzo? (*A fellow student who was good at sports*)

Why might you think Vicente might not like Ramos? (*He might envy Ramos his athletic ability; he also said Ramos acted like king of the class.*)

Why might you think Vicente is a smart boy? (*He invented a video game.*)

HOUGHTON MIFFLIN CRITERION TEST

Dictionary Guide Words

365. Alphabetical Order, Guide Words: Indicate the placement of a word: before, between, or after a pair of guide words.

DIRECTIONS:

These questions are about *guide words*. *Guide words* are at the top of each page in a dictionary. Use the *guide words* to answer each question.

SAMPLE:

deer   fog

Where would you find the word animal?   ANSWER:

A)   on this page
B)   before this page
C)   after this page

---

bog   ceiling

1. Where would you find the word able?

A)   on this page
B)   before this page
C)   after this page

lead   nap

2. Where would you find the word major?

A)   on this page
B)   before this page
C)   after this page

grace   habit

3. Where would you find the word frost?

A)   on this page
B)   before this page
C)   after this page

phrase   salt

4. Where would you find the word riddle?

A)   on this page
B)   before this page
C)   after this page

mole   nature

5. Where would you find the word oar?

A)   on this page
B)   before this page
C)   after this page

The Stanford Diagnostic Reading Test and the Stanford Diagnostic Math Test can be used in grades one to twelve. These tests measure the major components of the reading and math process. Alternate forms of the test, computerized scoring services, and easily interpreted reports on individual students are additional benefits of these testing services that appeal to many teachers.

Test results can be used to group students in flexible, or shifting, skill groups within classrooms or subject areas according to need. This approach is preferred by many teachers because it avoids segregating students into permanent ability groups that may harm the self-concept of some lower ability students. Computer print-outs even suggest which students should be placed in specific skill groups. The Diagnostic Test Printout on page 44 provides a simulated example of one of the student print-outs for these diagnostic tests. Teachers who are using a literature-based reading program, a process writing program, or a manipulative math program can also use these tests to measure competency. Accompanying record-keeping devices on file folders or computer data bases are available to teachers who need record-keeping forms without the headache that comes with mounds and mounds of individual student paperwork.

The Degrees of Reading Power Test, published by The Psychological Corporation, also offers a holistic approach to testing by measuring a student's ability to process and understand prose along a continuum of difficulty or readability. The test can be administered to students in grades three to twelve and provides a objective-referenced assessment of comprehension ability without the need to compare students with a norming sample. Optional and individual student reports are also available for this test.

These reports ease the interpretation of test results by providing detailed descriptions of students' independent and instructional reading levels. Additional holistic assessments are also available in the language arts, science and mathematics curriculum from The Psychological Corporation and other testing companies. Several of these companies provide teachers with management programs that help to organize a criterion-referenced approach to skill testing, skill grouping and skill instruction. For teachers who are unfamiliar with the management procedures and instructional strategies that can be used for this kind of flexible instruction, these management programs are an excellent starting point for the interested teacher.

ALTERNATIVES TO FORMAL PRETESTING

Although many teachers prefer to use a formal test to identify students' strengths and weaknesses, others prefer to ask students to demonstrate skills while they observe. This kind of performance-based assessment is becoming increasingly popular with educators because the *process* that the student goes through to arrive at an answer can be observed and assessed. Rapport is easily established with the student, and the procedure can be especially useful with younger children who are not yet ready for the more formal paper-and-pencil tests.

Performance-based assessment can also be used in place of pretesting. Students are usually assessed individually or in small groups through the use of conferences, interviews and portfolios of completed work. Like the use of formal pretests, performance assessment requires preplanning by the teacher who will use these assessments to modify instructional objectives. Time to locate or create these tests is a crucial

DIAGNOSTIC TEST PRINTOUT

(A) TEACHER CALLAN   GRADE 4   SCHOOL LINCOLN   DISTRICT SPRINGFIELD
LEVEL ELEMENTARY   FORM L   TEST DATE 10/86   MAT 6 NORMS 4.1

PUPIL OBJECTIVES ANALYSIS
FOR
JAMES MIGLIORE
AGE 10 YRS. 2 MOS

(C) SKILLS IN ORDER OF IMPORTANCE FOR THIS INSTRUCTIONAL READING LEVEL

	HIGH	SOME	LOW
VOCAB. IN CONTEXT		WORD PART CLUES	P / G CONSONANTS
RATE OF COMPREHENSION			P / G VOWELS

METROPOLITAN ACHIEVEMENT TESTS
MAT6 READING DIAGNOSTIC

(B) INDEPENDENT READINGLEVEL GRADE 5

INDEPENDENT READINGLEVEL
GRADE 6 OR HIGHER

FRUSTRATION READINGLEVEL ABOVE TEST RANGE

(D) READING COMPREHENSION

PERFORMANCE ??? GRADE ?????

	RS/MP
Grade 2	12/12
Grade 3	15/15
Grade 4	16/16
Grade 5	11/11
Grade 6	5/6

(F) PERFORMANCE ??? GRADE ??????

		RS/MP	CR
L4-01	Literal Comprehension	*17/17	✓
L4-0103	Detail & Sequence	17/17	✓
L4-02	Interential Comprehension	*28/28	✓
L4-0201	Inferred meaning/Figurative	10/10	✓
	language		
L4-0202	Cause and effect	7/7	✓
L4-0203	Main idea	5/5	✓
L4-0204	Character analysis	6/6	✓
L4-03	Critical Analysis	14/15	✓

(G)

RS/MP	59 / 60	NATL PR-S 99-9
CR/MP	59 / 60	NATL NCE 99-0
		SS 728
		GE PHS

(H) SIGHT VOCABULARY

(E) PHONEME/GRAPHEME: VOWELS

TEACHING SUGGESTION: APPLY

		RS/MP	CR
F0-01	Short Vowels	*15/15	✓
F0-0101	A	3/3	✓
F0-0102	E	3/3	✓
F0-0103	I	3/3	✓
F0-0104	O	9/9	✓
F0-0105	U	3/3	✓
F0-02	Long Vowels	*15/15	✓
F0-0201	A	3/3	✓
F0-0202	E	6/6	✓
F0-0203	I	3/3	✓
F0-0204	O	9/9	✓
F0-0205	U	13/3	✓
F0-03	Digraphs & Dipthongs	*0/12	✓
F0-0301	Digraphs	5/6	✓
F0-0302	Dipthongs	5/6	✓

RS/MP	40 / 42	NATL PR-S 87-7
CR/MP	12 / 12	NATL NCE 73.7
		SS 676
		GE 9.8

PHONEME/GRAPHEME: CONSONANTS

TEACHING SUGGESTION: APPLY

		RS/MP	CR
E0-01	Initail Consonants	*9/9	✓
E0-0101	Single Consonant	3/3	✓
E0-0102	Consonant cluster	3/3	✓
E0-0103	Consonant digraph	3/3	✓
E0-02	Final Consonants	9/9	✓
E0-0201	Single Consonant	3/3	✓
E0-0202	Consonant cluster	3/3	✓
E0-0203	Consonant digraph	3/3	✓
E0-04	Silent Letters	6/6	✓

RS/MP	24 / 24	NATL PR-S 95-8
CR/MP	7 / 7	NATL NCE 84.6
		SS 682
		GE 11.6

©1986 by Harcourt Brace Jovanovich, Inc.
ALL RIGHTS RESERVED PRINTED IN THE U.S.A.

PROCESS NO

The Psychological Corporation
Harcourt Brace Jovanovich, Inc.

Actual size 8 ½" x 11".
Simulated data.

variable in implementing this form of flexible instruction. Time is also required to assure that the assessment is reliable and valid and that it corresponds with the teacher's learning objectives.

THE POWER OF PRETESTS

Whether you use formal pretests, observations or samples of student work to assess mastery prior to instruction, the important point to remember is to use them! Although many schools have access to pretests through textbook publishers or testing companies, studies like those mentioned earlier suggest that few schools actually use them.

In one small Ohio school that was experimenting with the idea of using available pretests for modifying the language arts and math curriculum, norm-referenced reading and math subtest scores from a standardized achievement test were used to identify the above-average students. Thirty-four students of above-average ability were identified through this process. The eight classroom teachers of these students in grades four, five and six used pretests that measured the thirty most important learning objectives in the language arts and the math curriculum. These tests were administered to these students during the early autumn, prior to the onset of formal instruction. The results are shown below. All of the students pretested demonstrated mastery of *at least* fifty percent of the learning objectives prior to instruction. This information was a powerful tool for convincing other teachers in the district that compacting should become a major priority for curricular change.

Other districts that are interested in initiating curriculum compacting might consider the development of a pilot project such as this. By using volunteer teachers and available pretests, the results of pretesting and the procedures the teachers used to compact the curriculum can be documented. Their early experiences with the compacting process

PRETEST RESULTS
Compacting with Criterion-Referenced Tests

	4th Grade	5th Grade	6th Grade	TOTAL
Number of Talent Pool Students	10	9	15	34
Range of Language Arts Scores	60-79%	44-94%	31-84%	31-94%
Average Language Arts Competency	69%	77.3%	73.4%	69.9%
Range on Math Scores	44-78%	42-93%	44-76%	42-93%
Average Math Competency	55%	68.8%	59.6%	61.13%

can be shared with other interested teachers during building meetings or inservice sessions. In this way, the enrichment program can establish "grass roots" support and modeling for the compacting process.

THE IMPORTANCE OF PLANNING TIME

Compacting requires time to find or create the appropriate pretests, time to assess individual students or small groups of students, and time to analyze the results and make modifications in teaching strategies or learning options. Therefore, it is important that the teacher have sufficient planning time to locate, create and organize the components that are necessary to assure teacher and learner success. The time spent on this step will free time for more appropriate instruction by guaranteeing that worthwhile instruction is being offered to all students.

STEP THREE: IDENTIFY STUDENTS WHO SHOULD BE PRETESTED

After the teacher has become thoroughly familiar with the content and skill objectives to be covered during the school year and has had the opportunity to develop or locate appropriate pretests or assessment devices to measure mastery of these objectives, the teacher is in a position to begin the third step of the compacting process. In this step, the teacher identifies those students who *may* have mastered one or more of these objectives at an earlier point in time. In addition, those students who may have not yet demonstrated mastery, but may be capable of doing so with less instruction or practice time than is normally given to the other students must be identified. These students are most likely to receive pretesting and possibly compacting in their strength areas.

Identifying these students means identifying their specific curricular strengths first. It is perfectly normal for students to have peaks and valleys with respect to their academic performance in various content areas. Rather than assuming that all bright students are above average in all content areas, the third step in the compacting process can be used to identify each child's particular content area strengths. In this way you can be sure that if a student is excused from class participation in order to become involved in enrichment projects in the resource room, this child is doing so during a curricular strength time. This approach alleviates the need for the teacher to provide make up work for the students when they return to the classroom from the enrichment program. It also ensures that students are not missing necessary instruction when they are involved in enrichment program activities. General indications of strength in a subject area can be found in student records, standardized tests, classwork or through teacher observations. Questioning the teacher who had the student in his or her class the previous year can also provide this information.

USING OBSERVATIONS TO IDENTIFY STUDENTS' STRENGTH AREAS

By using skillful observation techniques, classroom teachers can train themselves to spot curricular strength areas of students in need of curriculum compacting. Teachers should watch for students who finish tasks quickly and well, who finish reading assignments first, or who appear bored during instruction time and consistently daydream in class. Some students with well above-average ability will tell their teacher that the assigned work is too easy or that they are bored. Some students will ask for extra reading assignments or request possible suggestions for independent study assignments. Others will carry extra reading material from home or the library to help them productively spend the spare minutes they have saved from finishing assigned work earlier than the rest of the class.

Sometimes classroom teachers will notice the need for curriculum compacting through anecdotal situations which arise in classrooms. In one case, a kindergarten teacher who had brought a novel with her to loan to another teacher, watched to her amazement as a girl in her morning class read word for word from the book jacket to two or three other classmates. When tested, the kindergarten-aged girl was found to be reading on a fifth-grade level and definitely required compacting. In a similar instance, a first-grade student, who was being administered an achievement test early in the school year, began reading aloud the teacher's instructions which were printed on the first page of every test. The teacher stopped suddenly when she realized that a girl in the back of the room was reading the rather complicated directions along with her. When tested, this first grader was found to be reading on a fourth-grade level and also needed to have her curriculum compacted. If the compacting of this first grader's language arts curriculum and subsequent acceleration into higher level reading material had not been accomplished, this child would might have spent her first grade in school repeatedly practicing redundant learning objectives.

ANALYZING STUDENT ABILITIES THROUGH TEST SCORE INFORMATION

Another method for identifying possible student strengths is to analyze the norm-referenced achievement and aptitude tests that are available to most teachers. By reviewing specific subtest scores for the students in a classroom, the teacher is able to identify which students are the more likely candidates for curriculum compacting in a particular subject. Student records such as those printed on page 48 are provided for teachers by many of the major testing companies. By analyzing the local or national norms using the most recent tests available, those students can be identified who performed in the above-average ranges on the test instrument. Since the "above average" designation usually means that a student either knows more or learns faster than their grade level peers, it seems appropriate to assume that many of these students will benefit from curriculum compacting.

It must be remembered that this information is used to identify only the *likely* candidates for compacting. It is not an assurance that all of these students could or do demonstrate prior mastery of the actual objectives being taught in a particular classroom. Although it may be fairly easy to locate norm-referenced tests for a subject, this does not preclude the need for the teacher to evaluate the contents of the tests to verify that the skills measured are indeed the relevant skills for a particular curriculum area. As we have mentioned earlier, a poor alignment often exists between district- or state-level subject area objectives, the objectives covered in a textbook series, and the objectives tested on a norm or criterion-referenced test.

The results of intelligence, achievement, aptitude and creativity tests may also be considered in helping to analyze students' strengths. Yet this is a difficult task for at least two additional reasons. First, all instruments, even so-called objective tests, are imperfect devices and therefore establishing "cut-off" scores to identify likely candidates

ITEM ANALYSIS REPORT

THE PSYCHOLOGICAL CORPORATION

METROPOLITAN ACHIEVEMENT TESTS
LEARNER OUTCOMES

TEACHER:
SCHOOL:
SYSTEM:

GRADE: 10
TEST DATE: 3/86

CLASS LIST REPORT
PAGE 19

PROCESS NO.
00-002041-011

NUMBER OF CASES   28

A. LEARNED OUTCOMES	B.	C. NATL % CORR	D.	Student data (NO / %)
READING				
10.1 Employ word attack skills in the continuing development of vocabulary	24	60	NO	17 16 16 12 11 12 11 22 20 8 20 19 14 18 3 20 9 14 11 11 16 16 11 18
			%	71 63 67 50 46 50 46 92 83 33 79 79 58 75 13 38 67 58 42 46 67 67 46 75
10.2 Use appropriate vocabulary skills in determining meaning for unknown words.	33	64	NO	25 24 24 18 19 18 13 31 28 13 29 26 21 26 4 13 21 18 17 25 23 20 24
			%	76 73 73 55 58 55 39 94 85 39 88 79 64 79 12 39 64 55 52 76 70 61 73
10.5 Apply reading skills to gain factual information.	15	84	NO	15 14 15 12 12 14 7 15 15 14 7 15 10 12 15 7 14 13 11 11 15 15 14 11
			%	100 93 100 80 80 93 47 100 100 93 47 100 67 80 100 47 93 87 73 73 100 100 93 73
10.7 Apply interpretive reading skills.	18	73	NO	16 16 10 14 11 7 18 16 8 18 14 13 3 18 6 14 11 11 16 14 15 9
			%	89 100 89 56 78 61 39 100 89 44 100 83 78 72 17 33 78 72 61 61 89 78 83 50
10.8 Make judgments about materials read.	17	63	NO	15 17 14 7 10 11 6 15 15 8 15 17 16 5 16 8 10 9 6 9 17 11 14 7
			%	88 100 82 41 59 65 35 88 88 47 88 100 88 29 94 47 59 53 35 35 100 65 82 41
10.10 Locate information using appropriate reference materials.	12	70	NO	12 12 10 8 8 10 5 11 12 3 10 11 12 10 9 6 4 1 0 10 11 8 5
			%	100 100 83 67 67 83 42 92 100 25 83 92 100 83 75 50 35 8 0 83 92 67 42
10.14 Adjust rate of reading to the purpose and difficulty of material.	50	73	NO	46 49 45 29 36 36 20 48 44 14 44 42 48 21 34 37 30 33 28 48 40 43 27
			%	92 98 90 58 72 72 40 96 88 28 90 84 96 42 68 74 60 66 56 96 80 84 54
10.15 Use graphic aids to gain information.	6	53	NO	3 5 3 4 2 2 1 3 4 2 3 2 3 2 3 2DNA 3 4DNA 2 6 3 1 1
			%	50 83 50 67 33 33 17 50 67 33 50 33 50 33 50 67 50 33 33 100 50 17 17

Actual size 8 ½" x 11".
Simulated data.

for curriculum compacting is always tenuous. Second, when it comes to test scores, psychologists and psychometricians have never been able to provide definitive answers to the age old question, "How high is high?" Does the fact that a particular student has achieved the 85th or 90th percentile in arithmetic computation, for example, justify that some form of action be taken to compact, accelerate or enrich his learning experiences? And does the 85th percentile on the *Stanford Achievement Test* mean the same thing as the 85th percentile on the *Iowa Test of Basic Skills*? Or suppose that a student scores at the 99th percentile on arithmetic computation but consistently gets C's and D's in arithmetic on his report card? Yet, a very high score on an IQ or achievement test generally indicates that a student is capable of mastering academic work more quickly than less able peers, and should be considered for compacting. Many very bright youngsters "underachieve" in school to avoid being assigned harder or extra work: providing an incentive to do one's best work in order to "earn time" for what one would like to do may help to motivate a bright student.

It is important to consider each student's background in relation to the prevailing culture and subculture. In schools that serve large populations of youngsters from educationally deprived and culturally different backgrounds, a score at the 85th or perhaps even 80th or 75th percentile (using national rather than local norms) may be remarkably high. Districts which serve children from high socioeconomic backgrounds often have large numbers of students who score in the top five or ten percent of the national standardization samples. Although it may seem trite to say, it remains true that in matters of individualized programming, it is the individual who must be studied. If we attempt to reduce the assessment process to a formula or predetermined set of cut-off scores, then we will have fallen back into the age-old trap of basing judgments on mechanical devices rather than on comprehensive professional judgment.

STEP FOUR: Pretest students to determine their mastery level of the chosen objectives

Once the learning objectives, the pretests, and students' strength(s) have been identified, a specific diagnosis of the students' strengths within the content area must be obtained. Diagnostic instruments in the basic skill areas (reading, language skills and mathematics) were identified in Step Two.

The identified students become those individuals in the classroom who are most likely to be excused from instruction or guided practice, or may be allowed to learn new material at a faster rate than whole group instruction allows.

SETTING THE CRITERION FOR MASTERY

The first issue that the teacher must address involves defining mastery. In other words, how good is good enough? In our experience, most teachers set a criterion level of eighty to eighty-five per cent for mastery. Yet mastery may mean different things to different teachers. Some will be more cautious than others to modify the regular curriculum for their brightest students and, consequently, set a very high level for mastery. They may feel hampered by administrative pressure to keep all students working together in a large group. Others may worry about repercussions from the teachers in later grades if their students miss any skills.

In view of the fact that students are graded on the *compacted regular* curriculum in this process, sensitivity to their feelings about grades is needed. If, for example, a student scores an eighty percent on a test of concept mastery, and the teacher considers this a clear indication of mastery, the assignment of a grade of B- may be devastating to a student who has never achieved a grade lower than A. The student should be given the opportunity to learn the skills that would earn the higher grade. Students who have their curriculum compacted usually receive top grades in those areas.

By analyzing the relevance of the objectives at each grade level and evaluating the quality of the pretests being used, teachers can identify potential problems with the criterion for mastery before they occur. If teachers work together and communicate their opinions about which objectives are most important for academic success in various grade levels, they can also decide which objectives must be emphasized at their own grade level. A joint agreement concerning the most important objectives at each grade level can ease fears about underemphasizing an objective that may be crucial to a fellow educator. In order to deal with these issues, we recommend scheduling a teacher's meeting to discuss and reach a consensus about the issue of skill mastery and selection of major curricular objectives.

SETTING THE MASTERY LEVEL FOR STUDENTS WITH SPECIAL NEEDS

Another point to consider is that the mastery level of the regular curriculum may not be the same for all students before they can participate in alternate learning activities. Without this kind of individual decision-making it is entirely possible that our ESL (English as a second language), LD (learning disabled), visually handicapped or hearing impaired students may never be allowed to participate in enrichment activities.

Consider a typical LD student who is working below grade level in spelling. This student may never be as good a speller as his or her peers. Does this mean that the student will never have the opportunity to participate in alternate learning activities? If opportunities for talent development are to be provided for as many students as possible, academic abilities must not be overemphasized. Most individuals are not high ability in every area, but have peaks and valleys with respect to their abilities in different content areas, yet their potential talents should still be developed.

One way to deal with this dilemma is to compact the student's strongest curriculum area even though the student may be performing below grade level in this area as well. The student can spend some classroom time in alternate activities, but also must be willing to use some recess, lunch or after-school time to accomplish this goal. Or the student may participate in alternate enrichment during the language arts period, since that skill is incorporated in nearly all student projects. Although the student may not necessarily be working on the same set of skills as those being taught in the classroom, the student will be asked to learn and apply other language arts skills during research, problem solving and product sharing. We have found that allowing a student who is working below grade level to participate in an interest-based project may restore damaged self-esteem and improve his or her attitude toward learning in general. Baum (1988) suggests that these benefits may, in turn, improve the child's academic performance.

Some teachers may encounter difficulties in trying to compact the curriculum for special-needs students. Teachers should gather as much information as possible about the special strengths, interests and needs of the students in question. Talking to the students themselves, conducting conferences with their parents or their former teachers, and considering the relative value of the content curriculum and the students' interests helps to achieve a better perspective on the problem and its solution. This case-study approach is much more advantageous than the development of a district policy concerning compacting for specific subpopulations of the student body. It also allows those who know the students best to decide how and when to compact.

SOLVING PROBLEMS CONCERNING THE CRITERION FOR MASTERY

If one or two teachers in a school consistently indicate that no students in their classrooms can or should have their curriculum compacted, then administrative involvement may be necessary. In this case a gap exists between the teacher's values or abilities to modify curriculum and the relative importance that the district places on student involvement in enrichment experiences. No amount of pressure is likely to change the minds of these individuals.

Instead, it may be more appropriate to help these teachers clarify not only their own values, but those of the school district as well, and ask administrators to attempt to mediate a compromise between the two positions. It may be that fear of change or an inability to manage the compacting process is at the root of the problem. Assuming good intentions on the teacher's part, a private conversation may be sufficient to unearth these problems and begin to work toward productive solutions.

By suggesting that the reluctant teachers begin slowly with a curriculum area that is most familiar, or with only one or two of the more self-reliant students in the classroom, the more hesitant participants can be encouraged to try the compacting process. This approach is more positive than a mandate from the district's central office. If we expect teachers to treat students as individuals, then we must help our teachers learn the compacting process at their own pace.

TECHNIQUES FOR ADMINISTERING PRETESTS

After deciding the criterion level for mastery, the teacher must decide how and when the actual pretests will be administered. Finding available pretests and deciding when or how to administer and correct them, are often two separate requirements. In order to minimize the time required to complete this step of the compacting process, we recommend that the teacher use as many short cuts as possible. One way is to maximize the number of students or objectives that are tested at one time.

Although a teacher could pretest individual students on single objectives, this approach can be time consuming. Instead, we recommend that, whenever possible, the teacher pretest small groups of students on several objectives at one time. For example, a future chapter in the math textbook might include ten objectives. Instead of pretesting students on each objective, students can be pretested on all ten at the same time. Multiple sets of objective-referenced tests could be used at the same time. A teacher who uses unit-based instruction can also use this procedure to save time and paperwork.

A teacher who has identified two or more students with strengths in a given content area might arrange to work with these students in a small group setting for fifteen or twenty minutes. During this time the teacher may explain to them that one or more of them might already know some of the material that is going to be covered in the unit or textbook, and they will be given the opportunity to "test out" of the unit. Students should be assured that they are not expected to show mastery of all objectives being tested, but will have an opportunity to receive a streamlined curriculum if they are able to demonstrate partial mastery. In addition, students should understand that they will not be labeled as "poor learners" if they are unable to pass one or more sections of the test.

If students agree to participate in the pretesting, the teacher can use the remaining time to explain the instructions and procedures for completing the pretests. Students can then be left to take the pretest. In this way the teacher is not forced to spend additional time monitoring a test that can be taken independently.

If small-group testing is not possible, the teacher can use the same procedure to pretest individual students on multiple objectives. It might even be possible to set up a permanent "testing table" in one corner of the room, and the purpose and procedures for pretesting can be explained to all students during the early weeks of the school year. In some classrooms, students have even been given the option of scoring and recording their own pretest results, thus saving the teacher time.

AN OPTION: PRETEST ALL STUDENTS IN THE CLASS

Based on the findings of the various field tests and research studies on the compacting process, we know that compacting can also be beneficial for many other students than those normally identified for gifted programs or those who are in a higher group (if ability group is used). In many instances, teachers indicated that they used compacting for as many as 50–60% of the students in their class. Therefore, a strategy that may prove useful is to pretest all students in the classroom on units or skills being introduced. If all students participate in the pretesting experience, teachers are able to administer tests in a large group setting. This process enables the teacher to determine (1) which students know all of the objectives in the unit, (2) which students know only some of the objectives in the unit, and (3) which students have not mastered the majority of skills in the unit. The use of a matrix of unit objectives such as the one depicted on page 53 enables the teacher to record pretest results and aids in the formation of flexible, small groups based on skill mastery for each unit introduced. The skill groups are often very different for each unit taught and are therefore less permanent than the ability groups used in some classrooms.

FINDING HELP TO ADMINISTER THE PRETESTS

In other districts, teachers and administrators have been able to use parent volunteers, aides or tutors to administer student pretests. Once others have been taught how to administer and score the pretest, they can work with students in a corner of the classroom or in a hallway or in a separate section of the school. Of course, the use of volunteers depends on their ability to be discrete with test results and to establish rapport with the students who will be working with them.

If a reading or math or other content specialist is available in the district, the teacher might ask that person to help with the compacting process. Since this person's job primarily involves testing and instruction within a content area, these professionals are

GRADE SIX MATH RESULTS—TEXTBOOK CHAPTER ONE

Student Name	Place Value: Billions	Round to Millions	Estimate Metric Measures	Estimate U.S. Measures	Problem Solving: 4 Step
Vanessa	80%	90%	80%	90%	80%
Tanya	70%	80%	20%	90%	90%
Patrick	30%	20%	40%	70%	80%
Dasha	0%	10%	20%	60%	60%
Enrico	100%	90%	100%	100%	40%
John	90%	100%	100%	100%	80%
Paul	40%	50%	60%	80%	80%
Morris	60%	30%	10%	40%	30%
Marla	20%	20%	40%	60%	60%
Bethany	0%	20%	50%	70%	70%
Nathan	100%	90%	80%	100%	60%
Birute	20%	30%	50%	60%	40%
Suleimann	100%	90%	80%	100%	60%
Prudence	90%	90%	60%	70%	70%
Chauncey	70%	80%	90%	100%	50%
Farah	80%	90%	100%	100%	30%
James	30%	20%	30%	50%	30%

usually comfortable working with individual students. The teacher might seek help in identifying the content objectives, locating the pretests, or in identifying the students who are likely to have strengths in the content area.

In a similar fashion, district consultants or the resource teachers of the gifted might be able to schedule one or two hours a week in a school to conduct pretests for teachers who are interested in their assistance. This service is extremely important during the first two or three years that the compacting process is implemented. By assisting teachers with the process during the implementation phase, the teachers are less likely to become frustrated with the time-consuming tasks that are necessary for the organization of any new curricular program.

It might be easy to dismiss these suggestions by saying, "Yes, that sounds like a good idea, but we don't have a content consultant, gifted education teacher, or any specialists." Yet to dismiss the need to find peer coaches or assistance in the early phases of the compacting process is to ignore the research on staff development that emphasizes the importance of guidance in helping teachers acquire new professional skills. Helping teachers with the pretesting phase of the compacting process is no less important than finding creative alternatives and innovative approaches for offering such assistance. In some districts we have seen principals, special education teachers, physical education teachers and librarians volunteer such assistance. Their willingness to help teachers get started, coupled with the teacher's willingness to assume greater responsibility as time goes on, may be another of the major factors that will ultimately affect the success of the compacting process.

PERFORMANCE-BASED TESTS

Performance testing, observations or work samples can be just as reliable as formal pretests in demonstrating student mastery of content objectives. In all likelihood, the teacher will need to schedule small group or individual conferences with the students in order to make accurate observations of the process they go through in demonstrating their knowledge of a content objective or their ability to use a skill objective. The teacher should monitor the student's performance closely, making notes and attempting to follow the student's thought processes. The teacher should ask the student several open-ended questions that will help to determine the extent of the student's expertise in that area.

For example, if students are expected to demonstrate proficiency in writing a persuasive essay, students who are being considered for compacting can submit such an essay for the teacher to analyze using appropriate criteria. Assuming that the essays are acceptable, the teacher can also ask the students to describe *how* they organized their thoughts in order to write the essay . The answers to these oral questions can help the teacher determine whether or not the student has acquired an understanding of the writing process as well as the ability to deliver an acceptable product.

Similar conferences can be used to assess student's ability to apply decoding rules, problem-solving abilities, science process skills, literary elements and a host of other learning objectives. In many cases, teachers may find that the use of student conferences and observations can provide more substantial information about students' ability than the use of formal pretests alone.

The field of performance testing is becoming more popular with educators. Teachers who are interested in learning more about how to use observations, conferences and questioning strategies to measure student mastery may want to examine strategies described in Berk (1986) and Stiggins' (1987) texts. These books provide a clear picture of how to conduct performance-based testing, process testing, and observations. The texts also discuss the use of student portfolios and work samples as another method for measuring growth.

RECORD KEEPING AND THE PRETESTING PROCESS

After the pretests have been administered and corrected, it is important that the teacher keep records to document student progress and any enrichment or accelerations options. We suggest the use of an individual student matrix, the Compactor form, or a whole-class, record-keeping device. (Examples of each of these can be found in Chapter 3.) Many textbook publishers provide student folders that can be used to document proficiency in a given grade level. These same publishers also furnish class charts and sometimes sell computer software that can be used to keep track of individual progress within the grade level curriculum. Catalogs can be obtained from textbook suppliers that include these records, folders and charts at very inexpensive rates.

Teachers who are using manipulative math, process writing, hands-on science thematic units, or the whole language approach can still use these records to keep track of the objectives that are taught through these innovative programs. It is quite possible that a teacher could use no textbooks whatsoever and still benefit from the record-keeping forms and pretests provided by these companies. But whether a textbook, a thematic unit or a novel selected by the student is used to teach reading, students still have strengths and needs. These charts and matrices can help us organize and plan.

In scoring the pretests and recording the results, teachers will frequently find that some of the most able students in a subject have mastered all objectives for the unit. Other students will demonstrate partial mastery and yet others will demonstrate little mastery. By recording these strengths and deficits on a class profile matrix, the teacher can easily scan the entire class list to identify possible groups for instruction.

STEP FIVE: ELIMINATE INSTRUCTIONAL TIME FOR STUDENTS WHO SHOW MASTERY OF THESE OBJECTIVES

Students who have mastered the objectives should have the opportunity to participate in alternate enrichment or acceleration activities. In this way class time can be used to expose them to more challenging material that is closely aligned to their learning abilities and learning rate. For example, if a bright language-arts student has shown mastery of three out of five of the objectives in a unit, it is easy to suggest that this student can be excused from instruction when the three mastered objectives are being taught. Subject area teachers might indicate that compacted students can be excused from the Monday-Wednesday-Friday sequence of instruction, but should participate in the Tuesday-Thursday sequence. Other teachers may indicate that the student will be excused from certain chapters or pages in the text. Others will name a unit of instruction or a special set of learning activities from which the student is excused.

STEP SIX: STREAMLINE INSTRUCTION OF THOSE OBJECTIVES STUDENTS HAVE NOT YET MASTERED BUT ARE CAPABLE OF DOING SO MORE QUICKLY THAN THEIR CLASSMATES

In the examples given above, some objectives have been successfully mastered and some have not. These unmastered objectives cannot be ignored, nor can it be assumed that the students will automatically learn them on their own. How to deal with these unmastered objectives has to be decided. It is important to remember that practice alone will not necessarily guarantee mastery.

WHEN MASTERY HAS NOT BEEN ATTAINED

How will the teacher offer instruction for the objectives not mastered by the students they know are eligible for curriculum compacting? One response is to require the student to participate in the same instruction, practice and assessment as the rest of the class. This can be both appropriate and practical for a unit of instruction that is unfamiliar to the bright students in the classroom.

The teacher will also encounter situations in which an above-average student is capable of mastering these objectives much more quickly than the other students in the class. If this occurs, the teacher might consider some form of "streamlining" that would allow the student to learn through a more individualized route. Many of the textbook or educational publishers provide teachers with "resource files" that offer numerous alternatives for providing such "streamlined" instruction. Practice worksheets, audio cassettes, computer software, videotapes, peer tutoring, cooperative learning, programmed instruction, conferences, independent reading or small group instruction are but a few of the ways that a teacher can help one or more students learn new objectives without the need to participate in the slower-paced large group instruction format.

Basic skills compacting involves curricular areas such as spelling, mathematics, or language arts (skills such as grammar or language mechanics) and is usually the easiest type of compacting to implement because pretesting is less difficult and mastery can be documented more efficiently. Students vary in amount and pace at which their curriculum can be modified when basic skills are being considered. If six students have mastered half of the basic skills in the fifth-grade math curriculum, the pace at which the remaining skills can be mastered will vary. Three of the students may be more interested, motivated and academically able in math than the other three students.

Content compacting requires different teacher efforts than basic skill compacting. Content compacting usually involves subjects such as social studies, science and literature. In some cases, students may have knowledge of the objectives without having to read the content materials. In other cases, students may be able to read the materials and master the objectives in a fraction of the time. A fifth grade student who loves history and has completed independent studies in American history, for example, may already know all of the objectives that the teacher has identified in the social studies curriculum. To enable the teacher to determine this, some type of assessment must be made. That may include an essay, an interview or a more formal assessment such as an open-ended, short-answer test. If the student knows the objectives, the teacher can decide whether or not the social studies textbook should be read by the student for some other purpose besides mastery of the objectives.

The use of any of these alternatives assumes that teachers are comfortable with students simultaneously working at various activities and that they have several instructional strategies in their professional repertoire. The ability to manage a classroom is also a prerequisite for curriculum streamlining. Last, the teacher must have the necessary resources (materials, books, access to the library, media, computers, physical space) to facilitate individual or small group instruction and the ability to teach students how to learn by themselves, with others, or working alone with the teacher.

For some teachers, and for many students, the opportunity to use alternative instructional strategies new. Teachers should be prepared to spend some time at the beginning of the school year teaching students how to use peer coaching, computer software, programmed instruction or other alternatives in order to acquire objectives independently. Programs or books highlighting methods of individualization for instruction such as *Tribes, Workshop Way, Change for Children,* or *One At A Time All At Once,* can all be used by the teacher to help students learn these new styles of learning and teaching.

To develop or adapt individualized instructional programs for students, an examination of what is currently available may be helpful. Different types of individualized instructional programs exist. Some require that all students learn the same content using the same procedures and materials at their own pace. Others encourage students to learn using different materials or methods but require them to demonstrate mastery in different ways. Good and Brophy (1987) believe that individualized instruction implies some degree of planned differentiation in the treatment of students in the same class.

TWO KINDS OF CURRICULUM COMPACTING

BASIC SKILL COMPACTING

1. Does the student already know the skills being covered in the classroom?

2. Can proficiency be documented?

3. Can certain skills be eliminated?

4. Will the student be allowed (and encouraged) to master missing skills at his/her own pace?

5. If skills can be mastered at a pace commensurate with a student's ability, will the student be able to help determine what he/she will do in the time earned by displaying mastery?

CONTENT COMPACTING

1. If the student already knows the content, will he/she have an opportunity to display competency of the subject or topic? (In English class, a teacher who has just distributed thirty copies of a novel to a sophomore class asks if anyone has already read the book.)

2. If students do not already know the content but have the ability to master the material at their own pace, will they be given that opportunity?

3. If content mastery can be demonstrated, will the student have the opportunity to select the work that will be substituted for previously mastered content?

INDIVIDUALIZING INSTRUCTION

Although reformers have called for individualized instruction in every educational era (Cuban, 1984) individualization has become easier to accomplish since the development of materials and methods specifically designed to allow teachers to modify their instruction to meet the needs of different students in the class. These methods and materials often provide instruction and practice opportunities for students who are not being taught or supervised directly by the teacher. Initial assessment determines where students should begin, and then the students work through the curriculum independently. In individualized programs, students receive more of their content instruction from the curriculum materials than from the teacher, who acts more as a materials manager, tester and progress monitor than as an instructor (Good & Brophy, 1987).

In the 1960's and 1970's, several individualized learning systems were developed for use in elementary and secondary schools (Talmage, 1975). In one such system, *Individually Prescribed Instruction* (IPI), students learn individually by using programmed packages. The teacher's role shifts from instructor to instructional manager. The teacher decides what programs are appropriate, monitors students' progress, and provides individualized help when needed. There is no worry about curriculum development because materials are supplied. IPI is often used in open classroom settings in elementary schools (Glaser & Rosner, 1975; Good & Brophy, 1987).

The *Primary Education Project* (PEP) emerged from IPI as a way to provide individualized instruction in the early elementary grades. PEP allows for more teaching of the class as a whole than IPI and includes more instruction and support designed to develop students' self-management of learning and independent work skills (Wang, 1981).

The *Program for Learning in Accordance with Need* (PLAN) was developed by the Westinghouse Learning Corporation, the American Institutes for Research in the Behavioral Sciences, and several public school systems. PLAN provides a collection of activities organized by goals and designed for individualized instruction. PLAN also provides students with opportunities to select their own goals and devise their plans for meeting them (Flanagan et al., 1973).

Individually Guided Education (IGE) is another system devised to help students learn at their own pace through activities suited to their individual needs. IGE is a strategy for managing instruction rather than a set of curriculum materials. Developed at the University of Wisconsin, the IGE model calls for both direct teacher instruction and student work on individualized assignments. However, the basic learning goals are specified by local teaching staffs rather than by the program's developers, and these local teaching staffs develop diagnostic tests to monitor student progress (Klausmeir, Rossmiller, & Sally, 1977). Teachers use tests, observation schedules and work samples to assess student achievement levels, learning styles and motivation, and then use this information to identify appropriate objectives and develop individualized instructional programs. Students are grouped according to perceived educational needs rather than age levels and are moved to new groups or new instructional sequences depending on mastery (Good & Brophy, 1987).

Information about student achievement in individualized programs at the elementary and secondary levels is difficult to evaluate because it is usually confined to scores on the criterion-referenced tests that accompany the programs. Such data usually show success in meeting the objectives of the program as formulated by its developers, but they do not permit conclusions about absolute effectiveness compared to traditional approaches. Part of the problem in evaluating individualized programs is that their implementation differs from classroom to classroom and from year to year. Teachers use the same program differently, and teachers using an individualized program may do just as much group-based instruction and no more individualized instruction than other teachers in traditional self-contained classrooms (Good & Brophy, 1987).

Consistent differences appear between individualized and traditional classes. Martin and Pavan (1976) reported that more individualized and small-group work was done in schools labeled nongraded or individualized than in other schools. Shimron (1976) found that slower students were off-task much more often than bright students in IPI classrooms. Tompson (1973) found that students in PLAN classes spent most of their time working on individual projects, whereas students in traditional classes spent most of their time in whole-class work. The key is the degree of implementation of the program developers' guidelines. Loucis (1976) found no general differences between IGE schools and other schools in second- and fourth-grade math and reading achievement. But when she classified schools according to the degree that they were actually implementing the program as designed, she found that high-implementation schools outperformed comparison schools on three of four achievement measures. Throughout all the approaches, the individualized programs worked well when implemented, but good implementation required staff competence and commitment to the innovation.

Slavin (1984) suggests that for any kind of instruction to be effective, four conditions must be satisfied: (1) the instruction must be high quality, (2) the instruction must be appropriate to the students' levels, (3) the students must be motivated to work on the tasks, and (4) the students must have adequate time to learn. Slavin argues that the individualized instructional programs of the 1960's and 1970's failed to work effectively in practice because they concentrated on increasing the appropriateness of instruction but did not address the other three essential conditions. Quality of instruction was reduced because the students were not taught directly by the teacher and were instead required to learn on their own. Students were also not adequately motivated because individualized instruction was often too boring and seldom offered incentives for moving through the curriculum rapidly (Good & Brophy, 1987).

Research shows that teachers have encountered difficulties in implementing individualized instructional programs in regular classrooms (Arlin, 1982; Carlson, 1982; Everhart, 1983). The main problem appears to be the student-teacher ratio. No individualized program is likely to be effective if it depends on the teacher to simultaneously provide individualized instruction to all the students in a class as well as develop the curriculum materials for the individualized instruction (Good & Brophy, 1987). Accordingly, a wide variety of books, curricular materials, and gifted program options need to be available for classroom teachers who are compacting curriculum.

FINDING IDEAS IN THE TEACHER'S MANUAL

Providing this kind of streamlining can require a great deal of preparation time for the teacher who has limited resources. The teacher must be creative both in finding alternative ways of providing instruction and in locating alternatives for instruction for those students who have demonstrated prior mastery. Some of these alternatives may be available in teachers' manuals. Many of the more current language arts, math, science and social studies programs provide the teacher with a quantity of suggestions, alternatives and options for instruction, enrichment, grouping and pacing.

Instead of assuming that the material in the teacher's manual has to be done by everyone, the teacher can view the activities as a menu from which a selection is to be made. In most manuals the author offers several suggestions for activities from which the teacher will select ones that are appropriate for individual students. Few authors intend for us to use all textbook activities with all of our students. In a similar vein, the teacher cannot be afraid to make decisions and must be willing to create or locate new materials. To aid in this process, we must insure that the teachers have the necessary materials available that allow the compacting process to proceed.

CHALLENGE LEVEL OF ACTIVITIES

In order to provide curriculum compacting, we must first believe that students have different learning needs and that they learn at different rates and through different teaching styles. The use of innovative curriculum in the classroom is not a substitute for pretesting, nor should it be a substitute for enrichment or acceleration alternatives.

Whether rote memory or manipulatives are emphasized in a math program, students still need to learn those mathematical skills and concepts at their developmental level. The same can be said for the spelling list, grammar book, or the process writing approach to language arts instruction. The use of these approaches does not preclude the need for the teacher to offer opportunities for the student to work with novels, manipulatives or writing assignments that *challenge* their abilities. Yet, we have often seen these innovative programs inaccurately used by some teachers. Some teachers allow students to select their own novel for independent reading, a good approach for encouraging recreational reading. However, if students always select novels that do not challenge them, is this the right strategy? The *challenge* level of activities must be considered when work is substituted, and teachers can most effectively challenge students by identifying their interests and encouraging them to pursue them.

STEP SEVEN: OFFER CHALLENGING OPTIONS FOR TIME PROVIDED BY COMPACTING

The most creative and challenging part of a teacher's role in curriculum compacting is to design alternatives for the students whose curriculum has been modified. If teachers have been successful in helping gifted youngsters master the regular curriculum efficiently, then they will have provided some time for these students to pursue advanced-level studies. Teachers will also have concrete evidence (test scores) that basic material has been mastered. Many alternatives can be considered for meeting the individual needs of students whose curriculum has been compacted. The list below includes some of the possibilities often discussed by both practitioners and researchers:

- Differentiated curriculum—higher level content
- Adaptation of classwork for individual learning styles
- Assignment of more challenging written work or reading material

- Independent or small group work on assigned topics
- Learning centers
- Small-group work on self-selected interests
- Use of contracts or management plans to facilitate independent study
- Self-directed learning and decision-making opportunities for students
- Provision for open-ended thinking and problem solving*

Deciding which of these techniques will provide the best alternatives for individual students or groups of students will depend on a variety of factors such as space, time, availability of resources, availability of a gifted program and local district policies. For example, if several mathematics curriculum units have been compacted for a student who displays high aptitude in mathematics, a teacher must decide what will be substituted. Although practical and organizational concerns may place certain restrictions on enrichment alternatives, the crucial consideration should be both the academic challenge level of the material to be substituted and the interests of the student. In the situation described above, without question, the student, if interested in math, should be provided with advanced mathematics instruction. However, a problem may arise if a student is taught advanced math who would rather pursue some other topic.

CURRICULAR MODIFICATIONS AND DIFFERENTIATION

What type of alternate programming do we want for our most able students? The term "qualitatively differentiated programs" has been used in state and national legislation throughout the history of the gifted education movement. Unfortunately, the term has not been precisely defined. Most educators would agree that the typical in-grade learning experiences are inappropriate for high-ability students by virtue of their ability to learn at a faster pace, to master high levels of content at an earlier age, and to handle abstract concepts with greater insight (Fox, 1979). The teacher faced with a group of thirty students of varying ability often finds it difficult to provide appropriate learning experiences for the gifted students in a regular classroom. Several practices for differentiating instruction, such as acceleration, individualized educational programs and curriculum compacting, are often suggested.

Certain common practices for providing instruction in regular classrooms have become well established and have continued to exist as the traditional model of classroom teaching: the lock-step curriculum with its grade-level sequencing; division of instruction in each subject matter into units and lessons; group pacing, in which the whole class is moved through the same curriculum at approximately the same pace using the same materials and methods; and whole-class instructional methods, in which the teacher usually begins a lesson by reviewing prerequisite material, then introduces and develops new concepts or skills, then leads the group in a recitation or supervised practice or application activity, and finally assigns seatwork or homework for students to complete on their own. The teacher may occasionally teach small groups rather than the whole class and may provide some degree of individualized instruction when checking progress of students during individual seatwork times. Overall, whole-class instruction with recitation and seatwork has existed as the dominant approach to public school instruction since it first became established, despite frequent criticism and cries

---

* Betts, 1986; Feldhusen & Kolloff, 1986; Renzulli & Reis, 1986; Starko, 1986; Tannebaum, 1986; Treffinger, 1986

for reform (Cuban, 1984; Goodlad, 1984). The fact that this traditional approach persists despite its weaknesses suggests that it has appeal. Since teachers must work with classes of twenty to forty students, the traditional method may be the only viable compromise (Good & Brophy, 1987). However, this is often criticized by those who believe that "brighter students who master the curriculum more quickly should get more enrichment or accelerated pacing, that slower students should get extra instruction or more time to master the material, and that students with special instructional needs should be taught using materials or methods different from those that are suitable for the majority" (Good & Brophy, 1987, p.353).

Curriculum differentiation for high-ability students has been debated since The Marland Report (1971) stated that gifted and talented children "require differentiated educational programs and/or services beyond those normally provided by the regular school program" if they are "to realize their contribution to self and society" (p.ix). Differentiation, however, does not mean "more of the same," as Barbe & Frierson (1975) have pointed out:

> There is belated awareness today that teaching the gifted does not mean merely exposure to more work or the expectation of completing the same work in a shorter period of time. Administrative provisions have been successful in many situations, but, except in the case of individual teachers, there has been no consideration of the possibility that the learning pattern followed by the gifted child is different from that of the average child (p.435).

Passow (1982) comments on the type of curriculum that must be designed for talented students: "The philosophy which underlies differentiated education is one which asserts that gifted/talented individuals, like all others, possess unique needs which can only be addressed through appropriately designed curricula" (p.5). All students need learning experiences appropriate to their "individual abilities, interests, and learning styles. Individual uniqueness should be respected and provided for, and every effort should be made to adapt learning experiences to their development (Keating, 1976). "Furthermore, differences in rate or pace can be so great that these necessitate differences in kind, not merely degree, of instruction" (Ward, 1980, p.177). Ward believes that high-ability students need a different curriculum. He urges, in considering a differentiated curriculum for the gifted, "a basis in child-centered fact for the educational program, as opposed to traditional curricular concepts and administrative practices" (Ward, 1980, p.82). Passow (1982) concurs, believing, "A differentiated curriculum embodies recognition of differing learning rates, styles, interests, and abilities. Curriculum differentiation aims at eliciting learner responses commensurate with gifts or talents" (p.6).

Parke (1989) provided the following guidelines for program planning in the regular classroom when considering differentiation:

1. The program should be characterized by its flexibility to respond to the individual needs of students.

2. Program options should be in place so that the varying skills, abilities, and interests of the students can be accommodated.

3. Patterns for grouping students should be based on the unique needs of the students and should allow students to progress at their own pace.

4. Decisions should be based on student needs. Individualized programs should be planned for all students (p.44).

Van Tassel-Baska (1989) related the understanding of gifted students' needs to curriculum modification in the regular classroom. She identified four aspects that needed to be addressed: deleting or compressing basic curriculum that has already been mastered or that can be mastered quickly; concentrating on higher level thinking skills to provide tools for the production rather than the consumption of knowledge; providing depth to the curriculum by concentrating on the interrelationships among bodies of knowledge; and encouraging self-directed learning so that the students can utilize more independent program options. She says, "...the content that the gifted receive is minimal compared to what they are capable of learning. If content were rearranged and restructured around a conceptual framework, the gifted could master whole content areas in half the time currently spent. This compression of content facilitates proficiency and learning of conceptual wholes" (p.179). In a later section, we will examine how to decide which available alternatives will provide an appropriate curriculum for these students.

STEP EIGHT: KEEP RECORDS OF THIS PROCESS AND THE INSTRUCTIONAL OPTIONS AVAILABLE TO "COMPACTED" STUDENTS

The teacher who initiates the compacting process in the classroom must understand that any kind of individualization for students is going to require additional record keeping. Unlike a teacher-directed class in which all students are on the same page of the same workbook on any given day, the teacher who provides a compacted curriculum is going to have different students doing different things, at different levels, and even perhaps working toward different goals. Keeping records of these differences can become quite time consuming unless planning and creativity are used before the process is initiated.

It is important to document more than just the names of the students who receive compacting or the subject in which they were compacted. Information must be recorded at several key times during the compacting process in order to communicate the process with other educators and parents. Initially, objectives which are being considered for instruction and the evidence that *suggests* that a student might be a candidate for compacting with respect to that objective is recorded. At a later phase, pretest information is documented and plans to eliminate or streamline corresponding instruction are recorded. The enrichment or acceleration options that replace the compacted curriculum are also noted. All of this information can be efficiently recorded on the Compactor, a form which was specifically developed for this purpose. Chapter 3 describes this form in detail and provides numerous examples of its use.

The Compactor

The best way to get an overview of the curriculum compacting process is to review "The Compactor." Conceived in 1978 by educators Joseph Renzulli and Linda Smith, the form is an easy-to-use, record-keeping device. Teachers usually complete one form per student or for a small group of students. Completed Compactors should be kept in students' academic files and updated regularly.

The Compactor is divided into three columns:

- The first column should list learning objectives followed by data on students' proficiency in that content area, including test scores, behavior profiles and past academic records.

- In the second column, teachers should detail the pretests they selected, along with test results. The pretest instruments can be formal measures, such as pencil and paper tests, or informal measures, such as essays, products or discussions. The amount of time saved for enrichment activities should be noted here also. Specificity is extremely important. Recording an overall score of 85% on ten objectives, for example, sheds little light on what portion of the material can be compacted, since students could show zero mastery of two objectives and perfect mastery of eight.

- Column three is for a description of acceleration or enrichment options that will be pursued during time that has been saved by the compacting process. These are based on students' interests and learning styles.

Sample Elementary Compactor

Eileen is a fifth grader in a self-contained classroom. Her school, which is very small, is located in a lower socioeconomic urban school district. While Eileen's reading and language scores range between two and five years above grade level, most of her 29 classmates are reading one to two years below grade level. This presented her teacher with a common problem: What was the best way to instruct Eileen?

He agreed to compact her curriculum. Taking the easiest approach possible, he administered all of the unit and level tests in the Holt Basal Language Arts program and excused Eileen from completing the activities and worksheets in the units where she showed proficiency (80 percent and above). If Eileen missed one or two questions, the teacher would quickly check for trends in those items; if an error pattern emerged, instruction would be provided to ensure concept mastery. Eileen usually took part in language arts lessons one or two days a week. The balance of the time she spent with alternative projects, some of which she selected.

This strategy spared Eileen six to eight hours a week of language arts instruction in skills that were below her level. She joined the class instruction only when her pretests indicated she had not fully acquired the skills.

In the time saved through compacting, Eileen engaged in several enrichment activities. First, she enjoyed as many as five hours a week in a resource room for high-ability students. This time was usually scheduled during her language arts class, benefiting both Eileen and her teacher; he didn't have to search for enrichment options because Eileen went to the resource room, and she didn't have make-up assignments because she was not missing essential work.

Eileen also visited a regional science center. Science was another strength area for her, and based on the results of an interest assessment (the Interest-A-Lyzer), famous women were a special interest. Working closely with her teacher, Eileen chose seven biographies of noted women. All of the books were extremely challenging and locally available. Three were adult books, but she had no trouble reading them.

Eileen's Compactor, which covered an entire semester, was updated in January. Her teacher remarked that compacting her curriculum had actually saved him time—time he would have spent correcting needlessly assigned papers! The value of compacting for Eileen also convinced him that he should continue the process.

INDIVIDUAL EDUCATIONAL PROGRAMMING GUIDE
The Compactor

Prepared by: Joseph S. Renzulli
Linda H. Smith

NAME ___Eileen___   AGE _____ TEACHER(S) _____   Individual Conference Dates And Persons Participating in Planning Of IEP

SCHOOL _____   GRADE __5__ PARENT(S) _____

CURRICULUM AREAS TO BE CONSIDERED FOR COMPACTING Provide a brief description of basic material to be covered during this marking period and the assessment information or evidence that suggests the need for compacting.	PROCEDURES FOR COMPACTING BASIC MATERIAL Describe activities that will be used to guarantee proficiency in basic curricular areas.	ACCELERATION AND/OR ENRICHMENT ACTIVITIES Describe activities that will be used to provide advanced level learning experiences in each area of the regular curriculum.
Language Arts: Holt 14: Units 2-6 Pre test Units 2-6 Decoding/encoding skills Language skills	Unit and level tests in Holt Language Arts. Eileen will participate in language arts activities in the classroom except those involving: decoding/encoding skills and Language skills already mastered and any kind of "seatwork" (repetitious work.)	Advanced Exposure in Language Arts: To read biographies for the purpose of enriching Eileen's background in literature and to see how the following human value applies to her selections: "Determination and courage are often necessary to achieve one's goals"
CTBS Scores Vocabulary 6.5 Language Mechanics 9.9 Comprehension 9.5 Language Expression 9.9 Total Reading 7.9 Total Language 9.8		Amelia Earhart Abigail Adams Phillis Whaitley Harriet Beecher Stowe Anne Bradstreet Mahalia Jackson Dolly Madison
	Time gained from this will go towards Eileen's enrichment activities in Language Arts.	Also, Eileen will choose novels from the Newberry Award series to increase vocabulary and deepen understanding of plot structure in terms of introduction, complication, climax, and resolution.
		Advanced Exposure in Science 8 trips to regional science center for extension, differentiated and intensive instruction in the area of computers and calculators, chronobiology and weather and time to
		instruct others in class on above areas. Resource room - 5 hours a week. Type I, II and III activities developing creative thinking, critical thinking, creative and critical problem solving.

☐ Check here if additional information is recorded on the reverse side.

Sample Group Compactor

Many of the teachers involved in our field tests of curriculum compacting have preferred to use group compacting. Group compacting is a practical approach to use if a teacher is interested in pretesting the entire class on units or skills that will be covered in a certain content area.

This group Compactor is an example of this practice. Students who displayed mastery of a unit in language arts did not have to do any of the exercises, activities or workbook pages related to the skills in the unit. Other students in the class were grouped together (for this unit only) by the number of skills they had yet to master. This enabled the teacher to compact for more students.

Sample Secondary Compactor

Bill's area of strength and interest was history. His sophomore U.S. history teacher knew him before he entered his class because Bill had often approached him asking to borrow textbooks or primary sources about the Civil War. His love for U.S. history in general, and his knowledge and fascination for the Civil War period, were well known to the entire history department. His history teacher had never requested help in the compacting process before, but Bill provided a good opportunity to field test it with a student who would obviously benefit.

INDIVIDUAL EDUCATIONAL PROGRAMMING GUIDE
The Compactor

Prepared by: Joseph S. Renzulli
Linda H. Smith

NAME _____ (Top Reading Group) _____   AGE _____ TEACHER(S) _____ S. Ksenych _____   Individual Conference Dates And Persons Participating in Planning Of IEP

SCHOOL _____ East _____   GRADE _4_ PARENT(S) _____   S. K.   S. L.   T. H.

CURRICULUM AREAS TO BE CONSIDERED FOR COMPACTING Provide a brief description of basic material to be covered during this marking period and the assessment information or evidence that suggests the need for compacting.	PROCEDURES FOR COMPACTING BASIC MATERIAL Describe activities that will be used to guarantee proficiency in basic curricular areas.	ACCELERATION AND/OR ENRICHMENT ACTIVITIES Describe activities that will be used to provide advanced level learning experiences in each area of the regular curriculum.
I. Language Arts Test: Holt Level: 13 Unit: 5	1. No reinforcement on exercises in the Holt reading series showing mastery. 2. No assignments in workbook pages of skills mastered. 3. Check proficiency by the Holt Unit tests.	1. Reading for pleasure 2. Creative writing (poetry, short stories, etc.) 3. Monthly book reports. 4. Participation in Talcott Mt. Science Center programs
II. As determined by the Holt Unit tests, these students consistently master over 85% in each skill area of the unit test.		5. RFU Reading Kit 6. Reading Comprehension Library--Level D 7. Research skills training in relation to Type III projects and classroom
III. Spelling These students continue to achieve a grade of 100 on all spelling tests.	Spelling The Economy Individualized Spelling Program will be utilized with this entire group.	projects 8. Letters from Santa (In conjunction with Mrs. Reiche) 9. Letter writing--related to Type III projects
		10. Type II Training activities in Resource Room 11. Mini-Course in Human Anatomy--with Mrs. Beck and Miss Towne "Bobby Bones" -- construction of human skeleton.
		12. "Be a Better Reader" Alison--Level C Eric--Level B 13. TYPE III Independent Study Projects in the Resource Room

☐ Check here if additional information is recorded on the reverse side.

As indicated in column one below, Bill is an excellent student. Besides having high achievement test scores, he also has read numerous texts and non-fiction books on American history, received top grades, and collects Civil War memorabilia as a hobby.

Bill took a mid-term exam in September—usually given in January—to determine his knowledge of American history and scored an A+. He was excused from most discussions and class assignments. Instead, he did independent reading, continued his research on Civil War Memorabilia, worked in the congressional campaign of a local candidate and conducted intensive research on the Kennedy/Nixon debates during the 1960 election. All of these alternative learning experiences were made possible because Bill's teacher was willing to assess his knowledge in September.

The Importance of Documentation

Whether you choose to use the Compactor, modify it, or use your own record-keeping device, these records should be kept in students' cumulative files and used to support the compacting process if parents, fellow teachers or administrators question a decision to modify the standard curriculum. Teachers can better explain why some students can be excused from selected instruction or practice when documentation is provided in a Compactor.

INDIVIDUAL EDUCATIONAL PROGRAMMING GUIDE
The Compactor

Prepared by: Joseph S. Renzulli
Linda H. Smith

NAME ___Bill___ AGE __15__ TEACHER(S) ___Hébert___

Individual Conference Dates And Persons Participating in Planning Of IEP

SCHOOL ___Canton High School___ GRADE __10__ PARENT(S) __Mr. Paul Jordan__

9/31   10/25   11/30   12/10

CURRICULUM AREAS TO BE CONSIDERED FOR COMPACTING Provide a brief description of basic material to be covered during this marking period and the assessment information or evidence that suggests the need for compacting.	PROCEDURES FOR COMPACTING BASIC MATERIAL Describe activities that will be used to guarantee proficiency in basic curricular areas.	ACCELERATION AND/OR ENRICHMENT ACTIVITIES Describe activities that will be used to provide advanced level learning experiences in each area of the regular curriculum.
U.S. History - Colonial History to Civil War 1. Reading 3 years above level- Achievement Test Results	1. Bill took an exam covering chapters 2-15 with a grade of A+ to A-	1. Bill will develop skills in museum research (related to Civil War memorabilia).
2. Bill's outside reading has allowed him to investigate many texts on history used in college courses.	2. Bill will write an interpretive paper on a self-selected topic.	2. Bill will develop poll- taking skills and work as a volunteer for a local Congressional candidate.
3. Hobby- collecting Civil War memorabilia. 4. Straight A's in Social Studies.	3. Student will not have to do regular curriculum work related to history.	3. Bill selected an interest area and will write a research paper on the political debates of 1960: Kennedy vs. Nixon.

☐ Check here if additional information is recorded on the reverse side.

Examining Curriculum Alternatives

The most challenging part of compacting is deciding what students should do with time that they have earned. In deciding which curriculum alternatives to use, teachers should first list all the enrichment and acceleration activities available in their school districts. These can be organized around five major topics:

1. Classroom Activities. Independent or small group study; escalated coverage of the regular curriculum; mini-courses; special interest groups; clubs; interest development centers; and special lessons for furthering cognitive and affective processes.

2. Resource Room and Special Class Programs. These include the same activities as above, but often held in locations outside of the classroom, and may be taught by special teachers.

3. Accelerated Studies. Grade-skipping; honors and advanced-placement courses; college classes; summer or evening classes; early admission to kindergarten or first grade; cross-grade grouping; continuous progress curricula; and special seminars.

4. Out of School Experiences. Internships; mentorships; work-study programs; and community programs such as theater and symphonic groups, artists' workshops and museum programs.

5. District, School or Departmental Programs. Encompasses the options above, plus correspondence courses, and programs for independent study, special counseling, career education and library studies.

Besides interests, teachers must take students' preferred learning styles into account. Learning styles may be discerned through observation, interview, or more formal means, such as the Learning Styles Inventory, devised by Joseph Renzulli and Linda Smith. This inventory identifies students' preferred learning modes.

Enrichment Materials in the Classroom

Gifted education teachers are excellent sources of enrichment activities. The services they provide can range from alternative teaching units or materials to mentoring student projects.

For teachers who don't have access to these specialists, there are a host of commercially published materials on the market. These kits, books and activity cards, which offer high quality enrichment at reasonable prices, can be adapted to individuals or small student groups of all ages.

Assessing Students' Interests

Student interests are key in choosing enrichment or acceleration options. When asked what they enjoy most about compacting, students consistently cite the freedom to select their own topics of study; conversely, their biggest objection to the regular curriculum is the limited opportunity to pursue their favorite subjects.

An interest assessment instrument called the *Interest-A-Lyzer* can be used to help students examine their present and potential interests (Sample pages of this instrument are on pages 106 and 107.) Items on the questionnaire include a variety of real and hypothetical situations in which students select their favorite options.

We sometimes assume that when a student excels in an area, he or she has a special interest in it. But often students perform well in a course because they've been directed and rewarded by parents and teachers. Students may also lean toward one academic area simply because they have had little exposure to others.

Still, if a youngster is outstanding in math, for example, the teacher should try to promote further interest in the subject. A good way to do this is to suggest an accelerated math activity; if the student and parents agree to it, they should proceed. If, however, the student would rather work in another subject area, then the teacher should try to accommodate those wishes while also considering how to provide an appropriate level of challenge.

Interest Development Centers

An interest development center allows children to explore a wide variety of options that are selected because of student interest and to pursue a new subject, and possible involvement in long-term research. These centers are stocked with manipulative materials, media and print materials, and many suggestions for experimenting and exploring specific topics that are presented as options for those students who have a genuine interest in learning more about a particular topic. Care is taken to preassess the general interest of the class prior to the construction of an interest center.

Interest centers also include resources that expose children to process or methodology skills that an adult would use in a career field. These research skills differ greatly from traditional reference skills such as note taking, outlining, and card-catalog skills.

An interest development center works best when it includes the following:

> *Narrative information.* Introductory books, magazines, professional journals, biographies, career pamphlets, video-tapes of public television specials, movies, records and filmstrips.

Suggestions for specific activities, experiments, or research. Recommended readings, investigations, experiments or activities for further study. These written suggestions should focus on the topic while stressing creative thinking, career exploration, higher level thinking, problem solving, moral dilemmas, imagination, or related academic concerns. Suggestions for writing letters or making phone calls, gathering data or developing a product are good possibilities for activity suggestions.

Community Resources. A list of phone numbers, names, or addresses of adults willing to let students visit their homes or places of business.

Display items. Slides, specimens, samples, photographs, tools, or raw materials. Poetry, art work, records, or picture books that deal with the subject may also make useful display items.

Decisions about the location of the center, the number of students who will use it, the hours of use, the kinds of students who will have access to it, and the way it will be introduced are all important. The teacher can create enthusiasm for the center's topics and activities through the use of an introductory film, speaker, book, or controversial classroom discussion. Current newspaper or magazine articles about the topic are also ideal for this purpose. Directions for using the center's audio-visual equipment also can be explained as it is introduced.

By praising and encouraging children to take risks and learn to gather information independently, the teacher will reinforce behavior that most likely will lead to a love for independent learning.

Guiding Students Through Independent Study

We've devised a 12-step process for teaching students how to produce quality enrichment projects. This process, which has evolved over several decades and countless activities, can be applied in classroom and resource room settings. Two comments on the steps themselves: First, they don't have to be followed in the order given. Second, some can be eliminated if students can accomplish the learning objectives in other ways.

1. Assess, Find or Create Student Interests

Students should select topics in which they have an intense interest. In some cases, teachers may have to spark an interest by introducing new fields of study or extending the regular curriculum. The Interest-A-Lyzer and scheduled speakers can also serve as motivators.

2. Conduct Interviews to Determine Interest Strength

Teachers should try to ascertain, through face-to-face interviews, how deeply committed students are to their interests. For example, if a youngster likes journalism and wants to produce a school newspaper, he or she might be asked these questions:

1. How long have you been interested in journalism?
2. What sources have you contacted to learn more about the subject?
3. Have you ever tried to publish a class or neighborhood newspaper? Why or why not?
4. Have your ever visited your local newspaper?
5. Do you know anyone else interested in this topic?
6. If I can help you find either books or people to talk to about your project, do you think it might give you some good ideas?
7. How did you become involved in journalism?

Posing these questions will reveal if the student has seriously considered how to go about producing a unique product and the amount of time that will be needed.

3. Help Students Arrive at a Question or Questions to Research

Most educators have little difficulty recognizing "families" of interest: scientific, historical, literary, mathematical, musical, athletic. Problems arise in fine tuning a broad area and focusing a specific interest into a research question.

The majority of teachers are not experienced in asking the right questions in a narrow field of study. Yet, this part of the process is critical. How it's handled will determine whether a student starts on the right or wrong track. Teachers can help students secure the "how to" books or resource people that routinely probe these important questions. Students who want to ask the right questions about problem focusing in anthropology, for instance, must begin by looking at the query techniques anthropologists apply.

4. Formulate a Written Plan

Once students have generated a question, they should draft a written plan for researching it. Many teachers employ contracts with students. Others prefer journals or logs, and still others use a Management Plan to organize ideas and develop time lines.

5. Help Students to Locate Resources

For advanced content and methodological aid, teachers should direct students to "how-to" books, as well as biographies and autobiographies, periodicals, atlases, letters, surveys, films, phone calls and personal interviews. Librarians and media specialists can also steer students to sources other than encyclopedic references.

6. Provide Methodological Assistance

In this step, the emphasis shifts from learning about topics to learning how one gathers, categorizes, analyzes and evaluates data. The teacher's role here is to show students how to identify and obtain the resources that explain how to properly investigate their topics.

Correct guidance during this phase almost guarantees that students will be first-hand investigators rather than reporters. Clearly, the caliber of instruction students receive here will differentiate their projects from those of their peers.

7. Help Students Choose the Question or Problem to Investigate

Students can often decide at this point which question or problem or area they want to research as a result of seeing how particular methodologies make it possible for them to pursue an interest.

8. Offer Managerial Assistance

Managerial assistance consists of helping students secure the information they need. Teachers can set up interviews with public officials, gain access to laboratories or computer centers, transport them to college libraries or help distribute questionnaires. At this stage, the student emerges as the leader and expert, while the educator assumes a more supportive role.

9. Identify Final Products and Audiences

A sense of audience is integral to students' concern for quality and commitment to their tasks. With that in mind, teachers should lead students to appropriate audiences and outlets for their work.

Teachers should also stress the impact creative efforts can have. Students should be aware that a job well done can bring more than individual expression and personal satisfaction; it benefits others by changing how they think or feel, or enhancing the quality of life in other, more tangible ways.

10. Offer Encouragement, Praise and Constructive Criticism

Almost every endeavor can be improved through revision, rewriting or closer attention to detail. Teachers must convey this fact to students as they review their projects with a sharp, yet sensitive eye. For their part, students should feel that the teacher's greatest concern is helping them achieve excellence, and that constructive feedback is vital to the process.

11. Escalate the Process

Critical feedback is highly successful in improving student projects. While progress is usually slow but sure, teachers can escalate the process by giving criticism that is as positive and precise as possible—an approach that also reaffirms students' confidence in their efforts.

Often bright students resort to simple or unimaginative research methods because they haven't been taught more advanced ones. Educators can change this by showing them how professionals work. Teachers, media specialists and librarians can assist students in phrasing their questions, designing research, gathering and analyzing data in an unbiased way, drawing conclusions and communicating their results.

12. Evaluate

Students always want to know how they're being "graded." However, we strongly discourage the formal grading of independent projects, since no letter grade, number or percent can accurately reflect the knowledge, creativity and commitment students develop during their individual study.

Nonetheless, evaluation and feedback do promote growth, and should be used. The ideal approach actively involves students and familiarizes them with the evaluative procedures. To help students appraise their own work, we suggest a short questionnaire, such as the one below:

1. How did you feel about working on the project?

2. What did you learn through your study?

3. Were you satisfied with the final product? In what ways?

4. How were you helped with your project?

5. Do you think you might like to undertake another project in the future? Do you have any ideas what that project would be like?

Curriculum compacting demands time and energy on the part of both teachers and students. Yet, over the years, we've discovered that it saves teachers precious hours once they're familiar with the process. Most educators who now compact effectively say that it takes no longer than normal teaching practices. More importantly, they tell us that the benefits to all students certainly make the effort worthwhile.

3 RECORD KEEPING AND ENRICHMENT OPTIONS

RECORD-KEEPING ON THE COMPACTOR FORM

The process of curriculum compacting is most simply explained by reviewing the form below called "The Compactor". The Compactor was developed to provide teachers with an easy-to-use, record-keeping device (Renzulli & Smith, 1978). It should be completed cooperatively by classroom teachers and resource teachers in order to serve as a means for joint planning, and should be maintained as part of the student's individual record. Every effort should be made to revise and update the form regularly.

The Compactor is divided into three columns: Curriculum Areas To Be Considered for Compacting, Procedures for Compacting Basic Material, and Acceleration and/or Enrichment Activities which provide space for documentation of strength areas, the skills within the strength area that have been mastered, and suggestions for appropriate enrichment and possible acceleration activities.

INDIVIDUAL EDUCATIONAL PROGRAMMING GUIDE
The Compactor

Prepared by: Joseph S. Renzulli
Linda H. Smith

NAME_____   AGE_____ TEACHER(S)_____   Individual Conference Dates And Persons Participating in Planning Of IEP

SCHOOL_____   GRADE_____ PARENT(S)_____   _____ _____ _____

CURRICULUM AREAS TO BE CONSIDERED FOR COMPACTING Provide a brief description of basic material to be covered during this marking period and the assessment information or evidence that suggests the need for compacting.	PROCEDURES FOR COMPACTING BASIC MATERIAL Describe activities that will be used to guarantee proficiency in basic curricular areas.	ACCELERATION AND/OR ENRICHMENT ACTIVITIES Describe activities that will be used to provide advanced level learning experiences in each area of the regular curriculum.
STEP ONE TO STEP FOUR	**STEP FIVE TO STEP SIX**	**STEP SEVEN**
←	**STEP EIGHT**	→

☐ Check here if additional information is recorded on the reverse side.

COMPLETING THE FIRST COLUMN OF THE COMPACTOR

The first column of the Compactor can be used to document the first three steps in the compacting process; naming the objective(s) being considered for compacting and citing information that indicates that the student is a good candidate for compacting with respect to these objectives. We recommend that teachers reduce the time needed to complete the form by using brief notes or some form of personal shorthand to record the relevant information. Using a code number or the page number of the Teacher's Manual on which the objectives appear will, in most cases, provide the reader with all of the relevant information.

The first sentence in this column might look like these examples:

- John's achievement test scores in math (99th percentile) indicate curriculum compacting is necessary.
- Tamara's grades in English have been "A"s for the last four years.
- Den-Mo's instructional reading level is four years above his grade placement.
- Sasha is an amateur ornithologist with the local Audubon association.

In each of these cases the writer has provided the reader with some tangible evidence of above-average ability in the subject area. Information from tests scores, classroom behaviors or the student's cumulative file has also been used to document curriculum strength.

The second sentence in this column should provide information about the objective(s) being considered for compacting such as the following examples:

- John will be pretested on the math computation objectives (B1- B21) in the fourth-grade math program (See Teacher's Manual, page A2-3).
- Grammar and sentence syntax objectives will be considered for compacting.
- It is likely that Den-Mo can be compacted from the word attack, vocabulary and comprehension objectives for this grade level.
- Sasha will be pretested on the objectives in Chapter 4 (Our Feathered Friends) of the science textbook series.

The teacher does not need to identify *all* possible objectives or subject areas to be considered for compacting during the first week of the school year. It is more likely that the process will start slowly with one student or in one content area. As the teacher and students become more proficient with the process, additional objectives for compacting will be identified and additional notations can be made in the remaining cells of column one of the Compactor. In most cases, compacting activity will vary during the course of the school year as students' proficiency or the availability of pretests increases or decreases.

COMPLETING THE SECOND COLUMN OF THE COMPACTOR

Information about *how* the specific objectives will be achieved should be documented in the second column of the Compactor. For example, if a student has shown mastery of seven of the ten objectives in a unit, the teacher must decide how to provide instruction in the remaining three objectives. The teacher may require that the student participate with the rest of the class, learn the objective through an individual tutorial, or become responsible for independent mastery of the unmet objectives. (Sample entries from this second column of the Compactor are included in subsequent examples in this chapter.)

The second column of the Compactor Form should also document how much time has been saved for enrichment or acceleration activities and just what is being eliminated from the classroom curriculum as a result of student mastery of tested objectives. If, for example, spelling pretests indicate that a student has mastery of six of the next eight units in the spelling curriculum, the writer might indicate the dates, the times of day or the days of the week when the six units are to be taught. The second column should include clarification of how much instructional time is being saved or which activities are being eliminated.

Column two of the Compactor can also be used to document the objectives and pretest results. First, the teacher should indicate which objectives were pretested for the student. The use of codes, numbered objectives or a reference to page numbers in the teacher's manual that contain the tested objectives are also acceptable. The reader should be able to understand the extent of the pretest and the specific skills or content objectives on which it is based. The teacher should attempt to record this information as succinctly as possible. The use of abbreviations, attached photocopies of the actual tests or objectives, or a computer-generated Compactor form can help to speed the record-keeping process for all involved. In documenting student performance on the pretest, more than an overall percentile score is needed. It does a reader little good to see that a student mastered eighty-five percent of ten objectives because an average score does not indicate which objectives were not mastered. It could mean that the student did not demonstrate mastery of two objectives and demonstrated perfect mastery of eight other objectives. Only by documenting the scores of *each* objective can objectives be identified which should be compacted.

COMPLETING THE THIRD COLUMN OF THE COMPACTOR

The third column, "Acceleration and/or Enrichment Activities," contains information about how time is to be spent that has been provided by the compacting process. More will be said about these enrichment options later in the chapter. Examples of third column entries can be found on pages 80–90.

ALTERNATIVES TO THE COMPACTOR

Some teachers might find that using the Compactor is redundant in light of the other record-keeping devices already being used. The decision to use or amend the Compactor is one that can and should be made by individual teachers or a committee of teachers within the building or school district. The use of the form enables the teacher to document all instances of change from the regular curriculum.

If you work in a state or province that has a mandate for gifted education, the Compactor might also be used to reduce some of the paperwork required for students who are receiving special, state-funded services. In many of these cases, gifted education is classified under the auspices of the special education program and the due process procedures that are required by Public Law 94-142. In these situations, the use of the

Compactor has often been used as a substitute for the Individual Education Plan (IEP) that is required. Since the Compactor documents all instances of curricular modification, it can easily be used to record the assessment information that led to compacting. It will also provide information about the enrichment or acceleration options that were offered to students who took advantage of the compacting procedure.

Some teachers prefer to keep track of students' pretest scores on a large matrix in which every student's name appears. Teachers might use checklists or matrices that are provided with their textbook series or adapt existing forms for their own purposes. Others prefer to keep records for each student in the class. The latter approach can also be combined with an individual student record (for the student's file) and a contract that describes required assignments and optional activities. The form on page 78 illustrates one of these group matrices in which the teacher records the number of correct items next to the total number (for example, 28 / 30).

THE IMPORTANCE OF DOCUMENTATION

Whether you choose to use the Compactor, to modify it, or to use your own record-keeping devices, we strongly recommend that some form of documentation be kept. These devices can also be used during parent-teacher conferences or by teachers in subsequent grade levels to continue the use of the compacting procedure. Students who move and transfer to a new school system should have documentation of compacting in their cumulative file. Without this information the student is likely to repeat inappropriate grade-level material. The existence of the Compactor allows teachers in the new school to identify the student's strengths without the need to repeat extensive testing procedures. Teachers can begin to compare these strengths and compacted skill objectives with the curriculum at the new school.

These records can also be used to support the compacting process. Robert Ringer (1973) believes in the power of the written word and contends that the individuals who come to a meeting or conference with information or a proposal *on paper* usually succeed in winning their case or furthering their cause. He further suggests that most people who attend such meetings come unprepared having given only cursory thought to the topics to be discussed. By preparing for the meeting through the development of a written plan or document, teachers are more likely to win the concessions that they are seeking.

This is especially true for the teacher who is trying to use the compacting process in a less than supportive situation. Consider the primary grade teacher who has been attempting to compact curriculum for her bright readers during the last two years. Her efforts have been thwarted several times by the district's reading supervisor. When the teacher asked for a single copy of the pretest that accompanied the district's reading series, she was told by the supervisor that the pretests were not to be used and that the post tests were to be given to the class as a large group after finishing each of the two required readers for their grade level. Teachers in the district were told to teach the reading series to the whole group and that no student should be using an out-of-level book or test. The situation was extremely frustrating. Finally, the teacher located a norm-referenced, diagnostic reading test that gave her the ammunition she needed to confront the supervisor about the policy of large-group instruction in the district's

GRADE SIX MATH RESULTS—TEXTBOOK CHAPTER ONE

Student Name: _____ Teacher: _____ Year: _____ **Student Profile**

Addison-Wesley Mathematics
Book 4

Chapter		Objectives	Multiple Choice Test Items Missed	Free Response Test Items Missed	Needs More Work	Accomplished
1 **Addition** **and** **Subtraction** **Facts**	1.1	Recalls addition and subtraction facts. Items 1–30	/30	/30		
	1.2	Add three 1-digit numbers using addition facts: Items 31–36.	/6	/6		
	1.3	Solve word problems using the 5-Point Checklist and cumulative computationaal skills. Items 37–41	/5	/5		
		Score:				
2 **Place** **Value**	2.1	Read, write, and compare numbers through four digits. Items 1–13	/13	/13		
	2.2	Round to the nearest ten, hundred, thousand, or dollar. Items 14–21	/8	/8		
	2.3	Read, write, and compare numbers through six digits. Items 22–26	/5	/5		
	2.4	Write standard sumbers for Roan numerals. Items 27–28	/2	/2		
	2.5	Read and write numbers through nine digits. Items 29–30	/2	/2		
	2.6	Count coins and dollars, make change, and use money notation through three digits. Items 31–35	/5	/5		
		Score:				
3 **Addition** **and** **Subtraction**	3.1	Add 2-, 3-, 4- and 5-digit numbers, including money. Items 1–12	/12	/12		
	3.2	Estimate ssums by rounding to the nearest ten, hundred, or dollar. Items 13–16	/4	/4		
	3.3	Add up to four 2-, 3-, and 4-digit numbers including money . Items 17–21	/5	/5		
	3.4	Subtract 2-, 3-, 4-, and 5-digit numbers, including money. Items 22–36	/15	/15		
	3.5	Estimate differences by rounding to the nearest ten hundred, or dollar. Items 37–40	/4	/4		
	3.6	Solve word problems using the 5-Point Checklost and cumulative computational skills. Items 41–45	/5	/5		
		Score:				
4 **Multiplication** **Facts**	4.1	Recall multiplication facts. Items 1–22	/22	/22		
	4.2	Identifiy multiples of 1-digit numbers. Item 23	/1	/1		
	4.3	Identify a missing factor given a product and one factor. Items 24–29	/6	/6		
	4.4	Solve word problems using the 5-Point Checklist and cumulative computational skills. Items 30–35	/6	/6		
		Score:				

Record Keeping

TRB 4

reading program. Armed with a printed set of objectives for the grade-level reading program and a set of tests scores from the diagnostic reading test, the teacher called a conference with the reading supervisor and her principal. As she expected, when she showed the supervisor the actual test scores for the able readers in her classroom and suggested that these students were wasting their time by participating in needless instruction and practice, the supervisor backed down. Although the teacher has still not been allowed to use out-of-level basal readers, she has been given permission to substitute trade books for the bright readers who have demonstrated skill mastery.

This teacher proved her case by using documentation to substantiate her students' content strength. This situation is not rare. Parents, fellow teachers and administrators may question a decision to modify the standard curriculum. Through attempts to define, preassess and document learning objectives, teachers can better explain why some students can be excused from selected instruction or practice. In the end, this documentation may even convince others to compact curriculum as well.

EXAMPLES OF CURRICULUM COMPACTING

We have found that it is often helpful to examine a number of completed Compactor forms to learn how other teachers have used this process. In this way, teachers may be able to use the process in various settings with various types of student strengths. Included in this chapter are Compactors for students of varying ages and educational settings. Some of the Compactors were completed by classroom teachers who also have the benefit of an enrichment teacher who works with targeted students on a weekly basis in their schools; others were completed by teachers who do not have this service.

SAMPLE ELEMENTARY GRADE COMPACTORS

Eileen's Compactor

Eileen is a fifth grader in a self-contained classroom in a very small school located in a lower socioeconomic urban school district. Most of her twenty-nine classmates are reading one to two years below grade level while Eileen's total reading and language arts scores range between two and almost five years above grade level. Eileen's classroom teacher faced a problem many other teachers face—he had thirty students in the class but no one was close to Eileen's reading level. The teacher agreed to compact curriculum but also insisted that he had to use the easiest possible approach. Eileen was asked to take all of the unit and level tests in the Holt Basal Language Arts program, and she was excused from doing the activities and worksheets from the units covered by the pretests on which she clearly indicated proficiency (85% and above). If Eileen missed one or two questions, her classroom teacher would quickly check for trends in those items missed and if a pattern of errors existed, instruction was provided to assure concept mastery. Eileen usually participated in language arts instruction for one or two days a week and the rest of the time was used for alternative activities, some of which were selected by Eileen.

This strategy saved Eileen as much as six or eight hours a week of basic skills activities in language arts that were simply too easy for her. She participated in group instruction only when her pretests indicated she had not mastered the skills. In the time saved, a number of alternatives were implemented for Eileen. First, she spent up to five hours a week in a resource room for above-average students. This time was almost always scheduled during Eileen's language arts class, thereby achieving two goals for her and her teacher. First, Eileen's teacher did not have to spend time looking for alternative activities during this time block because Eileen spent the majority of the time in the resource room. Second, the time that Eileen spent in the resource room did not result in a pile of make-up work that had to be completed when she returned to the classroom because she was not missing essential work.

The third column of the compactor includes information about the time Eileen spent in the resource room, as well as time spent on enrichment units in science, another of Eileen's strength areas. Based on the results of an Interest-A-Lyzer Eileen completed, the topic of famous women emerged as an interest. (More will be said about this assessment tool later.) Eileen and her classroom teacher identified seven biographies of famous women that were challenging and locally available. Three of those biographies were adult books that Eileen had no trouble reading.

This compactor covered the first semester and was updated at the end of January. Eileen's teacher indicated that learning how to compact curriculum had convinced him that he actually saved time that was usually spent correcting papers that should not have been assigned! The benefits to Eileen also convinced him of the value of continuing the compacting process.

INDIVIDUAL EDUCATIONAL PROGRAMMING GUIDE
The Compactor

Prepared by: Joseph S. Renzulli
Linda H. Smith

NAME Eileen   AGE ___ TEACHER(S) ___   Individual Conference Dates And Persons Participating in Planning Of IEP

SCHOOL ___   GRADE 5   PARENT(S) ___

CURRICULUM AREAS TO BE CONSIDERED FOR COMPACTING Provide a brief description of basic material to be covered during this marking period and the assessment information or evidence that suggests the need for compacting.	PROCEDURES FOR COMPACTING BASIC MATERIAL Describe activities that will be used to guarantee proficiency in basic curricular areas.	ACCELERATION AND/OR ENRICHMENT ACTIVITIES Describe activities that will be used to provide advanced level learning experiences in each area of the regular curriculum.
Language Arts: Holt 14: Units 2-6 Pre test Units 2-6 Decoding/encoding skills Language skills CTBS Scores Vocabulary 6.5 Language Mechanics 9.9 Comprehension 9.5 Language Expression 9.9 Total Reading 7.9 Total Language 9.8	Unit and level tests in Holt Language Arts Eileen will participate in language arts activities in the classroom except those involving: decoding/encoding skills and Language skills already mastered and any kind of "seatwork" (repetitious work.)	Advanced Exposure in Language Arts To read biographies for the purpose of enriching Eileen's background in literature and to see how the following human value applies to her selections: "Determination and courage are often necessary to achieve one's goals" Amelia Earhart Abigail Adams Phillis Whaitley Harriet Beecher Stowe Anne Bradstreet Mahalia Jackson Dolly Madison
	Time gained from this will go towards Eileen's enrichment activities in Language Arts.	Also, Eileen will choose novels from the Newberry Award series to increase vocabulary and deepen understanding of plot structure in terms of introduction, complication, climax, and resolution.
		Advanced Exposure in Science 8 trips to regional science center for extension, differentiated and intensive instruction in the area of computers and calculators, chronobiology and weather and time to
		instruct others in class on above areas. Resource room - 5 hours a week. Type I, II and III activities developing creative thinking, critical thinking, creative and critical problem solving.

☐ Check here if additional information is recorded on the reverse side.

Brad's Compactor

Brad displays strengths in language arts and mathematics. He attends a larger school than Alison which has the benefit of having a reading and math consultant on the staff. Both of these consultants helped with the pretesting administered to Brad and several other high potential students from the fourth grade. Brad's Compactor was completed by his classroom teacher who stapled the results of the pretest to the form. This explains why column one is less detailed than in other compacting examples. Brad's strengths are clearly noted, as are the strategies that will be used to eliminate content he already knows and the methods for guaranteeing proficiency in column two.

Brad did regular curricular work in language arts for only one or two days a week. In spelling, he was consistently able to skip all of the drill and review work necessary to achieve perfect scores on tests, and he used the time saved to pursue advanced reading in the Great Books program.

In mathematics, he was able to master all of his fourth grade curriculum in approximately two days each week. Brad worked with three other students of similar ability in a cooperative learning group (comprised of high ability math students who all liked math) to be able to master math at this pace. The group then selected alternatives listed in column three to pursue separately or as a group during mathematics instruction time.

INDIVIDUAL EDUCATIONAL PROGRAMMING GUIDE
The Compactor

Prepared by: Joseph S. Renzulli
Linda H. Smith

NAME ___Brad___   AGE __9__   TEACHER(S) ___Mrs. Scott___   Individual Conference Dates And Persons Participating in Planning Of IEP

SCHOOL _____   GRADE __4__ PARENT(S) _____

CURRICULUM AREAS TO BE CONSIDERED FOR COMPACTING Provide a brief description of basic material to be covered during this marking period and the assessment information or evidence that suggests the need for compacting.	PROCEDURES FOR COMPACTING BASIC MATERIAL Describe activities that will be used to guarantee proficiency in basic curricular areas.	ACCELERATION AND/OR ENRICHMENT ACTIVITIES Describe activities that will be used to provide advanced level learning experiences in each area of the regular curriculum.
1. Language Arts Text: Holt, Level 13 and novels.	1. Read independently at own pace. 2. Limited use of skills sheets and workbook. No reinforcedment or exercises showing mastery. 3. Emphasis on critical thinking, comprehension and literary skills. 4. Enrichment activities 5. Supplemental materials provided by the readingconsultant	1. Critical thinking - Talents Unlimited 2. USSR 3. Great Books 4. Process Writing 5. Story Mapping 6. Advanced research skills 7. Response-Oriented Projects:Writing, Arts, Geography 8. Time for Independent Study Project
2. Spelling	1. No reinforcement of words mastered. 2. Bonus words	
3. Math 　　Text: Addison-Wesley 　　Group: Enriched	1. Pace according to Brad's needs 2. No reinforcement on items that show proficiency 3. Limit extra practice - do just odd or just even examples. 4. Use supplemental materials provided by math consultant 5. Enrichment activities	1. Logical thinking 2. Probability and statistics 3. "Menu" learning center math 4. Puzzles and games—ex: tangrams, magic squares, number palindromes 5. Square One Videos 6. Geometry 7. Computer programs 8. Time for Independent Study Project

☐ Check here if additional information is recorded on the reverse side.

No gifted program existed in Brad's district, so his classroom teacher had to work much harder to provide appropriate instruction and alternatives for column three. However, assistance was provided by the math and language-arts consultants who worked with groups of either remedial or advanced students and who also provided enrichment materials and appropriately advanced content for targeted students. The media specialist directed the independent study of students whose curriculum was compacted.

Alison's Compactor

Alison's Compactor reflects strengths in three areas. In language arts, she mastered most of the comprehension skills for the levels that were to be introduced in first grade and all of the spelling levels. In math she received almost a perfect score on the placement test and the follow-up individual tests for each level. She is a very precocious student in a very small elementary school. She had few peers who were at a similar achievement level, and she was very interested in math and science. It was clear that she could master all of the rest of her language arts objectives in one day each week.

Column two includes a listing of skills Alison had *not* mastered in the first-grade language-arts program. She met with her first-grade group about one day each week or every other week to work on these areas. Her teacher also asked her to join the group whenever an enrichment lesson or an appropriate writing lesson was being taught. Because no other student in Alison's grade level was at a similar level, a decision was

INDIVIDUAL EDUCATIONAL PROGRAMMING GUIDE
The Compactor

Prepared by: Joseph S. Renzulli
Linda H. Smith

NAME_____Alison_____   AGE___6___ TEACHER(S)_____   Individual Conference Dates And Persons Participating in Planning Of IEP

SCHOOL_____   GRADE__1__ PARENT(S)_____   _____ _____ _____

CURRICULUM AREAS TO BE CONSIDERED FOR COMPACTING Provide a brief description of basic material to be covered during this marking period and the assessment information or evidence that suggests the need for compacting.	PROCEDURES FOR COMPACTING BASIC MATERIAL Describe activities that will be used to guarantee proficiency in basic curricular areas.	ACCELERATION AND/OR ENRICHMENT ACTIVITIES Describe activities that will be used to provide advanced level learning experiences in each area of the regular curriculum.
Holt Basic Reading Series - levels 3-6. As determined by Holt level tests, Alison has mastered most of the comprehension and phonetic objectives introduced in these levels.	Capital letters and periods - Teacher-made worksheets & Continental Press worksheets. She will participate in classroom activities dealing with these skills. Check proficiency by Holt level 6 test. Capital letters and periods - pg 27	Classroom Her classroom teacher will use the language experience approach. Achievement units on the Hoffman machine will be used with her (builds on Comprehension and incorporates handwriting.) Readers Digest Skill Builders will strengthen her comprehension, sequencing and higher level thinking skills. Scholastic Individual Reading Kit will provide opportunity to
Individualized Spelling Program by Economy - Alison has mastered levels 1-4. She will be placed in level 5.	Contractions - Level 7 Teacher's manual pages 81, 119, 175, 216, 217 and 255-256. Check proficiency by Holt Level 7 test (Contractions)	
Math - As determined by the first grade math placement test, Alison has mastered most of this curriculum. She will begin her math program in Miss Hirchak's 2nd grade classroom.	Change y to i and add es/and other plural forms: Level 9. Teacher's manual pages 202 and 293-294. Level 8 manual pages 222-223, 246, 311. Check proficiency by Holt Level 9 test and reading consultant-made test for these plural forms not covered in the Level 9 test.	read independently and use instructional games and records. Alison will be provided with time to work in her classroom on a Type III activity (independent study)
	Compound Words - Level 9 teacher's manual. Pages 77, 267. Check for proficiency - level 9 test page 9 (compound words)	Talcott Mt. Science Center Alison will participate in approximately seven field trips to the Center and will also take part in Talcott Mt. programs presented in school.
	Pronouns - Level 9 teacher's manual page 325. Check for proficiency - level 9 test (language skills) page 9	TAC resource room Critical thinking skills, creative thinking skills creative problem solving, critical problem solving, Type III independent study.

☐ Check here if additional information is recorded on the reverse side.

made to accelerate her to the second grade classroom for mathematics. It must be pointed out that Alison's first-grade teacher did not believe she could provide an individualized math program because of time restraints and other demands. It should also be noted that a move into the second grade classroom was not a panacea for meeting Alison's considerable strengths in math. For students who are precocious in mathematics, acceleration of only one grade is often not much more challenging than working on their own grade level material. In Alison's case, however, since she was so young, acceleration to grade two content did provide her with more challenge, and it also provided her with an opportunity to complete more advanced work on something she loved—mathematics. She was able to complete the regular second-grade math curriculum in half the time of other students, and the second-grade teacher worked to provide challenging content in the remaining time Alison was in the classroom.

It should also be noted that Alison was well suited to move into another classroom. Not only was she extremely intelligent, she was also quite mature for her age. She had already accepted her individual differences, often telling her teacher in the gifted program that she had realized from the time she was three or four years old that she was different from the children in her play group. Other very bright children are *not* happy when they are singled out for curriculum compacting. In fact, with some students, the process of helping them accept services is a slow and careful one because they consistently tell their teachers that they do not want to be different—they want to do the exact same work as their peers, *even if they have known the skills for years*. In this case, their anxieties and the type of whole-group instruction that has been standard in schools for so long must be recognized. If they had been taught to do work that was tailored to their needs, this particular problem would not exist. When it does, students must be helped to understand that requiring different assignments and work is appropriate. However, this process often takes time.

Alison's options in column three were many and varied. She worked on an Apple Computer in her classroom that provided advanced reading and writing options. She was offered independent, advanced reading opportunities and a regular opportunity to discuss these books with her teacher. She spent up to five hours each week in a resource room gifted program in her school. Time in the program resulted from specific instances of curriculum compacting in the classroom. During this time, she worked on a variety of experiences: independent study with close monitoring and guidance from her resource teacher, units designed to provide advanced content, critical and creative thinking skills, and other alternatives based on Alison's curricular strengths and interests. She also participated in science enrichment units taught by scientists from the regional science center. These units were designed to be presented to interested students with optional follow-up provided if students wished to pursue this option. Working with older students with whom she interacted quite well, Alison pursued two topics in which she was interested.

David's Compactor

David is a mathematically talented student who is a sixth grader in a school district which has a policy against vertical acceleration in mathematics. Many of the districts that have participated in field tests of curriculum compacting have stated policies that do not allow students to be accelerated past their chronological grade level in any content area. Obviously, this is a dilemma for talented students and their teachers.

However, it should also be noted that the dumbing down of textbooks and the ease with which talented students can master regular curriculum may result in little additional challenge being provided even when a student *is* moved into the next content level material. Accordingly, if an individual classroom teacher is willing and able to pursue appropriate alternatives, the program that is developed for talented students may be made more challenging than what a student would receive if a placement was simply made into the next grade level textbook.

In David's case, curriculum compacting resulted in the completion of his math work for the entire year in the first six weeks of school. His teacher decided to compact in this way instead of having David work with his group one day each week for the year. The teacher believed that this option worked in a more efficient manner for his very organized, structured classroom. Also, the identification of another student with abilities similar to David's enabed David and her to work as learning partners throughout the year.

The classroom teacher selected various mathematics enrichment activities, as described in the district's math curriculum guide for David's grade. He also selected several math alternative enrichment activities for David's work in the classroom. David also spent two hours a week of his mathematics instructional time in the gifted and talented program resource room with a teacher who further enriched his math program with computer skills.

INDIVIDUAL EDUCATIONAL PROGRAMMING GUIDE
The Compactor

Prepared by: Joseph S. Renzulli
Linda H. Smith

NAME __David__   AGE __11__   TEACHER(S) _____   Individual Conference Dates And Persons Participating in Planning Of IEP

SCHOOL _____   GRADE ____   PARENT(S) _____

CURRICULUM AREAS TO BE CONSIDERED FOR COMPACTING Provide a brief description of basic material to be covered during this marking period and the assessment information or evidence that suggests the need for compacting.	PROCEDURES FOR COMPACTING BASIC MATERIAL Describe activities that will be used to guarantee proficiency in basic curricular areas.	ACCELERATION AND/OR ENRICHMENT ACTIVITIES Describe activities that will be used to provide advanced level learning experiences in each area of the regular curriculum.
Math 6th Grade Health test with 6th Grade Math Curriculum objectives.	Major check-ups: pg. 62, 94, 120, 150, 174, 198, 224, 258, 278, 300 and 316	Advanced Exposure to Math: Inductive thinking skills: Open Ended Problems by A. Harnadek. Logic skills: Classroom Quickies by A. Harnadek; What Are My Chances? by A Shulte; Aftermath II by M. Laycock
CTBS Score in Math 10/78 8.7 OGE	Concentrated activities to develop mastery in multiplying by a 3-digit number, dividing with fractions, operations with decimals, finding percents, integers	Using above references, he will increase his ability to understand problems using probability induction, deduction, spatial perception, inferences, cause and effect, analogy, relevant information and logic.
Skills test at the end of 6th Grade test Mastery of all skills except for: multiplying a number by a 3-digit number dividing by a 2 or 3 digit number <u>dividing with fractions</u>	+ Recommended and additional activities in Math as outlined by district's Mathematics Curriculum objectives for Grade 6.	
operations with decimals finding percents integers		

☐ Check here if additional information is recorded on the reverse side.

Liza's Compactor

Liza is such an advanced student that compacting is needed in almost every content area. As with the other Compactors, documentation from pretests is provided to demonstrate the need for the service and a wide variety of alternatives is provided in column three in language arts and mathematics. Liza's interests in journalism resulted in the creation of a fifth-grade classroom newspaper which was developed by Liza with the help of volunteers from her classroom. No gifted program existed in Liza's school, so without a great deal of flexibility and effort on the part of her classroom teacher, these creative alternatives would not have been provided.

In October, Liza had completed all of the spelling in the advanced individualized program that her teacher provided, so her spelling work became spell-checking and editing the fifth-grade newspaper. She was accelerated into grade six, and subsequently, grade seven mathematics and did extremely well in both areas.

The compacting in social studies demonstrates the difference between basic skills and content compacting. Liza did not know the curriculum in social studies because she had not studied these specific areas. However, because she was so bright and has attained some general knowledge in geography and social studies, she learned the year's content in one month. Content compacting provides students who do not know the objectives the opportunity to master them in a time frame which matches their potential.

INDIVIDUAL EDUCATIONAL PROGRAMMING GUIDE
The Compactor

Prepared by: Joseph S. Renzulli
Linda H. Smith

NAME Liza   AGE 10   TEACHER(S) _____   Individual Conference Dates And Persons Participating in Planning Of IEP

SCHOOL _____   GRADE 5   PARENT(S) _____   _____ _____ _____

CURRICULUM AREAS TO BE CONSIDERED FOR COMPACTING Provide a brief description of basic material to be covered during this marking period and the assessment information or evidence that suggests the need for compacting.	PROCEDURES FOR COMPACTING BASIC MATERIAL Describe activities that will be used to guarantee proficiency in basic curricular areas.	ACCELERATION AND/OR ENRICHMENT ACTIVITIES Describe activities that will be used to provide advanced level learning experiences in each area of the regular curriculum.
English Unit on adjectives (identification, proper adjectives, comparing adjectives) Unit on nouns (proper, common, possessive plurals, identification) Unit on Capital Letters	Teacher-made tests in all areas described Continental Press dittos used as test Will work on individual tests on articles (a, an, the) and possessive adjectives.	Start a school newspaper to be published once a month Liza will edit the Geography and Travel section of the school newspaper. Liza will also write a monthly column.
Math Unit on fractions (adding, subtracting, multiplying, dividing)	Teacher-made tests Unit 7 test Macmillan Mathematics 5 Math curriculum post-tests	Will be able to move to multiplying and dividing since mastery was shown in other areas. Acceleration.
Spelling Words in Ecomony Press Kit on Individualizing Spelling—one week. Next week—works with teacher in directed activities from Harper/Row Basic Speller 5.	Is on highest level in spelling kit. Daily work Teacher-made tests where she shows knowledge of spelling rules.	School newspaper (see above) – independent study project
Social Studies U.S. Geography - Geography and the history of New England	Teacher-made tests to show basic understanding of geography, production, colonial history	Individual project work on history and geography of New England (specifically Rhode Island.)

☐ Check here if additional information is recorded on the reverse side.

In the case of a very bright student, the activities listed in column three should offer appropriately challenging content. However, it is also important that a student does not perceive that he or she is being punished because of high ability. This often occurs when harder and more math problems replace the regular math curriculum and then the old refrain often emerges:

Slow down - you're working too fast

You've got to make the regular work last

Or else - you'll get harder work as a reward.

This scenario occurs in classrooms across our country each day. Students like Liza do their very best work and are "rewarded" with countless repetitions of more work. In this Compactor, it should be noted that the replacement activities for Liza are based on her interests. The replacement activities listed in column three will encourage her to do her best work in order to have the time to pursue these alternatives.

Group Compactor

Many of the teachers involved in our field tests of curriculum compacting have preferred to use group compacting to address the needs of students of similar ability in math, language arts, or other content areas. Through our research studies (Reis et al., 1992), we also learned that if one or two students were targeted to have their curriculum compacted, the classroom teacher often extended this service to other students who

INDIVIDUAL EDUCATIONAL PROGRAMMING GUIDE
The Compactor

Prepared by: Joseph S. Renzulli
Linda H. Smith

NAME High Reading Group   AGE_____ TEACHER(S)____S. Ksenych_____

Individual Conference Dates And Persons Participating in Planning Of IEP

SCHOOL _____East_____   GRADE__4__ PARENT(S) _____   S. K.   S. L.   T. H.

CURRICULUM AREAS TO BE CONSIDERED FOR COMPACTING Provide a brief description of basic material to be covered during this marking period and the assessment information or evidence that suggests the need for compacting.	PROCEDURES FOR COMPACTING BASIC MATERIAL Describe activities that will be used to guarantee proficiency in basic curricular areas.	ACCELERATION AND/OR ENRICHMENT ACTIVITIES Describe activities that will be used to provide advanced level learning experiences in each area of the regular curriculum.

I.   Language Arts
    Test: Holt
    Level: 13
    Unit: 5
	1. No reinforcement on exercises in the Holt reading series showing mastery.
	2. No assignments in workbook pages of skills mastered.
	3. Check proficiency by the Holt Unit tests
		1. Reading for pleasure
		2. Creative writing (poetry, short stories, etc.)
		3. Monthly book reports.
		4. Participation in Talcott Mt. Science Center programs
		5. RFU Reading Kit
		6. Reading Comprehension Library--Level D
		7. Research skills training in relation to Type III projects and classroom projects

II. As determined by the Holt Unit tests, these students consistently master over 85% in each skill area of the unit test.		
III. Spelling These students continue to achieve a grade of 100 on all spelling tests.	Spelling The Economy Individualized Spelling Program will be utilized with this entire group.	8. Letters of various types (In conjunction with Mrs. Beck) 9. Letter writing--related to Type III projects 10. Type II Training activities in Resource Room 11. Mini-Course in Human Anatomy--with Mrs. Beck and Miss Towne "Bobby Bones" -- construction of human skeleton. 12. "Be a Better Reader" Alison--Level C
		Eric--Level B 13. TYPE III Independent Study Projects in the Resource Room

☐ Check here if additional information is recorded on the reverse side.

displayed strengths in the curriculum area. Group compacting is a practical approach to use if a teacher is interested in pretesting the entire class on units or skills that will be covered in a certain content area.

This group Compactor is an example of this practice. Students who displayed mastery of a unit in language arts did not have to do any of the exercises, activities or workbook pages related to the skills in the unit. Other students in the class were grouped together (for this unit only) by the number of skills they had yet to master. This enabled the teacher to compact skills for more students.

The targeted group described in this Compactor had several options listed in the third column. During the time the other students in the class were working on skills they had not yet mastered, the students in this group were working on alternative tasks. Some days, the teacher would meet with the group during regular language arts instructional time, give an assignment such as a group reading from the Junior Great Books program, followed by a discussion later in the week. Other times, students were able to select one of the alternative assignments listed in column three based on their own interests. During language arts instructional time, some of the students were also allowed to go to the resource room in the district to work with a facilitator on an interest-based independent or small group project. This group Compactor indicates that many students can benefit from curriculum compacting beyond those normally identified and placed in gifted and talented programs. In research studies on curriculum compacting, most participating teachers indicated that they could use curriculum compacting with other students than those formally identified for the gifted program.

SAMPLE SECONDARY GRADE COMPACTORS

As mentioned earlier, it is a more challenging task to implement curriculum compacting in a secondary school. More classes, more preparations for different classes, a large variety of student needs and a restrictive schedule all contribute to the challenges faced by secondary teachers who want to modify curriculum for their most able students.

Secondary teachers consistently indicate that it is easier to compact curriculum for students of similar ability. Several grouping alternatives and programming suggestions are available for those who want to examine *The Secondary Triad Model* (Reis and Renzulli, 1986). Several group compacting and classroom organization strategies are provided within this model.

For secondary teachers who are interested in implementing curriculum compacting, the strategies and steps outlined in this book can be used as described. Assessment may take longer, however, since there are many more students to test. Secondary teachers may want to select one student who obviously needs the service from one to two of their classes and begin with those students. The sample secondary compactors (Juanita, Caitlin and Bill) should be helpful to secondary teachers.

Caitlin's Compactor

Caitlin is a sophomore who excels in science. She is particularly interested in biology, and her teacher has been able to compact her curriculum because Caitlin can cover basic concepts in biology three to four times faster than most students. She is also interested in ecology and has indicated that she would like to pursue an ecological examination of an area near the high school.

The teacher, Donna Johnson, encouraged Caitlin to read her biology textbook at an appropriate pace, and Caitlin usually read three or four chapters in the same time her peers read one. Ms. Johnson made chapter tests available to Caitlin so that as she completed each chapter she could take a test. Occasionally, Ms. Johnson would involve Caitlin in the classroom discussions, but usually Caitlin was encouraged to work on her advanced lab work or her independent study in ecology. Ms. Johnson also sent a form asking whether compacting could be accomplished to all of Caitlin's other teachers to let them know about her independent study. Caitlin's English teacher responded by indicating that she would allow Caitlin to use her findings from her ecology study as her term paper instead of choosing from a predetermined list of English topics. In this way, she was able to pursue her interests in ecology and also meet her English term paper requirements. Her English teacher's objectives in assigning the term paper was to have students learn the mechanics and form of writing a paper—footnotes, references, formatting—and learn the skills of note taking and using primary sources.

Caitlin's biology teacher later indicated that monitoring Caitlin's independent study in ecology was among her most exciting and rewarding teaching experiences. She also was delighted that Caitlin had become so interested in this area of science that she decided to pursue a major in this area in college.

INDIVIDUAL EDUCATIONAL PROGRAMMING GUIDE
The Compactor

Prepared by: Joseph S. Renzulli
Linda H. Smith

NAME __Caitlin__   AGE __15__   TEACHER(S) __D. Johnson__   Individual Conference Dates And Persons Participating in Planning Of IEP

SCHOOL __De Soto High School__   GRADE __10__   PARENT(S) _____

CURRICULUM AREAS TO BE CONSIDERED FOR COMPACTING Provide a brief description of basic material to be covered during this marking period and the assessment information or evidence that suggests the need for compacting.	PROCEDURES FOR COMPACTING BASIC MATERIAL Describe activities that will be used to guarantee proficiency in basic curricular areas.	ACCELERATION AND/OR ENRICHMENT ACTIVITIES Describe activities that will be used to provide advanced level learning experiences in each area of the regular curriculum.
Biology I Terrestrial Ecology-Chapter 2 BSCS text Has no trouble in grasping basic concepts, and can master material 3 to 4 times faster than most students.	After reading each chapter, Caitlin will take chapter test or teacher-made test of material.	Independent study option: Ecology study of the area north of football field. Species diversity of herbs, birds, mammals.
Modern Biology Text First semester's work chapters 1-19	Chapter test and/or teacher made test to be taken after individual study in area is completed.	Possible study of how local area farming practices have changed basic ecology of area in the last 300 years.
Laboratory Techniques Mastered or will be able to master all necessary skills in a short period of time.	Teacher directed quiz on Lab equipment, uses, and applications to ecology.	Independent laboratory experiments and projects under the guidance of D. Johnson.
	As soon as Caitlin has mastered material for each chapter, she will be excused from class to work on activities described in column three.	

☐ Check here if additional information is recorded on the reverse side.

Juanita's Compactor

Juanita was a freshman in high school who had been an avid reader all her life. She had scored the highest percentile nationally (99%) on the Iowa Test of Basic Skills and had already read two of the novels to be covered in ninth-grade English. She was an excellent writer who had published two poems and a short story in a local junior-high-school literary journal. Juanita never failed to seek additional help on her writing and was an independent worker who often wrote several drafts of the same story. Her use of vocabulary exceeded her peers, as did her mastery of basic mechanics of writing.

Juanita's teacher learned of her motivation and love of writing during the first week of school when Juanita asked her if she would be willing to read a draft of one of her stories and offer critical suggestions. During the first month of school, Juanita's teacher was asked to read four short stories and a selection of her poems.

Juanita had previously read most of the American fiction and non-fiction that was assigned in this class, so an assessment was conducted to determine if she understood the themes and the vocabulary in these works. Her spelling and vocabulary work was substituted for more advanced work in the other period novels she had selected to read. She was occasionally asked to participate in class lectures or discussions either to introduce materials she did not know or to discuss more advanced themes or issues. Juanita would often come to class to check in and then leave to spend time in the library working on the alternative assignments listed in column three of her Compactor.

INDIVIDUAL EDUCATIONAL PROGRAMMING GUIDE
The Compactor

Prepared by: Joseph S. Renzulli
Linda H. Smith

NAME ___Juanita___   AGE __14__ TEACHER(S) ___C. Cooper___   Individual Conference Dates And Persons Participating in Planning Of IEP

SCHOOL ___Concord High___   GRADE _9_ PARENT(S) _____

CURRICULUM AREAS TO BE CONSIDERED FOR COMPACTING Provide a brief description of basic material to be covered during this marking period and the assessment information or evidence that suggests the need for compacting.	PROCEDURES FOR COMPACTING BASIC MATERIAL Describe activities that will be used to guarantee proficiency in basic curricular areas.	ACCELERATION AND/OR ENRICHMENT ACTIVITIES Describe activities that will be used to provide advanced level learning experiences in each area of the regular curriculum.
1. Vocabulary 2. Mastery of grammar- subordinate and verbal classes 3. Has mastered mechanics of basic writing skills (has publishing in local literary journal) 4. Has read two books covered in the English curriculum such as Huckle-berry Finn	1. Give a pretest to determine which vocabulary words student already knows-student studies only words he doesn't know and takes quiz to demonstrate mastery. 2. Use mastery tests from Warner's English Grammar review to see if she has mastered grammar skills--individualize practice for problem areas.	1. Juanita can work on individual research on a self-selected topic in American literature during the time the rest of the class spends on vocabulary and grammar. 2. Juanita can read other books by the author of books she has already read ... another book by Mark Twain.
Achievement Test Scores (ITBS) 99% (national) score in Reading, Vocabulary, Spelling	3. Evaluate writing sample based on books already read such as Huckleberry Finn. Evaluate for mechanics, organization and thesis development. If mechanics are mastered, focus on thematic content.	3. Juanita can use the resource library provided by classroom teacher and librarian to focus on historical and biographical material during this literary period.
Juanita will continue to write fiction independently and her teacher will critique her efforts.	4. Make sure student reads and attends class when covering new literature--historical background could be attained from primary source material.	

☐ Check here if additional information is recorded on the reverse side.

Bill's Compactor

Bill's area of strength and interest was history. His sophomore U.S. history teacher knew Bill before he entered his class because Bill had often approached him asking to borrow textbooks or primary source books about the Civil War. His love for U.S. history in general, and his knowledge and fascination for the Civil War period, were well known to the entire history department. His history teacher had never requested help in the compacting process before, but Bill provided a good opportunity to field test it with a student who would obviously benefit from it.

As indicated in column one below, Bill is an excellent student. Besides having high achievement test scores, he also has read numerous texts and non-fiction books on American history, received top grades, and collects Civil War memorabilia as a hobby.

Bill took a mid-term exam in September—usually given in January—to determine his knowledge of American history. He scored an A+. He was excused from most discussions and class assignments (such as answering the questions at the end of every chapter, outlining each chapter, doing group work related to concepts he already knew). Instead, he did independent reading, continued his research on Civil War Memorabilia, worked in the congressional campaign of a local candidate and conducted intensive research on the Kennedy/Nixon debates during the 1960 election. All of these alternative learning experiences were made possible because Bill's teacher was willing to assess his knowledge in September.

INDIVIDUAL EDUCATIONAL PROGRAMMING GUIDE
The Compactor

Prepared by: Joseph S. Renzulli
Linda H. Smith

NAME __Bill__   AGE __15__   TEACHER(S) __Hébert__   Individual Conference Dates And Persons Participating in Planning Of IEP

SCHOOL __Canton High School__   GRADE __10__   PARENT(S) __Mr. Paul Jordan__   __9/31__ __10/25__ __11/30__ __12/10__

CURRICULUM AREAS TO BE CONSIDERED FOR COMPACTING Provide a brief description of basic material to be covered during this marking period and the assessment information or evidence that suggests the need for compacting.	PROCEDURES FOR COMPACTING BASIC MATERIAL Describe activities that will be used to guarantee proficiency in basic curricular areas.	ACCELERATION AND/OR ENRICHMENT ACTIVITIES Describe activities that will be used to provide advanced level learning experiences in each area of the regular curriculum.
U.S. History - Colonial History to Civil War 1. Reading 3 years above level-Achievement Test Results	1. Bill took an exam covering chapters 2-15 with a grade of A+ to A-	1. Bill will develop skills in museum research (related to Civil War memorabilia).
2. Bill's outside reading has allowed him to investigate many texts on history used in college courses.	2. Bill will write an interpretive paper on a self-selected topic.	2. Bill will develop poll-taking skills and work as a volunteer for a local Congressional candidate.
3. Hobby- collecting Civil War memorabilia. 4. Straight A's in Social Studies.	3. Bill will not have to do regular curriculum work related to history.	3. Bill selected an interest area and will write a research paper on the political debates of 1960: Kennedy vs. Nixon.

☐ Check here if additional information is recorded on the reverse side.

EXAMINING AVAILABLE ALTERNATIVES WITHIN THE SCHOOL DISTRICT OR COMMUNITY

One of the best ways to provide challenging replacement alternatives which will be recorded in the Compactor's third column is to develop a list of all available enrichment and acceleration activities within your school district. This list may be modest to begin with; however, as resources and special services to advanced-level students expand, the list can serve as an important part of the planning and program development process. The following list has been developed around five major organizational topics. Although each topic has a general characteristic, additional enrichment or acceleration options can be planned by combining various elements from among the five major topics.

1. Enrichment in the regular classroom: independent study, small-group investigations, accelerated coverage of the regular curriculum, mini-courses, special interest groups, learning centers, clubs, interest-development centers, use of computer software, learning modules or simulation activities and special lessons that emphasize the development of cognitive and affective processes.

2. Resource room, full and part-time special class (same activities as above): this cluster also includes itinerant teachers who serve as resource persons or special teachers to groups of advanced ability students.

3. Acceleration: grade skipping, honors and advanced placement courses, college courses, summer or evening courses, early admission to kindergarten or first grade, and special seminars, advanced content replacing traditional textbooks at each grade level.

4. Off-campus experiences: internships; mentorships; work-study programs; and participation in community programs such as theatrical groups, symphonies, artists' workshops, and museum programs.

5. Districtwide programs, schoolwide programs or departmental programs: any of the options above, plus independent study programs, correspondence courses, special counseling programs, career education programs, and library-based programs.

A final consideration in providing alternatives is the degree of structure that students generally prefer in learning activities. Students' preferred learning style or mode can be identified formally or informally. One instrument, the Learning Styles Inventory (Renzulli & Smith, 1978b) yields individual student data about preferences for learning under nine types of instructional techniques. Some of these scores reflect a preference for structured activities (such as lecture, programmed instruction, drill and recitation), others imply a greater need for interactive experiences (such as simulation, discussion, peer teaching, teacher games), and still others reflect a preference for an unstructured learning environment (such as projects, independent study). Teachers may also determine preferences by observing or interviewing students. Determining both interests and learning styles can help determine the activities that will be substituted during compacted time: activities that students will *want* to pursue and *enjoy* doing.

ENRICHMENT MATERIALS TO USE IN CLASSROOMS

Many strategies have been successfully used by classroom teachers to substitute more challenging and interesting work for students during time saved through compacting. The simplest strategy is to use commercial materials. Teachers sometimes are able to rely on the services of an enrichment specialist (sometimes called a gifted education teacher). In addition, this teacher is frequently responsible for mentoring a student's projects, investigations and research. In other situations, enrichment teachers provide the classroom teacher with alternative teaching units or supplemental materials. These specialists can be a big help to the busy classroom teacher who has numerous obligations to all of the students in the classroom.

What happens to a classroom teacher who is interested in curriculum compacting but has no "extra pair of hands" to work with students who have time for enrichment or acceleration? How can this teacher provide alternative learning options without relying on meaningless drill or busywork assignments? It might be appropriate to suggest the development of alternative curriculum units, learning centers, or out-of-level assignments, but the creation of enough new lessons and curricular materials are not always feasible. Teachers' and students' needs might be better served through the acquisition of commercially published enrichment and acceleration materials. Numerous publishers and distributors offer high quality materials that can be used successfully by individual or small groups of students at all grade levels. Many of these materials are available at reasonable prices and can be easily reproduced for use with one or more students. In order to save teachers the time required to locate such materials, a list of the more popular materials has been prepared and is reprinted here, providing the following information:

Column	Describes
1	The grade level for whom these materials were designed (P=Primary; I=Intermediate; S=Secondary)
2	The name of the enrichment or acceleration material
3	The content area covered in the materials
4	The size of the group with which the materials can be used. (I=Individual; S=Small group; L=Large group)
5	An indication as to whether the materials are intended for use by teachers (professional) or by teachers and students (instructional)
6	A price code (A=currently less that $15.00; B=between $15.00 and $35.00; C=more than $35.00)
7	The name of the publisher, or at least one distributor from whom these materials are available

Publishers' addresses are included following the list of materials.

Although this is by no means a definitive list of enrichment and acceleration materials, it does represent some of the better known kits, books and activity cards in the field. All of the materials listed in the matrix have been used by one or more of the gifted education specialists at The University of Connecticut and have been useful in providing meaningful alternative assignments for high-ability students. Of course the teacher's teaching style and students' learning style will also determine how best to use the materials in the matrix. Teachers may wish to obtain examination copies of materials that seem appropriate in order to evaluate the materials' components. Criteria for evaluation might include the following:

1. Clearly stated learning objectives
2. A comprehensive teacher's guide
3. The appropriateness of the reading level
4. The need for additional materials or equipment
5. An appealing format
6. Motivating student activities
7. Options for self-directed study or practice
8. Suggestions for using the materials with individuals or small groups.

We also recommend that funds be budgeted every year for the purchase of appropriate enrichment and acceleration materials. Some districts may wish to allow individual teachers to select those materials that best meet the needs of the students in a particular classroom. Other schools find that the creation of a large lending library that serves all of the teachers in a school can better meet the changing needs of the staff and students. Whatever the approach, we have found that the availability of these materials increases the likelihood that classroom teachers will be able to compact the curriculum for students consistently.

Enrichment Materials to Use in Classrooms

Grade Level	Name	Content	Group Size	Audience	Price	Publisher
Adult	Workjobs for Parents	Math	NA	Professional	A	Addison-Wesley
All	Providing Opportunities for the Mathematically Gifted, K-12	Math	NA	Professional	A	A. W. Peller
All	Creative Problem Solving: The Basic Course	Thinking	S, L	Instructional	B	Center for Creative Learning
All	Tangram Patterns	Math	I	Instructional	A	Creative Publications
All	Tangramath	Math	I, S, L	Instructional	A	Creative Publications
All	NCTM Curriculum & Evaluation Standards for Sch. Mathematics	Math	NA	Professional	B	Creative Publications
All	Guiding Gifted Readers	Language Arts	I, S, L	Professional	B	GCT
All	A Whack on the Side of the Head	Thinking	NA	Professional	A	GCT
All	A Kick in the Seat of the Pants	Thinking	NA	Professional	A	GCT
All	Conceptual Blockbusting: A Guide to Better Ideas (3rd Edition)	Thinking	NA	Professional	A	GCT
All	DeBono's Thinking Course	Thinking	NA	Professional	B	GCT
All	SCAMPER	Thinking	S, L	Instructional	A	GCT
All	Creative Kids	Thinking	S, L	Instructional	B	GCT
All	My Family Tree Workbook: Genealogy for Beginners	Social Studies	I, S	Instructional	A	Geode
All	Drawing With Children	Arts	I, S, L	Instructional	A	Geode
All	Bookcrafts for Children	Language Arts	I, S, L	Instructional	A	Geode
All	Six Thinking Hats	Thinking	S, L	Professional	B	Geode
All	Philosophy for Young Thinkers	Thinking	S, L	Instructional	B	Geode
All	Leadership: A Special Type of Giftedness	Social Studies	S, L	Instructional	A	Geode
All	The New Games Book	Social Studies	S, L	Instructional	A	Geode
All	More New Games	Social Studies	S, L	Instructional	A	Geode
All	Writing the Natural Way	Language Arts	S, L	Instructional	A	Geode
All	One at a Time All at Once	All	L, S	Professional	A	Goodyear Books
All	Evaulating Critical Thinking	Thinking	NA	Professional	B	Midwest
All	Techniques For Teaching Thinking	Thinking	NA	Professional	A	Midwest
All	Ideas for Teaching Gifted Students: Science	Science	S, L	Instructional	B	Opportunities for Learning
All	Ideas for Teaching Gifted Students: Mathematics	Math	S, L	Instructional	B	Opportunities for Learning
All	Ideas for Teaching Gifted Students: Visual Arts	Arts	S, L	Instructional	B	Opportunities for Learning
All	Paper Projects for Creative Kids of All Ages	Arts	I, S	Instructional	A	Stevens and Shea
All	Ideas for Teaching Gifted Students	All	I, S, L	Professional	C	Sunburst
All	How to Make Pop-Ups	Arts	I, S, L	Instructional	A	Synergetics
All	Writing: Teachers & Children at Work	Language Arts	I, S, L	Professional	B	Teachers & Writer Collaborative
All	The Art of Teaching Writing	Language Arts	NA	Professional	B	Teachers & Writer Collaborative
I	Reader's Theater: Whole Lang. Approach to Reading & LA Instr.	Language Arts	I, S, L	Instructional	A	A. W. Peller
I	Learning to Think and Choose	Thinking	S, L	Instructional	A	Center for Creative Learning
I	Who Put the Cannon in the Courthouse Square?	Social Studies	I, S, L	Instructional	A	Creative Learning Press
I	My Backyard History Book	Social Studies	I, S, L	Instructional	A	Creative Learning Press
I	Ecology in Your Community	Science	I, S, L	Instructional	A	Creative Learning Press

Enrichment Materials to Use in Classrooms

Grade Level	Name	Content	Group Size	Audience	Price	Publisher
I	Introduction to Chemistry	Science	I, S, L	Instructional	A	Creative Learning Press
I	Small Creatures	Science	I, S, L	Instructional	A	Creative Learning Press
I	The Young Naturalist	Science	I, S, L	Instructional	A	Creative Learning Press
I	Pollution	Science	I, S, L	Instructional	A	Creative Learning Press
I	Your Senses	Science	I, S, L	Instructional	A	Creative Learning Press
I	Steven Caney's Invention Book	Science	I, S, L	Instructional	A	Creative Learning Press
I	Carpentry for Children	Arts	I, S, L	Instructional	A	Creative Learning Press
I	Extra Cash for Kids	Social Studies	I, S, L	Instructional	A	Creative Learning Press
I	Intermediate Jobcards Puzzles With Unifix Cubes	Math	I	Instructional	B	Creative Publications
I	Fraction Factory Jobcards Series	Math	I	Instructional	B	Creative Publications
I	Junior High Jobcards Pattern Blocks	Math	I	Instructional	B	Creative Publications
I	Thinker Tasks Jobcards Series	Thinking	I	Instructional	C	Creative Publications
I	Aftermath Series	Math	I, S, L	Instructional	B	Creative Publications
I	Aftermath 1, 2, 3, 4	Math	I, S, L	Instructional	A	Creative Publications
I	Mathematics: A Way of Thinking	Math	NA	Professional	B	Creative Publications
I	Number Sense and Arithmetic Skills	Math	S, L	Professional	C	Creative Publications
I	Statistics and Information Organization	Math	S, L	Instructional	C	Creative Publications
I	Geometry and Visualization	Math	S, L	Instructional	C	Creative Publications
I	Pentomino Lessons	Math	S, L	Instructional	A	Creative Publications
I	Statistics: The Shape of the Data	Math	S, L	Instructional	A	Dale Seymour
I	Statistics: Prediction and Sampling	Math	S, L	Instructional	A	Dale Seymour
I	Statistics: Middles, Means, and In-Betweens	Math	S, L	Instructional	A	Dale Seymour
I	Developing Skills in Estimation	Math	S, L	Instructional	A	Dale Seymour
I	Anywhere, Anytime, Individualized Speller	Language Arts	I, S	Instructional	A	Dandy Lion
I	Blueprints: A Guide for Independent Study	Research	I, S	Instructional	A	Dandy Lion
I	Investigator	Research	I, S	Instructional	A	Dandy Lion
I	Explorations	Social Studies	I, S	Instructional	A	Dandy Lion
I	Talent Scout	Thinking	S, L	Instructional	A	Dandy Lion
I	Asking Questions, Finding Answers	Research	S, L	Instructional	A	Dandy Lion
I	No Problem!	Math	S, L	Instructional	A	Dandy Lion
I	The Future Traveler	Thinking	S, L	Instructional	A	Dandy Lion
I	Inventions, Inventors and You	Science	S, L	Instructional	A	Dandy Lion
I	Options	Thinking	S, L	Instructional	A	Dandy Lion
I	Creative Problem-Solving for Gretel and Hansel	Thinking	S, L	Instructional	A	DOK
I	Create an Autobiography: Writing from Experiences	Language Arts	I, S	Instructional	A	Educational Impressions
I	Geography Mini-Center Series	Social Studies	I	Instructional	A	Engine-Uity
I	$Money$	Math	I	Instructional	B	Engine-Uity
I	Author! Author!	Language Arts	I	Instructional	B	Engine-Uity

Enrichment Materials to Use in Classrooms

Grade Level	Name	Content	Group Size	Audience	Price	Publisher
I	Mini-Center Kits	Research	I	Instructional	A	Engine-Uity
I	Earth Mysteries	Science	I	Instructional	B	Engine-Uity
I	Junk Food	Science	I	Instructional	B	Engine-Uity
I	Inventors and Inventions	Science	I	Instructional	B	Engine-Uity
I	Solar System	Science	I	Instructional	B	Engine-Uity
I	Under Your Hat: The Human Mind	Science	I	Instructional	B	Engine-Uity
I	Weather	Science	I	Instructional	B	Engine-Uity
I	Reptiles	Science	I	Instructional	B	Engine-Uity
I	Volcanoes and Earthquakes	Science	I	Instructional	B	Engine-Uity
I	Robots	Science	I	Instructional	B	Engine-Uity
I	Oceanography	Science	I	Instructional	B	Engine-Uity
I	The Explorers	Social Studies	I	Instructional	B	Engine-Uity
I	Great Disasters	Social Studies	I	Instructional	B	Engine-Uity
I	Knights and Castles	Social Studies	I	Instructional	B	Engine-Uity
I	Ancient Egypt	Social Studies	I	Instructional	B	Engine-Uity
I	Product Pouch	Research	I	Instructional	B	Engine-Uity
I	Inventors Workshop	Science	I, S	Instructional	A	GCT
I	The Research Project Book	Research	I, S	Instructional	A	GCT
I	Investigator	Research	I, S	Instructional	A	GCT
I	Project Planner	Research	I, S	Instructional	A	GCT
I	Pot Pourri	Research	I, S	Instructional	A	GCT
I	Research without Copying	Research	I, S	Instructional	A	GCT
I	The Research Almanac	Research	I, S	Instructional	A	GCT
I	Classroom Ideas for Encouraging Thinking & Feeling	Thinking	I, S, L	Professional	A	GCT
I	2nd Vol. Classroom Ideas for Encouraging Thinking & Feeling	Thinking	I, S, L	Professional	A	GCT
I	The Poetry Corner	Language Arts	I, S, L	Instructional	A	GCT
I	Where in Europe is Carmen Sandiego?	Social Studies	I, S, L	Instructional	C	GCT
I	Where in the USA is Carmen Sandiego?	Social Studies	I, S, L	Instructional	C	GCT
I	Future Traveler	Science	I, S, L	Instructional	A	GCT
I	Change for Children	All	I, S, L	Professional	A	GCT
I	The Map Corner	Social Studies	I, S, L	Instructional	A	GCT
I	Calculation Capers	Math	I, S, L	Instructional	A	GCT
I	Math Doins for High Achievers	Math	I, S, L	Instructional	A	GCT
I	Solving Problems Kids Care About: Math Skills & Word Prob.	Math	I, S, L	Instructional	A	GCT
I	CPS for Kids: Resource Bk for Teach. Creative Prob. to Children	Thinking	S, L	Instructional	A	GCT
I	I Believe in Unicorns	Thinking	S, L	Instructional	A	GCT
I	Fact, Fantasy, and Folklore	Language Arts, Thinking	S, L	Instructional	A	GCT
I	Naturewatch: Exploring Nature with Your Children	Science	S, L	Instructional	A	GCT

Enrichment Materials to Use in Classrooms

Grade Level	Name	Content	Group Size	Audience	Price	Publisher
I	Harry Stottlemeier's Discovery: Basic Reasoning Skills	Thinking	S, L	Instructional	C	GCT
I	Reader's Theater	Language Arts	S, L	Instructional	A	GCT
I	Building Toothpick Bridges	Math	I, S, L	Instructional	A	Geode
I	My Backyard History Book	Social Studies	I, S, L	Instructional	A	Geode
I	Great Bridge Lowering	Thinking	S, L	Instructional	A	Geode
I	Inventioneering	Thinking	S, L	Instructional	A	Geode
I	Ethic Pride	Social Studies	S, L	Instructional	A	Geode
I	My Backyard History Book	Social Studies	S, L	Instructional	A	Geode
I	The Book of Where	Social Studies	S, L	Instructional	A	Geode
I	Beastly Neighbors: All About Wild Things in the City	Social Studies	S, L	Instructional	A	Geode
I	Everybody's a Winner	Social Studies	S, L	Instructional	A	Geode
I	Learning Contracts 1	All	I	Instructional	B	Interact
I	Science Fair	Science	I	Instructional	C	Interact
I	Shopping Spree	Math	S, L	Instructional	C	Interact
I	Flight	Social Studies	S, L	Instructional	B	Interact
I	Book 2 Building Thinking Skills	Thinking	S, L	Instructional	B	Midwest
I	Critical Thinking Activities to Improve Writing Skills	Language Arts	S, L	Instructional	A	Midwest
I	Organizing Thinking (Graphic Organizers)	Thinking	S, L	Instructional	B	Midwest
I	Castles, Pirates, Knights, and Other Learning Delights	Language Arts	I, S, L	Instructional	A	Opportunities for Learning
I	Ideas for Teaching Gifted Students: English	Language Arts	S, L	Instructional	B	Opportunities for Learning
I	Drama Workbooks	Language Arts	S, L	Instructional	B	Opportunities for Learning
I	The Creativity Catalog	Research	I, S	Instructional	A	Stevens and Shea
I	Puzzle Thinking	Thinking	S, L	Instructional	A	Stevens and Shea
I	Discovering Science: Projects for Everyone	Science	I, S	Instructional	C	Sunburst
I	Think Tank: Problem Solving for Today's World	Social Studies	I, S	Instructional	C	Sunburst
I	Creative Problem Solving: Be an Inventor	Thinking	I, S	Instructional	C	Sunburst
I	Have I Got a Problem for You	Math	I, S,	Instructional	C	Sunburst
I	You're the Author	Language Arts	I, S, L	Instructional	C	Sunburst
I	Newbery Books for Grades 3 to 5	Language Arts	I, S, L	Instructional	C	Sunburst
I	Newberys: The Latest Winners	Language Arts	I, S, L	Instructional	C	Sunburst
I	Propaganda: What Can You Believe?	Thinking	S, L	Instructional	C	Sunburst
I	Creative Problem Solving: Planning New Worlds	Thinking	S, L	Instructional	C	Sunburst
I	Self-Starter Kit for Independent Study	Research	I	Instructional	B	Synergetics
I	Leadership Unit: Use of Teacher-Scholar Teams to Develop					
I	Units for Gifted	Social Studies	S, L	Instructional	A	Trillium
I	Challenge	Math			B, C	Addison-Wesley
I	Scienceworks	Science			A	Delta Education, Inc.
I	The Science Book	Science			A	Delta Education, Inc.

Enrichment Materials to Use in Classrooms

Grade Level	Name	Content	Group Size	Audience	Price	Publisher
I	Science Fare	Science			A	Delta Education, Inc.
I	Great Investigations....One Step at a Time	Science			B	Delta Education, Inc.
I, Adult	Paper Engineering	Thinking	I, S	Instructional	A	Geode
I, Adult	Chi Square, Pie Charts, and Me	Math	S, L	Instructional	A	Geode
I, S	So You Want To Do a Science Project!	Science	I, S	Instructional	A	Creative Learning Systems
I, S	How to Tape Instant Oral Biographies	Social Studies	I, S, L	Instructional	A	Creative Learning Press
I, S	The Writing Workshop	Language Arts	I, S, L	Instructional	A	Dale Seymour
I, S	Exploring Data	Math	S, L	Instructional	B	Dale Seymour
I, S	Project Banner	Thinking	I, S	Instructional	A	Dandy Lion
I, S	Idea Machine	Social Studies	I, S	Instructional	A	DOK
I, S	How to Open Their World With Letters	Language Arts	I, S, L	Instructional	A	DOK
I, S	Be a Problem Solver	Thinking	S, L	Instructional	A	DOK
I, S	Straight From the Source: Nine Research Projects	Research	I, S	Instructional	A	Educational Impressions
I, S	Roots For Kids	Social Studies	I, S, L	Instructional	A	Free Spirit Publishing
I, S	Straight from the Source: Nine Research Projects	Research	I, S	Instructional	A	GCT
I, S	At the Grass Roots Level: A Community Research & Writing Proj.	Research	I, S, L	Instructional	A	GCT
I, S	Stocks and Bonds	Social Studies	I, S, L	Instructional	B	GCT
I, S	Stock Market	Social Studies	I, S, L	Instructional	B	GCT
I, S	Discovering Anthropology	Social Studies	I, S, L	Instructional	A	GCT
I, S	Discovering Economics	Social Studies	I, S, L	Instructional	A	GCT
I, S	Discovering Philosophy	Social Studies	I, S, L	Instructional	A	GCT
I, S	Discovering Psychology	Social Studies	I, S, L	Instructional	A	GCT
I, S	I Know That Building	Social Studies	I, S, L	Instructional	B	Geode
I, S	Great Ancestor Hunt	Social Studies	I, S, L	Instructional	B	Geode
I, S	What Would You Do?	Thinking	S, L	Instructional	A	Midwest
I, S	Moral Reasoning: Teaching Handbk for Adapting Kohlberg Classrm	Thinking	S, L	Instructional	A	Opportunities for Learning
I, S	Reader's Theatre Starter Packets	Language Arts	S, L	Instructional	C	Opportunities for Learning
I, S	Chi Square, Pie Charts and Me	Research	I, S	Instructional	A	Trillium
I, S	Like It Was	Language Arts	S, L	Instructional	A	Teachers & Writer Collaborative
I, S	The Unconventional Invention Book	Thinking	I, S, L	Instructional	A	GCT
I, S	Hippogriff Feathers	Thinking	S, L	Instructional	A	GCT
I, S	Sunflowering	Thinking	S, L	Instructional	A	GCT
I, S	Learning Through Science: A Twelve Part Series	Science			B each	Teacher's Laboratory, Inc.
I, S	Builde Your Own Polyhedra	Math			B	Addison-Wesley
I, S, Adult	Films and Special Effects	Research	I, S	Instructional	A	Creative Learning Systems
I, S, Adult	Baking Chemistry	Science	S, L	Instructional	A	Geode
P	Frog and Toad Thinking Book	Thinking	S, L	Instructional	A	Book Lures
P	Thinker's Mother Goose	Thinking	S, L	Instructional	A	Book Lures

Enrichment Materials to Use in Classrooms

Grade Level	Name	Content	Group Size	Audience	Price	Publisher
P	Workjobs and Workjobs II	Math, Language Arts	I	Instructional	B	Creative Publications
P	Teddy Bear Jobcards Starter Set	Math	I	Instructional	C	Creative Publications
P	Kindergarten Jobcards Unifix Cubes Starter Set	Math	I	Instructional	B	Creative Publications
P	Primary Jobcards: Patterns with Unifix Cubes	Math	I	Instructional	B	Creative Publications
P	Kindergarten Jobcards Tangrams Starter Set	Math	I	Instructional	B	Creative Publications
P	Tangram Primary Jobcards Starter Set	Math	I	Instructional	B	Creative Publications
P	Geoboards Jobcards Starter Set	Math	I	Instructional	C	Creative Publications
P	Primary Jobcards for Rainbow Cubes	Math	I	Instructional	A	Creative Publications
P	Money Jobcards	Math	I	Instructional	B	Creative Publications
P	Hands On Unifix Cubes	Math	I, S, L	Instructional	B	Creative Publications
P	Measuring: From Paces to Feet	Math	S, L	Instructional	A	Dale Seymour
P	Counting: Ourselves and Our Families	Math	S, L	Instructional	A	Dale Seymour
P	Sorting: Groups and Graphs	Math	S, L	Instructional	A	Dale Seymour
P	Pictograms: Graphing Pictures for a Reusable Classroom Grid	Math	S, L	Instructional	A	Dale Seymour
P	Graphing Primer	Math	S, L	Instructional	A	Dale Seymour
P	Primarily Research	Research	I, S	Instructional	A	Dandy Lion
P	Primarily Problem Solving	Thinking	S, L	Instructional	A	Dandy Lion
P	Future Pathways	Thinking	S, L	Instructional	A	Dandy Lion
P	Our Town	Social Studies	S, L	Instructional	A	Dandy Lion
P	A Monster's Shoe and the Cat Kangaroo	Thinking	S, L	Instructional	A	DOK
P	Creative Problem-Solving For an Eency Weency Spider	Thinking	S, L	Instructional	A	DOK
P	Bac Packs	Language Arts	I	Instructional	A	Engine-Uity
P	Creepy Crawlies	Science	I	Instructional	B	Engine-Uity
P	Dinosaurs	Social Studies	I	Instructional	B	Engine-Uity
P	Poetry Power!	Language Arts	I	Instructional	B	Engine-Uity
P	Product Booklet 1	Research	I	Instructional	B	Engine-Uity
P	Product Booklet 2	Research	I	Instructional	B	Engine-Uity
P	Product Booklet 3	Research	I	Instructional	B	Engine-Uity
P	Bears	Math, Language Arts	I	Instructional	B	Engine-Uity
P	Peanut Butter and Jelly	Math	I	Instructional	B	Engine-Uity
P	Prima Study Packet 1	Research	I	Instructional	A	Engine-Uity
P	Prima Study Packet 2	Research	I	Instructional	A	Engine-Uity
P	The Age of Dinosaurs	Science	I	Instructional	B	Engine-Uity
P	First Research Projects	Research	I, S	Instructional	A	GCT
P	Our Town: A Guide for Studying Any Community	Social Studies	I, S	Instructional	A	GCT
P	Future Think	Research	I, S, L	Instructional	A	GCT
P	Primarily Creativity	Thinking	S, L	Instructional	A	GCT
P	Primary Problem Solving	Thinking	S, L	Instructional	A	GCT

Enrichment Materials to Use in Classrooms

Grade Level	Name	Content	Group Size	Audience	Price	Publisher
P	Foodworks: Over 100 Science Act. that Explore Magic of Food	Science	S, L	Instructional	A	GCT
P	Kio and Gus Wondering at the World	Thinking	S, L	Instructional	C	GCT
P	Pixie	Thinking	S, L	Instructional	C	GCT
P	Anno's Math Games	Math	I, S	Instructional	B	Geode
P	Anno's Math Games II	Math	I, S	Instructional	B	Geode
P	Anno's Mysterious Multiplying Jar	Math	I, S	Instructional	B	Geode
P	Put Your Mother on the Ceiling: Children's Imagination Games	Thinking	S, L	Instructional	A	Geode
P	New Way to Use Your Bean	Thinking	S, L	Instructional	A	Geode
P	A Young Child Experiences	All	I, S	Professional	A	Goodyear Books
P	Run, Run	Research	S, L	Instructional	A	Interact
P	Primary Thinking Skills, B1, B2, B3, B4	Thinking	S, L	Instructional	A	Midwest
P	Primary Building Thinking Skills	Thinking	S, L	Instructional	A	Midwest
P	Book 1 Building Thinking Skills	Thinking	S, L	Instructional	B	Midwest
P	Bringing Out the Best	Social Studies	NA	Professional	A	NAGC
P	Hug a Tree and Other Things To Do With Young Children	Social Studies	S, L	Instructional	A	Stevens and Shea
P	Primary Independent Study Student Workbook	Research	I	Instructional	A	Synergetics
P	Primary Independent Study	Research	I	Instructional	A	Synergetics
P	Creativity 1, 2, 3	Thinking	S, L	Instructional	A	Trillium
P	Workjobs	Math			B	Addison-Wesley
P	Workjobs II	Math			A	Addison-Wesley
P	Bugplay	Science			B	Addison-Wesley
P, I	Independent Study Folders	Research	I	Instructional	A	Center for Creative Learning
P, I	Individualized Teaching of Gifted Children in the Regular Classrm	All	I, S	Professional	A	Center for Creative Learning
P, I	Starter Sets for Base Ten Blocks Jobcards	Math	I	Instructional	C	Creative Publications
P, I	Animal Attribute Tiles Jobcards	Math	I	Instructional	B	Creative Publications
P, I	Intermediate Jobcards: Puzzles with Tangrams	Math	I	Instructional	B	Creative Publications
P, I	Intermediate Jobcards: Puzzles with Geoboards	Math	I	Instructional	B	Creative Publications
P, I	Creative Expressions: An Art Curriculum	Arts	S, L	Instructional	C	Dale Seymour
P, I	Pocketful of Projects	Research	I, S	Instructional	A	DOK
P, I	Individualized Teaching of Gifted Children in Regular Classrooms	All	I, S	Professional	A	DOK
P, I	Once Upon a Time (CPS Through Fairy Tales)	Thinking	S, L	Instructional	A	DOK
P, I	Creative Problem-Solving for the 4th Little Pig	Thinking	S, L	Instructional	A	DOK
P, I	What Would You Do?	Thinking	S, L	Instructional	A	Educational Impressions
P, I	ABCs of Thinking with Caldecott Books	Language Arts	S, L	Instructional	A	GCT
P, I	Asking Questions, Finding Answers	Research	S, L	Instructional	A	GCT
P, I	Drinking Straw Construction	Science	I, S	Instructional	A	Geode
P, I	Bubbles	Science	I, S	Instructional	A	Geode
P, I	Raceways: Having Fun With Balls and Tracks	Science	I, S, L	Instructional	A	Geode

Enrichment Materials to Use in Classrooms

Grade Level	Name	Content	Group Size	Audience	Price	Publisher
P, I	Tops: Building and Experimenting With Spinning Toys	Science	I, S, L	Instructional	A	Geode
P, I	Wheels At Work	Science	S, L	Instructional	A	Geode
P, I	Water-Pumps and Siphons	Science	S, L	Instructional	A	Geode
P, I	Clocks	Science	S<L	Instructional	A	Geode
P, I	Dinosaur	Social Studies	S, L	Instructional	B	Interact
P, I	Enchanted Castle	Language Arts	S, L	Instructional	B	Interact
P, I	Ideas for Teaching Gifted Students: Language Arts	Language Arts	S, L	Instructional	B	Opportunities for Learning
P, I	Science on a Shoestring	Science	S, L	Instructional	B	Synergetics
P, I	Trillium Basal Mathware	Math	I, S, L	Professional	C	Trillium
P, I	Making Theatre	Arts	S, L	Instructional	B	Teachers & Writer Collaborative
P, I	Sportsworks	Science			A	Addison-Wesley
P, I	Outdoor Biology Instruct. Strategies (OBIS)	Science			B	Delta Education, Inc.
P, I	Creative, Hands-On Science Experiences	Science			A	Opportunities for Learning, Inc.
P, S	Ideas for Teaching Gifted Students: Social Studies	Social Studies	S, L	Instructional	B	Opportunities for Learning
S	Photosearch: A Library Skills Detective Game	Research	I, S, L	Instructional	C	A. W. Peller
S	National Council of Teachers of Mathematics Books	Math	NA	Professional	A	A. W. Peller
S	Problem Solving and Comprehension	Thinking	S, L	Instructional	A	Center for Creative Learning
S	Junior High Jobcards	Math	I	Instructional	C	Creative Publications
S	Mathematics in Science and Society	Math	S, L	Instructional	C	Creative Publications
S	Ratio, Proportion and Scaling	Math	S, L	Instructional	C	Creative Publications
S	Can You Find It?	Research	I, S, L	Instructional	A	Dale Seymour
S	Writing Down the Days	Language Arts	I, S, L	Instructional	A	Free Spirit Publishing
S	Lisa: Reasoning in Ethics	Thinking	S, L	Instructional	C	GCT
S	Suki: Reasoning in Language Arts	Thinking	S, L	Instructional	C	GCT
S	Mark: Reasoning in Social Studies	Thinking	S, L	Instructional	C	GCT
S	Leadership Education: Developing Skills for Youth	Social Studies	S, L	Instructional	A	Geode
S	Book 3 Figural Building Thinking Skills	Math	S, L	Instructional	B	Midwest
S	Book 3 Verbal Building Thinking Skills	Language Arts	S, L	Instructional	B	Midwest
S	Critical Viewing	Thinking	S, L	Instructional	A	Midwest
S	Critical Thinking Book One	Thinking	S, L	Instructional	A	Midwest
S	Critical Thinking Book Two	Thinking	S, L	Instructional	A	Midwest
S	Critical Thinking in American History	Social Studies	S, L	Instructional	A	Midwest
S	Evaluating Viewpoints: Critical Thinking in United States History	Social Studies	S, L	Instructional	A	Midwest
S	The Art of Science Writing	Language Arts, Science	S, L	Instructional	A	Teachers & Writer Collaborative

List of Publishers of Enrichment Materials

A. W. Peller & Associates, Inc.
P.O. Box 106
Hawthorne, NJ 07507

Addison-Wesley Publishing Company
Route 128
Reading, MA 01867

Book Lures, Inc.
P.O. Box 9450
O'Fallon, MO 63366

Center for Creative Learning
P.O. Box 619
Honeoye, NY 14471

Creative Learning Press, Inc.
P.O. Box 320
Mansfield Center, CT 06250

Creative Learning Systems, Inc.
9899 Hibert, Suite C
San Diego, CA 92131

Creative Publications
5040 West 11th Street
Oak Lawn, IL 60453

D.O.K. Publishers
P.O. Box 605
East Aurora, NY 14052

Dale Seymour Publications
P.O. Box 10888
Palo Alto, CA 94303

Dandy Lion Publications
3563—L Sueldo
San Luis Obispo, CA 93401

Delta Education, Inc.
P.O. Box 915
Hudson, NH 03051

Educational Impressions
P.O. Box 77
Hawthorne, NJ 07507

Engine-Uity, Ltd.
P.O. Box 9610
Phoenix, AZ 85068

Free Spirit Publishing, Inc.
123 N. Third Street, Suite 716B
Minneapolis, MN 55401-9967

GCT Inc.
P.O. Box 6448
Mobile, AL 36660

Geode Educational Options
P.O. Box 106
West Chester, PA 19381

Good Year Books
Scott, Foresman and Company
1900 East Lake Avenue
Glenview, IL 60025

Interact
P.O. Box 997-Y90
Lakeside, CA 92040

Midwest Publications
P.O. Box 448
Pacific Grove, CA 93950

National Association for Gifted Children
4175 Lovell Road, Suite 140
Circle Pines, MN 55014

Opportunities for Learning, Inc.
20417 Nordhoff Street, Dept. S9RF
Chatsworth, CA 91311

Sunburst Communications
39 Washington Avenue
Pleasantville, NY 10570-9971

Synergetics
P.O. Box 84
East Windsor Hill, CT 06028

Trillium Press
P.O. Box 209
Monroe, NY 10950

Teachers & Writers Collaborative
5 Union Square West
New York, NY 10003

Teachers' Laboratory, Inc.
P.O. Box 6480
Brattleboro, VT 05302-6480

Tools for Thinking
Stevens & Shea Publishers
Dept. 7, 325 E. Wyandotte Street
Stockton, CA 95204

OTHER COMPACTING STRATEGIES

Three other strategies have also been very helpful in enabling teachers to offer high quality alternatives for students whose curriculum is compacted: (1) interest assessment, (2) interest development centers, and (3) independent study options. Included below are instructions for assessing interests, developing interest centers, and step-by-step instructions for guiding bright students through independent study projects.

INTEREST ASSESSMENT

Building educational experiences around students' interests is probably one of the most recognizable ways in which schoolwide enrichment programs differ from the regular curriculum. In numerous evaluation studies when bright students were asked what they liked best about being in a special program, the first response almost always dealt with the greater freedom allowed for selecting topics of study. Conversely, when asked about their greatest objection to the regular curriculum, students' comments frequently referred to the limited opportunities to pursue topics of their own choosing. Indeed, high-ability students' views of the regular curriculum so far as freedom of choice is concerned are extremely negative. As one youngster so ably put it, "They tell us what book we have to use, what page, paragraph, and problem we should be on, and how long we should spend on that problem." While many group activities in special programs do require whole class teaching and similar involvement for each student, we must raise some serious questions about freedom of choice when every youngster in a group is preparing a ritualized report on "Houses of the Future," "Life in a Colonial Village" or "The Rocks and Minerals of Colorado." This is not to say that every independent study situation should be without limits. The teacher's own strengths and interests may lead him or her to place certain restrictions on general areas of study (for example, futuristics, colonial history, geology), but *within* these broad areas a great deal of freedom should be allowed in the selection of specific topics or problems. In other words, there is nothing wrong with focusing on a general theme such as futuristics, but there are numerous topics, issues, and methodologies within futuristics that should be explored by individuals or small groups. If every student is designing a house of the future, the teacher may be guilty of predetermining and prescribing in the same way the regular curriculum often does.

The intensity and manner of a student's interest in a particular topic should also be considered. One of the teachers' major responsibilities in identifying interests is to make certain that they do not push a student into an independent study or other educational activity at the first sign of interest. No matter how much initial enthusiasm a youngster displays, the possibility of following up such interest with more intensive study should be handled with great delicacy. Students should be encouraged to do further independent *exploratory* work about various ways that an area of interest can be investigated, the amount of time, materials and resource personnel that might be required for such an investigation, and, most importantly, whether or not the interest is powerful enough to sustain an in-depth involvement with a particular problem area.

As an example, take the case of two youngsters who became interested in genealogy as a result of watching the television program, *Roots*. This was an assigned "exploratory experience" that was part of their general enrichment program. Both youngsters were aware that if the program were particularly interesting to them, they would be provided with an opportunity to doing some type of follow-up study. Working together, both youngsters began to look through books on genealogy. One of these was *How To Trace Your Family Tree* (AGRI, 1975). This magnificent little book describes in great detail the methodological procedures followed by genealogists in carrying out investigations. It provides several types of how-to information such as how to construct individual and family worksheets, the names and addresses of all offices in the United States where birth and death records are stored, the types of information that should be addressed to such offices, and the types of questions that should be asked of relatives in order to obtain accurate information about ancestors. The book also includes a glossary of terms used in wills and birth and death records and the types of information that are available from the various U.S. censuses that have been conducted over the years.

One thing that became readily apparent from these additional explorations was that a great deal of time-consuming and laborious work is involved in such an investigation. This type of detective work actually served to sharpen the interest and increase the enthusiasm of one student, and she began immediately to organize and develop a plan of attack. The other student, however, seemed to drag her feet in getting started on a genealogical investigation. Further discussion revealed that this student was more interested in the literary aspects of *Roots* and the social injustice that was conveyed through the dramatic portrayal of the treatment of slaves in the 1800's. This student obtained a copy of *Roots*, read and reread it several times, and was referred to additional books dealing with the same topic. She did not, however, express the same enthusiasm toward carrying out a genealogical study.

The lesson to be learned from this example is obvious. Although both students expressed an interest in the same exploratory activity, their interest were different. Had both students been forced to engage in genealogical research as a result of their early interests, what turned out to be an exciting follow-up study for one student may well have turned into a dreary and forced exercise for the other. Perhaps some alternative follow-up activities might have been explored with the second student such as writing a story about the lives of early American slaves; preparing a presentation about some local points of interest (such as stops on the underground railroad, slaves' quarters, or early schools for black children), or perhaps interviewing the descendants of slaves to discover their reaction to *Roots*, their degree of familiarity with their own backgrounds, or their feelings and attitudes toward this particular time in our nation's history.

The teacher's role in promoting student interest is especially crucial. He or she must be able to spot areas of sincere or unusual interest and help the student explore the various ways that such an interest might be developed or expressed in a creative and productive follow-up study. In other words, teachers must help students identify not only *what*, but *how* they want to pursue an interest. Merely being interested in, for example, rock music, mystery stories or U.S. history does not necessarily mean that the student will automatically want to become a musician, writer or historian. Such interests do, of course, represent *possible* points of entry into the more obvious modes of creative expression associated with these particular fields, and therefore these modes should be explored. It also is important, however, to explore several of the other creative modes of expression possible within a given topic. To elaborate on the above example, a student (with or without musical ability) who is interested in rock music might explore the possibility of being a radio announcer or the producer of a rock concert; a youngster interested in mysteries might enjoy telling about them in the book review section of the school newspaper or on a school radio program; and an interest in U.S. history might be manifested in writing a novel, play, travel brochure or doing a photographic essay. Thus our role as teachers is twofold in promoting students' interests: we must help youngsters to identify both areas of interest and ways in which these interests can be expressed creatively and productively.

A word of caution should be mentioned at this point. It is a common practice in our culture to reward persons for superior performance. Teachers give A's and gold stars for good work and parents sometimes give their children money for good grades. Such practices may reinforce good study habits, but they may also lead students and teachers to think that the student is interested in a particular area because he or she happens to perform well in it. Therefore, teachers need to use information about student interests and learning styles to make decisions about substitute activities. This requires teachers to devote some time to helping students explore their interests. A student may very well think that he or she likes a particular area of study, but this conclusion may be based on limited exposure to other areas of knowledge which may actually hold far more fascination for the student than the area in which he or she has received straight A's.

The Interest-A-Lyzer

A planned strategy for helping students to examine their present and potential interests is based on an instrument called the *Interest-A-Lyzer*. (Sample pages of this instrument are on pages 106 and 107.) This thirteen-item questionnaire is designed to help students explore their individual areas of interest. The Interest-A-Lyzer has been used with students in grades four to nine, and it has also been adapted for use with students in grades three to eight (McGreevey, 1982) and adults. The items consist of a variety of real and hypothetical situations to which students are asked to respond in terms of the choices they would make (or have made) were they involved in these situations.

Field tests using the Interest-A-Lyzer have shown that it can serve as the basis for lively group discussions or in-depth counseling sessions with individual students. It also is designed to facilitate discussion between groups of children with similar interests who are attempting to identify areas in which they might like to pursue advanced level studies. Field tests have also shown that the self-analysis of interests is an ongoing process that should not be rushed, and that steps should be taken to avoid peer pressure that may lead to group conformity or stereotyped responses. An attempt has been made to overcome some of these problems by developing a careful set of directions for the instrument; however, teachers should allow students maximum freedom in choosing how and with whom they would like to discuss their responses. A free and open discussion should lead students to the conclusion that the instrument is indeed an honest attempt to help them both explore a wide variety of interests and subsequently focus on a particular topic.

The teacher may also want to suggest that students discuss the instrument with their parents, emphasizing that it is students' rather than parents' opinions that are being sought. It is also a good idea to suggest that students do not discuss their thoughts with other children. Remind students that opportunities for group discussion and sharing will be provided *after* the Interest-A-Lyzers have been completed, and that at this initial stage of the process the goal is to find out how they respond on their own.

SAMPLE ITEMS FROM THE INTEREST-A-LYZER

Cover Page

The Interest-A-Lyzer

by
Joseph S. Renzulli
University of Connecticut

Name _____   Age _____

School _____   Grade _____

Date _____

The purpose of this questionnaire is to help you become more familiar with some of your interests and potential interests. The questionnaire is not a test and there are no right or wrong answers. Your answers will be completely confidential. You may want to talk them over with your teacher or other students, but this choice is entirely up to you.

Some of the time that you spend in the special program will be devoted to working on individual or small-group projects. We would like for you to work on projects that are of interest to you, but sometimes we have to do a little thinking before we really know what some of our interests might be.

A good way to get in touch with our interests is to think about some of the things we like to do now and also some of the things we might like to do if given the opportunity. Some of the questions that follow will be "Let's pretend" questions; but keep in mind that their only purpose is to see what choices you would make in an imaginary situation.

As you read the questions try not to think about the kinds of answers that your classmates might write or how they might feel about your answers. Remember, no one will see your answers if you want to keep them confidential.

Do not try to answer the questions now. Read them over and think about them for a few days and then write your answers. Please do not discuss the questionnaire with others at this time. Sometimes we can be influenced by the opinions of others and this influence may prevent you from exploring some of your own interests. Remember, the major purpose of The Interest-A-Lyzer is to get YOU to THINK about YOUR OWN INTERESTS.

SAMPLE ITEMS FROM THE
INTEREST-A-LYZER
(continued)

Sample Items

- Pretend that your class has decided to put on a play to raise money for a class trip. Each person has been asked to sign up for his or her first, second, or third choice for one of the jobs listed below. Mark your first choice with a 1, second choice with a 2, and third choice with a 3.

    _____ Actor/Actress   _____ Playwright

    _____ Director   _____ Musician

    _____ Design Costumes   _____ Dancer

    _____ Make Costumes   _____ Singer

    _____ Light/Sound Person   _____ Business Manager

    _____ Design Scenery   _____ Design Advertisements

    _____ Build and Paint Scenery _____ Photographer (to prepare photos for newspapers, bulletin boards, and other advertisements)

- Pretend that you can invite any person in the world to be a teacher in the special program for two weeks. Who would you invite?

    First Choice_____

    Second Choice_____

    Third Choice_____

- Are you a collector? Do you collect stamps, sea shells, baseball cards, or other things? List the things that you collect and the number of years you have been collecting.

Things I Collect	Number of Years I Have Been Collecting
_____	_____
_____	_____
_____	_____
_____	_____
_____	_____

- What are some of the things you would like to collect if you had the time and money?

    _____

    _____

Interpreting the Interest-A-Lyzer

The Interest-A-Lyzer is not the type of instrument that yields a numerical score, but rather is designed in a way that allows for *pattern analysis*. The major interest area patterns that might emerge from the instrument are as follows:

1. Fine Arts and Crafts
2. Scientific and Technical
3. Creative Writing and Journalism
4. Legal, Political and Judicial
5. Mathematical
6. Managerial
7. Historical
8. Athletic and Outdoor Related Activities
9. Performing Arts
10. Business
11. Consumer Action and Ecology Related Activities

Remember first that the above items represent *general* fields or families of interest and second that an individual's interest might be expressed in numerous ways. Identifying general patterns is only the first step in interest analysis. General interests must be refined and focused so that students will arrive at specific problems within a general field or a combination of fields. This is often more difficult than identifying general patterns, because in moving from general to specific, there is the danger of steering students to such an extent that a problem may be imposed on them rather than be determined by them. Steps are included in a later section for helping youngsters pursue topics that they may become interested in exploring in more depth.

INTEREST DEVELOPMENT CENTERS

Interest development centers differ in purpose and content from traditional learning centers. Instead of providing a means for mastering basic curriculum skills, an interest development center allows children to explore a wide variety of individually selected topics. Topics are selected because of student interest and are pursued to expand students' understanding of the world around them, to explore a new subject, and to invite involvement in long-term research. Specific behavioral objectives, task cards, or pre- and post tests typically are not found in an interest development center. Instead, the centers are stocked with manipulative materials, media and print materials, and many suggestions for experimenting and exploring specific topics. These open-ended, activity-oriented materials are then presented as options for those students who have a genuine interest in learning more about a particular topic.

For this reason, teachers who create interest development centers must stock it with a wealth of information and appropriate materials about the selected topic. This is essential if students are to be exposed to a new area. Films, pamphlets, magazine articles, library books, slides, display items, and newspaper clippings are all standard fare in most interest development centers created by teachers. Care is taken to preassess the general interest of the class prior to the construction of an interest center. In this way, teachers are more likely to spend valuable time designing a center that will be used.

Interest centers also include resources that expose children to process or methodology skills that an adult would use in a career field. For example, a teacher who constructed an interest development center about bicycling included a few introductory texts from a bookstore or library on how to create a bike path or how to approach the city council for permission to erect bike racks near businesses catering to students.

With this approach, the student who is interested in pursuing a long-term project or investigation in a related area will already be familiar with appropriate research skills. These research skills differ greatly from traditional reference skills taught by most librarians or classroom teachers. Although note taking, outlining, and card-catalog skills are essential for good research, the student who becomes involved in genuine research, rather than report writing, must also learn more advanced research skills.

It must be remembered that interest development centers will be used by students of varying abilities. Although they allow all students, including those of above-average ability, to develop or elaborate on an existing interest by providing activity options with different levels of sophistication, they will not guarantee a differentiated curriculum for bright students. A creative product that develops from a child's involvement in center activities is as much the result of the child's task commitment as it is the teacher's ability to modify students' curricular experiences.

How To Plan an Interest Development Center

In planning an interest development center you may want to discuss the topic to be covered with another teacher. Their ideas, suggestions, and personal materials may add to the breadth and depth of a center.

Another item to consider is the outside shell. *Change for Children* (Kaplan, 1982) offers suggestions for construction of the shell. Fabric cutting boards, lamp shades, bulletin boards, or venetian blinds can be modified as the backdrop or collection center for materials. Many teachers found that a trifold of colorful posterboard often works best as the center's skeleton. This trifold is made with two pieces of posterboard and two-inch adhesive tape. By cutting one of the pieces of posterboard in half, these halves can serve as the left and right sides of the center. Then, by taping each half sheet to the central piece one has constructed a portable center that can be carried under the arm or stored, with its boxed components, in a cupboard.

Catchy titles, appealing graphics, and colorful pictures may be added. Later, the activity and research suggestions that are a part of each interest development center can be mounted to index cards and attached to the posterboard using rubber cement. Laminating a center helps extend its lifetime. Because each center requires several hours to complete, only a few can be created in a school year so some teachers share centers within schools or districts as part of a traveling lending library. That way, available centers in each classroom can be changed every six to eight weeks.

After the skeleton for the center has been assembled, teachers collect display items, audio-visual aids, and narrative information that comprise the heart of the center. Materials listed on the planning sheet or mentioned in the brainstorming session become important during this phase of center planning. In our experience, a quality interest development center works best when it includes the following:

Narrative information. Introductory books, magazines, professional journals, biographies, career pamphlets, video-tapes of public television specials, movies, records and filmstrips are excellent ways to introduce students to interest areas. An interest development center on photography might contain pamphlets from the Kodak Company, old issues of *Photography Today* or *Popular Photography*, and filmstrips or library books. Many teachers also use newspapers as a source of community talent or current events. Related news articles can be clipped and attached to the interest development center as they are found. Issues of *National Geographic, 3-2-1 Contact, Ranger Rick, Discovery, Your Big Backyard* and *Science Digest* are also excellent sources for pictures and articles.

Many publishers of educational materials offer compendia of ten to twenty chapters, each dealing with an interest area for a particular age group. *Kid's America* (Carey, 1978); *M.A.G.I.C. K.I.T.S.* (Heuer & Koprowicz, 1980); *Mission: Possible* (Toovey & Nizgorski, 1982); *The Great Perpetual Learning Machine* (Blake & Ernst, 1976); *Castles, Pirates, Knights and Other Learning Delights* (Glassock & Weber, 1980); *Earthpeople* (Abruscato, 1978); *Thumbs Up* (Holmes & Christie, 1978); *Bright Ideas* (Johnson, 1981); *Aaahs* (Dallas, 1977); and *Whole Cosmos* (Abruscato, 1977) have been useful in various interest centers. These books are stocked with information, activities, addresses, pictures, and experiments in hundreds of topics. Women's history, solar energy, dinosaurs, nutrition, and electronics have been popular with intermediate-age students. Teachers might also introduce the arrival of a new center with a lecture by a community speaker. This approach adds interest and motivation for the center's suggested activities.

Suggestions for specific activities, experiments, or research. Even if students are interested in a topic, they may not have sufficient expertise to devise their own exploration or research tasks. Because they may have difficulty perceiving real-life problems or societal issues related to this topic, it is appropriate that the teacher recommend readings, investigations, experiments or activities for further study. But the choice for a long-term investigation should be the student's and not part of a class or individual assignment. Written suggestions about future study should focus on the topic and stress creative thinking, problem solving, career exploration, higher level thinking, moral dilemmas, imagination, or related academic concerns. Survey ideas, suggestions for writing letters or making phone calls, gathering data or developing a product are good possibilities for activity suggestions.

A center that allows fourth- though sixth-grade students to explore education of the hearing impaired or sign language might contain twenty or thirty suggestions which vary in complexity like these:

- Find out about the difference between American sign language and signed English. How would you prefer to learn? Which do deaf students and teachers of the deaf prefer?

- Visit a class for the hearing impaired. What is similar and what is different from your classroom?

- What is our community doing or not doing to remove communication barriers for deaf people?

- Contact a rehabilitation center and arrange an interview with a deaf client. What are some of the problems faced as a result of being deaf? Can you do anything to alleviate one of these problems?

- Use the sign language dictionaries on this table to learn a few basic signs for the members of your family.

These suggestions are typed on index cards and mounted to the center's shell near pictures or narrative information. Another center on bicycling, developed by Karen Conwell, contained over twenty suggestions like these:

- Map an original bicycle trip across your state. Include historical stops along the journey.
- Plan a bicycle safety rodeo for your community.
- Develop a bicycle safety talk to present to your class.
- Find a book, film, or pamphlet that deals with the gear ratios for your ten-speed bike. Can you draw a chart or graph that explains this gear system?
- Try your hand at designing a bicycle storage unit for commuters.
- Compare bicycles on the market costs, features, use, etc.
- Design safety clothing and gear to be worn on a bike trip.

The age of students and intensity of their interests will ultimately influence a teacher's choice of topics and suggestions for further study. Yet, the more ideas one proposes, the more likely it is that one suggestion will spark a student's interest.

Community Resources. Students frequently enjoy having a list of phone numbers, names, or addresses of adults willing to let students visit their homes or places of business. Students might also undertake written correspondence with a practicing professional or use the addresses to request brochures and documents about the topic. A weather center we created contains addresses of the town's airport-based weather station, the phone number of a local principal who served as a meteorologist in the Armed Forces, and a suggestion to interview a local celebrity and store owner named Brownie who had been accurately predicting our county's number of snowfalls for over forty winters. A professor of meteorology also volunteered to demonstrate weather forecasting equipment.

Display items. The collection of slides, specimens, samples, photographs, tools, or raw materials housed in the center are often prime motivators for students. Good sources for these materials are other teachers, parents, community agencies or clubs, and the children themselves. Students who have completed projects in related areas are usually happy to loan their materials to other children. Poetry, art work, records, or picture books that deal with the subject may also make useful display items. Once the center is dismantled, these items can be returned to the original owners or stored in an accompanying container.

The components described above comprise most of the necessary ingredients for stimulating the curiosity of students with interest centers. The most important stimulation is how the teacher presents this opportunity to students.

Using Centers in Your Classroom

Although the actual design and construction of the interest center usually takes the majority of the teacher's preparation time, one cannot minimize the importance of the relatively few minutes it takes to display and introduce the new center to students.

Decisions about the location of the center, the number of students who will use it at a time, hours of use, and the kinds of students who will have access to it cannot be ignored.

It has been our experience that centers have the greatest effect when they are introduced to the class during a fifteen to twenty minute overview session conducted by the teacher. During this time, the teacher can create enthusiasm for the center's topics and activities through the use of an introductory film, speaker, book, or controversial classroom discussion. Current newspaper or magazine articles about the topic are also ideal for this purpose. Directions for using the center's audio-visual equipment can be explained at this time, and demonstrations of some of the center's optional activities can be conducted. Additional special suggestions can be found in *Using Learning Centers with Not-Yet Readers* (Judy & Steely, 1978) and *Secondary Learning Centers* (Bee, 1980).

We have also found it useful to make student memo blanks called "Action Information Messages" available for those who wish to pursue the topic in greater detail. These "lightbulb" messages, an identification and communication device used within The Enrichment Triad Model, can be given to the resource room teacher to alert him or her to the student's interest in a long-term investigation. Examples of these lightbulbs are on page 113. Teachers should be alert to the student who displays great enthusiasm and knowledge about the center's topic. With teacher intervention and motivation, students can and should become prime candidates for long-term projects. The steps to help students pursue these projects are explained in the next section.

Not all students whose curriculum has been compacted may be interested in exploring the center's topics, and even fewer will have the necessary task commitment to become involved in long-term projects. This should not be construed as lack of motivation or independence, but more likely a lack of interest in, exposure to, or experience with self-initiated projects. With the introduction of several centers over the school year, we found that most students become involved in at least one center's activities. In addition, the use of information from students' interest inventories should help focus future center design on topics of greatest interest to the majority of students.

Even more important is the teacher's attitude and behavior toward the use of the interest development center. If, on introducing the new center, the teacher is adamant that it may only be used by students who consistently finish all their work, students will perceive that interest development centers are based on basic skill development. Students may conclude erroneously that activities involving interest exploration and creative production are not as valuable as time spent in textbook assignments and worksheet completion. On the other hand, the teacher who allocates some regularly scheduled amount of time to interest exploration is conveying yet another nonverbal message—one that more closely parallels the philosophy behind child-centered learning.

By praising and encouraging children to take risks and learn to independently gather information, the teacher has reinforced behavior that most likely will lead to a love of independent learning. The opportunity for children to explore interests and solve real-world problems, rather than to be merely involved in acquiring basic skills at a superior level, seems the most likely way to foster habits that will help our bright children actualize their potential for creativity and problem solving.

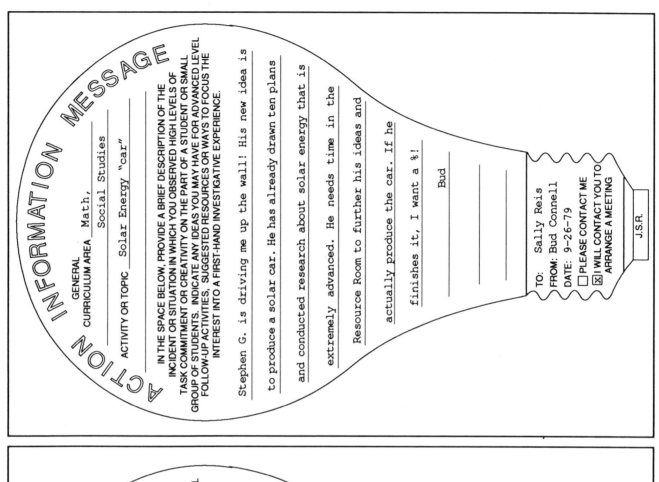

ACTION INFORMATION MESSAGE

GENERAL
CURRICULUM AREA Math,
                 Social Studies

ACTIVITY OR TOPIC Solar Energy "car"

IN THE SPACE BELOW, PROVIDE A BRIEF DESCRIPTION OF THE
INCIDENT OR SITUATION IN WHICH YOU OBSERVED HIGH LEVELS OF
TASK COMMITMENT OR CREATIVITY ON THE PART OF A STUDENT OR SMALL
GROUP OF STUDENTS. INDICATE ANY IDEAS YOU MAY HAVE FOR ADVANCED LEVEL
FOLLOW-UP ACTIVITIES, SUGGESTED RESOURCES OR WAYS TO FOCUS THE
INTEREST INTO A FIRST-HAND INVESTIGATIVE EXPERIENCE.

Stephen G. is driving me up the wall! His new idea is

to produce a solar car. He has already drawn ten plans

and conducted research about solar energy that is

extremely advanced. He needs time in the

Resource Room to further his ideas and

actually produce the car. If he

finishes it, I want a %!

Bud

TO: Sally Reis
FROM: Bud Connell
DATE: 9-26-79
☐ PLEASE CONTACT ME
☒ I WILL CONTACT YOU TO
   ARRANGE A MEETING

J.S.R.

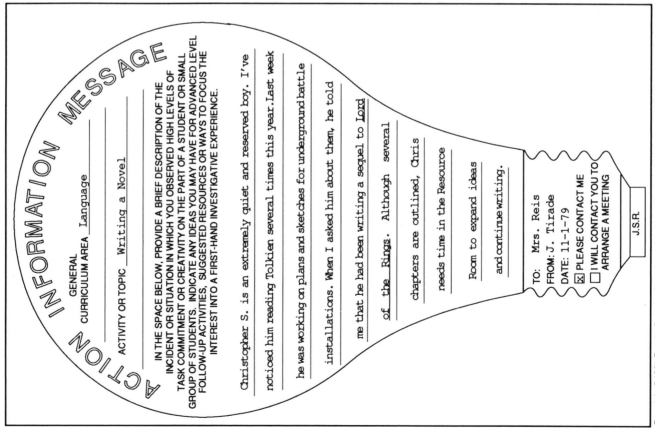

ACTION INFORMATION MESSAGE

GENERAL
CURRICULUM AREA Language

ACTIVITY OR TOPIC Writing a Novel

IN THE SPACE BELOW, PROVIDE A BRIEF DESCRIPTION OF THE
INCIDENT OR SITUATION IN WHICH YOU OBSERVED HIGH LEVELS OF
TASK COMMITMENT OR CREATIVITY ON THE PART OF A STUDENT OR SMALL
GROUP OF STUDENTS. INDICATE ANY IDEAS YOU MAY HAVE FOR ADVANCED LEVEL
FOLLOW-UP ACTIVITIES, SUGGESTED RESOURCES OR WAYS TO FOCUS THE
INTEREST INTO A FIRST-HAND INVESTIGATIVE EXPERIENCE.

Christopher S. is an extremely quiet and reserved boy. I've

noticed him reading Tolkien several times this year. Last week

he was working on plans and sketches for underground battle

installations. When I asked him about them, he told

me that he had been writing a sequel to Lord

of the Rings. Although several

chapters are outlined, Chris

needs time in the Resource

Room to expand ideas

and continue writing.

TO: Mrs. Reis
FROM: J. Tirade
DATE: 11-1-79
☒ PLEASE CONTACT ME
☐ I WILL CONTACT YOU TO
   ARRANGE A MEETING

J.S.R.

GUIDING STUDENTS THROUGH INDEPENDENT STUDY

Twelve steps are provided here to teach students how to produce high quality products using the time saved in the compacting process. These steps have emerged from many years of working with above-average students in classroom and resource room settings in a program based on focusing student interests into manageable products. The steps are not necessarily sequential and some may be eliminated if students have previously accomplished the objective.

Teachers or media specialists may first instruct students in these steps. They can be modified for use with primary students or introduced in a written format for upper elementary or secondary students. In a heterogeneous classroom, the methodology of independent research can be taught to students whose curriculum has been compacted or it can be introduced to the top reading group (usually above-average students) or even the entire classroom. When the latter approach is used, a student's positive response and desire to follow through is an excellent indication that this student is capable of independent work. Various degrees of response come from students of various ability levels. Our experience has shown that students in the upper ability range have the most potential for developing high quality differentiated products, but that should not deter us from teaching the process to all students in a regular classroom setting.

STEP ONE: ASSESS, FIND OR CREATE STUDENT INTERESTS

First, students should be encouraged to select a topic in which they have an intense interest. Too often, independent study is mistakenly confused with doing a research or term paper based on the subject area in which the paper is assigned. We cannot expect a student to become actively involved in a topic in which little or no interest is displayed. For example, a student who has a passionate interest in artificial intelligence and spends all of her free time devouring books on that topic probably will not expend high energy or commitment on a report or term paper on Shakespeare for an honors English class.

Students' interests may need to be sparked by exposure to new topics or disciplines of study or by extensions of the regular curriculum. An interesting observation about student interests is that they often decline as students get older. Primary-aged students have many intereststhey would like to pursue; junior- and senior-high-school students indicate interest in fewer topics. In some cases, interests can be created by administering an open-ended instrument such as the Interest-A-Lyzer, scheduling high-interest speakers, or introducing high-interest topics into the regular curriculum.

Casual interest may or may not be appropriate for independent study. If a student's interest and questions about a topic can be addressed in a brief review of available references, it probably will not result in an extensive research project. Whether it is a casual or long-term interest can often be ascertained by interviewing the student.

STEP TWO: CONDUCT AN INTERVIEW TO DETERMINE
THE STRENGTH OF THE INTEREST

Several important topics should be dealt with in a student interview. The teacher or a media specialist or librarian should try to assess how much interest is really present for further pursuit of the topics. Several questions may be asked that will lead the teacher to determine whether or not a true interest is being pursued. If the interest involved journalism, for example, and the student wanted to produce a monthly school newspaper, the following questions might be asked at an initial interview:

1. How long have you been interested in journalism?
2. What sources have you contacted to learn more about this subject?
3. Have you ever tried to publish a class or neighborhood newspaper? If not, why?
4. Have you ever tried to visit our local newspaper?
5. Do you know any other students or adults who are interested in this topic?
6. Have you looked at any books or talked with anyone who might help you get started on a monthly newspaper? If I can help you find some books or someone to talk to about this project, do you think this might give you some ideas?
7. How did you become interested in journalism?

Questions such as these will help to assess interest and commitment. The last question is especially important because we want to be certain that the interest is, in fact, the student's. If the student responded that he had not contacted any sources or read any books or made any attempt in any way to learn more about journalism, one might question whether or not this would be an appropriate topic to pursue. Every attempt should be made to encourage the interest and assist the student in finding information about the interest. If, however, these attempts do not generate the type of follow-up that should be required to produce a high quality product, it is unreasonable to expect that a student should or would want to continue in this endeavor. Questions such as these will help to determine if the student has really considered the amount of work involved in the actual completion of the independent study. If the student indicates that he has only an hour a month outside of school to spend on this project, suggestions should be provided for how more time might be spent pursuing this idea both at home and in school. Curriculum compacting frees up several hours a week for bright students in their classroom which might be spent producing a differentiated product. A student often will not know *how* to develop a newspaper that is different from other student efforts. This is the crucial step in producing a differentiated product; at this time, the methodology of how to produce something qualitatively better can be introduced.

STEP THREE: HELP STUDENTS FIND A QUESTION (QUESTIONS) TO RESEARCH

This step in teaching the process of independent study is also referred to as problem finding and focusing. Most educators have little difficulty recognizing general families of interest: scientific, historical, literary, mathematical, musical, athletic. However, problems arise when they attempt to capitalize on these general interests and use them as the starting point for (1) focusing in on a specific manifestation of general interests, and (2) structuring specific interests into researchable problems. How teachers deal with interests, both general and specific, is crucial and if handled improperly will undoubtedly get students off on the *wrong* track.

We know of one youngster, for example, who expressed an unusual interest in sharks. The teacher appreciated the child's enthusiasm and reacted in what he thought was an appropriate fashion: "I'm glad that you have such a great interest in sharks. Why don't you do a report about sharks?" Those words, "do a report..." lead to an inevitable end result—yet another summary of facts and drawings based entirely on information copied from encyclopedias and "all-about" books. While the student prepared a very neat, accurate report, her major investigative activity was looking up and summarizing already existing information. Although gathering background information is always an important starting point for any investigative endeavor, one of the goals of independent study is to help youngsters extend their work beyond the usual kinds of *reporting* that result when teachers and students view this process as merely looking up information. Some training in reporting is a necessary part of good education for all students. Indeed, the pursuit of new knowledge should always begin with a review of what is already known about a topic. The end result of independent study for gifted students, however, should be a creative contribution that is beyond the already existing information typically found in encyclopedias and "all-about" books.

How can we help students learn to focus problems and become involved in more advanced types of creative and productive involvement? The first step is to help students ask the right kinds of questions: those routinely raised by those who do investigative research within particular fields of knowledge. At this point, however, we are faced with a practical problem. Because most teachers are not themselves well-versed in asking the right questions about all fields of study, they cannot be expected to generate appropriate questions in any field of study their students might want to investigate. Teachers, therefore, can assist students in obtaining the methodological books (or resource persons, if available) that routinely list these important questions. In other words, if a student wants to ask the right questions about focusing a problem in anthropology, then he or she must begin by looking at techniques used by anthropologists.

Every field of organized knowledge can be defined, in part, by its methodology. In every case, this methodology can be found in certain guidebooks or manuals. These "How-to" books are the keys to escalating studies beyond the traditional report-writing approach, and therefore we will devote a later section of this chapter to procedures for identifying and making the best use of "How-to" books. Unfortunately, some of these books are not ordinarily included in elementary or high school libraries because of their advanced nature, but that does not mean that able students cannot make appropriate use of at least selected parts of advanced materials. A listing of relatively inexpensive how-to books is included in the enrichment materials listed earlier in this chapter.

How-to books can help a teacher to find appropriate research questions for students. Jason's teacher was aware of his special interest in anything and everything having to do with science. (Keep in mind that science is an area rather than a problem.) She provided him with several copies of *Popular Science* and asked him to pick out the articles he liked best. This is a good example of an exploratory activity because these magazines include many topics not ordinarily covered in the science curriculum. When the teacher asked Jason if he would like to follow-up any articles by doing some research of his own, he selected hydroponic gardening. (The general area of science has now been narrowed somewhat, but hydroponic gardening is a topic rather than a problem.) The teacher obtained the following book from the media specialist, and Jason practically "devoured" it in one night: Birdwell, R. (1974). *Hydroponic Gardening*. Santa Clara, CA: Woodbridge Press Publishing Co.

Through discussion with his teacher, Jason came up with the idea of growing corn under varying conditions. His research question became: Will corn grow at different rates when certain macronutrients are varied while other conditions stay constant? He constructed several growing trays using paper milk cartons and obtained the necessary nutrients from his chemistry set, a high school chemistry teacher and a university extension agent with whom he made contact through assistance from his teacher. By varying the amount of certain macronutrients (nitrogen, phosphorous, potassium) and keeping other conditions constant [good research procedures] he was able to observe different rates of growth. Meticulous records were kept and weekly measurements of growth rates and plant "health" [data] were recorded. He also photographed plants grown under varying conditions by placing a standard growth-grid chart behind each plant [visual data]. Graphics and statistical summaries were prepared [data summary and analysis] and a written report was developed [communication of results]. Jason also organized an audio-visual presentation of his work [another mode of communication].

STEP FOUR: DEVELOP A WRITTEN PLAN

Once students have generated a question or a series of questions, they should be encouraged to develop a written plan. Some educators who have been successful in facilitating independent projects like to use a contract with students; others prefer the use of a student journal or log. The Management Plan (see page 118) (Renzulli & Smith, 1977) has also been an effective way to help organize ideas and develop a time line.

The Management Plan is an educational device containing a format that is not very different from the procedures followed by the first-hand inquirer. The adult inquirer intuitively engages in certain activities described on the Management Plan. For example, a sociologist working on an attitude survey may not actually list her intended audiences; however, she usually has a fairly good idea of the journals to which her results may be submitted and of the professional societies or organizations to whom such a research paper might be presented. After the student has identified a general area in which to do advanced level work and has used appropriate problem-focusing techniques, the student can begin to fill in the material requested in the box entitled "Specific Area of Study." A great deal of careful thought should be given to completing this box because all subsequent activities will reflect the degree of clarity with which the problem is focused and stated. The teacher and student(s) should answer the two questions listed in the box by using a frame of reference that characterizes the actual thinking of a real investigator in this field. If such a frame of reference is not apparent to teacher or student, a community resource person who knows that field or a methodology book will help to start them on the right track.

The two boxes labeled "Intended Audiences" and "Intended Products and Outlets" are designed to help steer the student toward thinking about the final form that the investigation will take and about the audiences potentially interested in the results. The questions and information sought in these boxes are derived from the role and purpose of the first-hand inquirer discussed above.

The two larger boxes on the Management Plan (Getting Started and Methodological Resources and Activities) are intended to provide a running account of the procedures and resources that will be used during an investigative activity. Both of these boxes should be completed cooperatively by the educator and student and modification should

Sample

MANAGEMENT PLAN FOR INDIVIDUAL AND SMALL GROUP INVESTIGATIONS
(Actual Size: 11" x 17")

Prepared by: Joseph S. Renzulli
Linda H. Smith

NAME _____

TEACHER _____

GRADE _____

SCHOOL _____

Beginning Date _____

Estimated Ending Date _____

Progress Reports Due on Following Dates _____

GENERAL AREA(S) OF STUDY (Check all that apply)

___ Language Arts/Humanities   ___ Science   ___ Personal and Social Development

___ Social Studies   ___ Music   ___ Other (Specify) _____

___ Mathematics   ___ Art   ___ Other (Specify) _____

INTENDED AUDIENCES
Which individuals or groups would be most interested in the findings? List the organized groups (clubs, societies, teams) at the local, regional, state, and national levels. What are the names and addresses of contact persons in these groups? When and where do they meet?

1. _____
2. _____
3. _____
4. _____
5. _____

INTENDED PRODUCT(S) AND OUTLETS
What form(s) will the final product take? How, when, and where will you communicate the results of your investigation to an appropriate audience(s)? What outlet vehicles (journals, conferences, art shows, etc.) are typically used by professionals in this field?

SPECIFIC AREA OF STUDY
Write a brief description of the problem that you plan to investigate. What are the objectives of your investigation? What do you hope to find out?

METHODOLOGICAL RESOURCES AND ACTIVITIES
List the names & addresses of persons who might provide assistance in attacking this problem. List the how-to-do-it books that are available in this area of study. List other resources (films, collections, exhibits, etc.) and special equipment (e.g., camera, transit, tape recorder, questionnaire). Keep a continuous record of all activities that are a part of this investigation.

GETTING STARTED
What are the first steps you should take to begin this investigation? What types of information or data will be needed to solve the problem? If "raw data," how can it be gathered, classified, and presented? If you plan to use already categorized information or data, where is it located and how can you obtain what you need?

be made as new activities are followed through and as a greater variety of resources are brought to the student's attention. A "mushrooming effect" often takes place as resources become more familiar and the greater variety of resources, in turn, advance the level of sophistication that is brought to bear on a particular problem.

The completion of the "Getting Started" and "Methodological Resources" boxes will often be dependent on the availability of appropriate resource guides. For example, if a youngster is studying the attitudes of other students about an issue such as dress code regulations, an interviewer's manual or guidebook for constructing attitude questionnaires will be a key resource. In many cases these types of references provide the step-by-step procedures that will assist students in completing the "Getting Started" box and the activities section of the "Methodological Resources" box.

In certain respects, the two larger boxes on the Management Plan should parallel each other. In the "Getting Started" box, the student should list the early steps necessary for beginning an investigation and the types of information that will be needed to pursue the study, at least in the initial stages. Since early success is an important factor for continued motivation to complete the study, teachers must work very closely with youngsters in helping them to complete this box. The information in the box can serve as a checklist for determining whether the student is heading in the right direction. It can also assist in setting target dates for progress reports. In certain instances a student may want to lay out the entire plan in the "Getting Started" box, and, in other cases, the plan may begin here and be continued in the "Methodological and Resources and Activities" box. In view of the wide variety of topics that students may choose to pursue and the many variations in methodology that characterize various areas of study, a rigid prescription for completing these two boxes of the Management Plan is difficult to outline. In some instances, students may wish to use a flow chart and record their activities in a log or notebook. Whenever space does not permit the recording of necessary information, the reverse side of the Management Plan can be used, additional pages can be appended or a separate notebook may be maintained.

STEP FIVE: HELP STUDENTS LOCATE MULTIPLE RESOURCES AND CONTINUE WORKING ON THE TOPIC

In addition to helping students focus their problem through the methods described earlier, how-to-do-it books should be located to help provide advanced content and methodological assistance. Students should also be directed to the numerous resources at their disposal *beyond* encyclopedic references. These resources include but are not limited to textbooks, biographies and autobiographies, how-to books, periodicals, films, letters, surveys, phone calls and personal interviews, almanacs, and atlases. Educators should encourage students to use many different types of resources. Librarians and media specialists are also able to help students with this.

STEP SIX: PROVIDE METHODOLOGICAL ASSISTANCE

Methodological assistance means helping students to acquire and make appropriate use of the specific data-gathering tools and investigative techniques that are the standard and necessary methods for authentic research in particular fields of study. If a problem is well defined and focused, the correct guidance by teachers, media specialists or librarians during this phase of a study can almost guarantee that students will be first-hand investigators rather than reporters. This step of the process involves shifting the emphasis from learning *about* topics to learning *how* one gathers, categorizes, analyzes, and evaluates information in particular fields. During this crucial time of independent research, we can almost guarantee that student products will be differentiated by the methodological assistance and instruction they receive.

Every field of knowledge is characterized in part by certain kinds of raw data. New contributions are made in a field when investigators apply well-defined methods to the process of synthesizing previously random bits and pieces of information. Although some investigations require levels of sophistication and equipment that are far beyond the reach of younger students, almost every field of knowledge has entry level and junior level data gathering opportunities. At this stage of the independent study process, the teacher's role is to help students identify, locate and obtain resource materials or persons that can provide assistance in the appropriate use of investigative techniques. In some cases, teachers may have to consult with librarians or professionals within a field for advice about where and how to find resource materials. Professional assistance also may be needed to translate complex concepts into ideas students can understand. Although methodological assistance is a major part of the teacher's responsibility, to expect teachers to have mastered a large number of investigative techniques is neither necessary nor realistic. That is one reason that a critical role can be played by media specialists and librarians. A good general background and orientation toward the overall nature of research is necessary, but the most important skills are the ability to know where and how to help a student obtain the right kind of material and the willingness to locate the necessary resources for students.

For elementary classroom and secondary subject area teachers, the first step in learning about methodologies involves identifying the disciplines within the subject being taught, the "-ologies" and "-ographies" of the field. Following are some examples:

Social Science—history, geography, economics, sociology, political science, anthropology, psychology, theology, philosophy

Sciences—biology, microbiology, botany, zoology, ornithology, herpetology, entomology, oceanography, ecology, biochemistry, chemistry, physics, astronomy, geology, meteorology

Language Arts (Modes of Communication)—fiction writing, journalism, play writing, literary criticism, poetry, cartooning, drawing, graphics, photography, cinematography, drama, oratory, debate, story telling, mime, dance, song writing, music

Mathematics—number theory, statistics, probability, geometry, topology, logic, calculus, mathematical modeling.

Once the disciplines have been identified, teachers or students can be helped to focus on areas that are of interest to many students (based on information from an interest inventory). One example of a process skill that would prove useful in almost any independent project is research methodology, including such aspects as problem finding and focusing, research question and hypothesis generation, research design, data gathering and analysis, and dissemination of results.

Once an interest is chosen, the teacher should help the student to identify methodologies used within the particular discipline. This can be accomplished by obtaining "How-to" books that explain the methodologies of practicing professionals in terms that students and teachers can understand. A few are texts, but most are published as trade books, intended for a general audience.

Using a "How-to" book as a source of professional expertise for students who have already identified an area of potential investigation is an excellent way of upgrading the quality of independent study products. Depending on the ability of the student and the readability of the book, the teacher may choose to have the student work with the book independently, teach the techniques, or work with the student using the book as a resource. The book might provide suggestions for research or real-world problems to be solved. The book should provide guidance and instruction in professional-level methodologies that the student can use to carry out the project after a problem has been brought into focus. Finally, the book might have information about appropriate audiences and formats for communicating findings.

STEP SEVEN: HELP STUDENTS DECIDE WHICH QUESTION (S) TO ANSWER

Once students have learned about the disciplines, become more aware of their interests and identified the methodology, they are then able to decide which question or area they want to research. Students often begin investigations when they see how particular methodologies make it possible for them to pursue an interest.

STEP EIGHT: PROVIDE MANAGERIAL ASSISTANCE

Managerial assistance consists of helping students make arrangements for obtaining the data and resources necessary for independent investigations. Setting up an interview with a public official, arranging for the distribution of a questionnaire to students or parents, and providing transportation to a place where data will be gathered are all examples of managerial functions. Additional activities might include gaining access to laboratories of computer centers, arranging for the use of a college library, helping students gain access to a telephone or photocopying machine and driving to pick up some photographic materials or electronic parts. Our responsibilities concerning this are similar to the combined roles of research assistant, advocate, ombudsman, campaign strategist and enthusiastic friend. At this stage of product development, the student should be the leader and emerging expert while the teacher or librarian assumes a supportive rather than authoritative posture. The teacher's typical comments should be: "What can I do to help you? Are you having any problems? Do you need to get a book from the university library? Would you like to bounce a few ideas off me? Are there some ways that we might explore raising the money for solar cells?"

The major purpose of the managerial role is to help the student stay on track and move toward each intermediate goal. A planned strategy for up-to-date progress reports between meetings such as a log, notebook or annotated time line will create a vehicle for fulfilling the managerial role. And of course, this procedure should involve a review and analysis of the Management Plan or any other written plan being kept by the student.

STEP NINE: IDENTIFY FINAL PRODUCTS AND AUDIENCES

Finding an audience is regarded by some theorists (Renzulli, 1977) as the key to improving the quality of products and developing effective ways of communicating their results with interested others. A sense of audience is a primary contributor to task commitment and the concern for excellence and quality that we have witnessed in many high quality products resulting from independent study projects.

Attention must be given to helping students find appropriate outlets and audiences for their most creative efforts. This concern is once again modeled after the *modus operandi* of creative and productive individuals. If we could sum up in as few words as possible the *raison d'etre* of highly creative artists and scholars, it would certainly be *impact on audience*. Creativity is a source of personal satisfaction and self-expression, but a good deal of the rewards come from bringing about desired changes in the human condition. The writer hopes to influence thoughts and emotions, the scientist carries out research to find better ways to contribute to the knowledge of their field, and artists create products to enrich the lives of those who view their works. Teachers can help young people to acquire this orientation by encouraging them to develop a sense of audience from the earliest stages of an independent investigation.

It is the teacher's role to help students take this one small but often neglected step in the overall process of product development: selecting an outlet and an audience. How people typically communicate results or products within a field should be considered. The final product should be decided by the student based on that student's interests. Students who are interested in media or film should not be forced to write an article. Once a type of product has been chosen, audiences should be explored. For teachers to have the names of all possible audiences and outlets at their fingertips is neither necessary nor practical; however, classroom teachers need to find out about the existence of audiences and outlets. What historical societies or conservation groups are in your community? Do they publish newsletters or have regularly scheduled meetings? Would they be receptive to including a student's article in their newsletter or perhaps having a student present the research results at one of their meetings? "How-to" books may also be used to provide guidance for identifying products and audiences.

Although school and local audiences are an obvious starting point, teachers should help students gain a perspective for more comprehensive outlet vehicles and audiences. Many organizations, for example, prepare newsletters and journals at the state and national levels. These organizations usually are receptive to high quality contributions by young people. Similarly, state and national magazines often carry outstanding work by young people. Whenever a student product achieves an unusually high level of excellence, encourage the student to contact one of the publishing companies and magazines that specialize in or are receptive to the contributions of young writers, artists and researchers. Just as gifted athletes extend their involvement into larger and larger fields of competition, so should young scholars and artists be encouraged to reach out beyond the local levels of success they have achieved. This involves an element of "risk-taking" and the chances of not having one's work accepted in the wider arenas.

STEP TEN: OFFER ENCOURAGEMENT, PRAISE AND CRITICAL ASSISTANCE

Even the most experienced researchers, writers and creative producers need feedback from persons who can reflect objectively on their work. For students beginning the often frustrating task of first-hand inquiry, feedback must be given firmly but sensitively. The major idea underlying the feedback process is that almost everything can be improved through revision, rewriting, and attention to details, both large and small. This message must be conveyed to students without harsh criticism or discouraging comments. Each student must be made to feel that your most important concern is to help the aspiring artist or scholar reach the highest possible level of excellence. Just as a champion athlete or dancer knows that a rigorous coach has the performer's best interests at heart, so must students learn that critical feedback is a major service that good teachers must offer.

Bright students often are unaccustomed to any criticism of their work. Therefore, encouragement must be given throughout the process, and students must understand that all professionals regard feedback as a necessary, although sometimes unpleasant, way to improve their work.

STEP ELEVEN: ESCALATE THE PROCESS

The teacher, media specialist or librarian should view his or her role in the feedback process as that of a "resident escalator." Sensitive and specific recommendations about how particular aspects of the work can be improved will help the aspiring scholar to progress towards higher and higher levels of product excellence. Every effort should be made to pinpoint specific areas for suggested changes. This will help avoid student discouragement and reconfirm a belief in the overall value of their endeavors.

How many of us have encouraged students to do research only to have them return with a synthesis of magazine articles (at best) or encyclopedia references? Even when we encouraged students to go one step further and do surveys, how often have we found that each polled the same ten friends or classmates? Bright students should not be blamed for using simple or unimaginative methods when they are not taught more advanced or appropriate ones. If teachers want students to act like first-hand researchers, they must teach them how these professionals work. Media specialists and librarians can also help in this process. Students need to understand how to identify and phrase research questions and hypotheses, design research that will answer their research questions appropriately, gather and analyze data without bias, draw conclusions, and communicate their results effectively. While the specifics change from discipline to discipline, all professionals use the research process in their work. Authors may state their premises less formally than scientists and may gather data through observations and introspection rather than experimentation, but the underlying processes are similar.

STEP TWELVE: EVALUATE

An almost universal characteristic of students at all ages is a desire to know how they will be evaluated or "graded." We would like to begin by saying that we strongly discourage the formal grading of products resulting from independent study. No letter grade, number or percent can accurately reflect the comprehensive types of knowledge, creativity and task commitment developed within the context of independent study. At the same time evaluation and feedback are important parts of the overall process of promoting growth through this type of enrichment experience and therefore students should be thoroughly oriented in the procedures that will be used to evaluate their work.

We believe students and teachers should both be involved in the evaluation process. Additionally, if an outside resource person or mentor has been involved in the development of the product, this person should be asked to provide evaluation input.

Numerous forms have been developed to help students evaluate their own work. An effective and simple questionnaire which has successfully been used for ten years in an enrichment program includes these questions:

1. What were your feelings about working on your project?

2. What were some of the things you learned while working on your project?

3. Were you satisfied with your final product? In what ways?

4. What were some of the ways you were helped on your project?

5. Do you think you might like to work on another project in the future? What ideas do you have for this project?

CONCLUSION

While no panacea exists for adjusting or modifying the regular curriculum for high-ability students, curriculum compacting provides clear direction and specific examples of what can be accomplished. Our field tests and research indicate that compacting *can* be implemented by teaching staffs. And when a *group* of teachers decides to use this system, it is easier to do than if one or two teachers try to compact without the support of their peers.

Deciding what replacement activities to use is often the most challenging part of this process for teachers, and, as we have stated, three basic concerns should guide these decisions: (1) the appropriate level of challenge for the students; (2) the individual content strengths, interests and learning styles of the student; and (3) the availability of advanced content and other enrichment and/or acceleration alternatives.

Many classroom teachers have not been exposed to methods of differentiating curriculum or providing for the needs of high-ability students in the regular classroom setting, and, accordingly, as much assistance and support as possible should be provided. There is more than one way to compact curriculum. The goal is effective, appropriate instruction for all students and many methods, materials and strategies can be employed to reach this goal. By tapping the creativity of many teachers, diverse methods that fit the individual styles of both teachers and students can be used to adjust the regular curriculum to meet the needs of high-ability students.

Challenges and Problems Associated with Compacting

Problem 1: *Spiraled Curriculum*

This approach works well for heterogeneous classrooms because students at various developmental levels can achieve mastery of these objectives over an extended period of time, but bright students end up repeating material they have previously mastered.

A quick glance at the scope and sequence chart of a curriculum guide or the teacher's manual of a textbook series will reveal the extent of curriculum spiraling in your own curriculum.

In order to deal with this problem, rather than assuming that every objective in a textbook's scope and sequence chart represents new or relevant learning, the teacher must decide which objectives are most appropriate for a given group of students. In deciding this, the teacher must determine the grade level at which the skill or content objective is first introduced. Students can then be pretested on these objectives to determine to what extent they have already mastered them.

Problem 2: *Poor Curricular Organization*

When districts do not have clear-cut guidelines, the adopted textbook series usually becomes the curriculum guide and the teacher's guide that accompanies this series must be used to identify the most relevant objectives. In other situations, the skills being tested at the end of a unit and the objectives listed for that unit in the teacher's guide often have such gaps that it appears as if two different people wrote the objectives and the tests.

When the objectives of the curriculum guide that is provided do not align with the objectives in the textbook series nor the skills that are tested on the district's standardized achievement test series, curriculum compacting cannot proceed without a satisfactory solution.

When courses of study are implemented without the use of curriculum guides, curriculum compacting becomes difficult at best. In this case, the interested teacher can begin the compacting process with a content area such as the math or reading. This step can be a help in at least *beginning* the compacting process.

Problem 3: *Attitudes of Co-workers*

The negative attitudes of co-workers can dampen the enthusiasm of teachers who support curriculum compacting. The reading supervisor who will not allow a classroom teacher to use out-of-level testing, the principal who evaluates teachers negatively if all students are not working on the same learning objective, or the fourth-grade teacher who objects when a third-grade teacher wants to accelerate bright students into fourth-grade math will all have a negative impact on a teacher who is trying to implement the curriculum compacting process.

To avoid this problem, a task force of parents, administrators, teachers, and building level curriculum specialists needs to be involved in the decision to adopt curriculum compacting. If it is formally adopted and creatively communicated to all who are concerned, negative attitudes will be minimized.

Problem 4: Insufficient Enrichment Resources

It is of little benefit to compact six months of lessons for a child if the teacher has no enrichment or acceleration options to offer. To provide these options, a classroom or building library of enrichment and acceleration materials can be set up to loan to classroom teachers who are implementing curriculum compacting, and the resources of the library can be expanded annually as the budget permits.

Problem 5: The Need for Flexible Classroom Management

The use of curriculum compacting requires that teachers use multiple teaching strategies and good classroom management techniques. Teachers with little knowledge of curricular objectives or a lack of experience balancing more than one student activity at the same time or who is accustomed to large group instruction is apt to resist or have difficulty with the compacting process. These teachers must be helped on an individual basis, ideally by a peer coach or a gifted education teacher who can serve as a consultant or mentor.

Problem 6: The Need for Staff Development

Teachers can learn most of what they need to know about the compacting process by reading this book. But before they are interested enough to read a book like this, they must be introduced to the concept through staff development.

Research shows that, rather than training sessions changing teachers' attitudes so that they change their teaching methods, the training does nothing to change teachers' views. It is not until they have applied what they have learned and seen positive results that any real change in beliefs and attitudes takes place.A review of the literature on staff development research reveals the following:

1. What a teacher *thinks* about teaching determines how teaching is done.
2. Almost all teachers can take useful information back to their classrooms when training consists of the following: (1) presentation of theory, (2) demonstration of the new strategy, (3) initial practice in the workshop, and (4) prompt feedback about their efforts.

3. Teachers are likely to use new strategies if they receive coaching (either expert or peer) while they are trying them out in their classrooms.

4. Competent teachers with high self-esteem benefit more from training than less competent, less confident colleagues.

5. Teachers who are flexible learn new skills and incorporate them into their repertoires of methods.

6. Teachers' styles and values do not affect their abilities to learn from staff development.

7. A basic level of knowledge or skill is necessary before teachers can "buy into" a new approach.

Joyce and Showers (1983) reviewed a number of research studies to determine the elements of training needed to enable teachers to implement new teaching practices. These are the necessary components for training teachers:

1. The study of the theoretical basis or the rationale of the teaching method;

2. The opportunity to observe the model being demonstrated by persons who are relatively expert in the model;

3. Practice and feedback in relatively protected conditions (such as trying it out on each other and then on children who are relatively easy to teach); and

4. Coaching one another as they work the new model into their repertoire, providing companionship, helping one another to learn to teach the appropriate responses to their students and to figure out the optimal uses of the model in their courses, and providing one another with ideas and feedback).

Recommendations Based on Current Research

During the 1990-1991 academic year, The University of Connecticut site of The National Research Center on the Gifted and Talented conducted a study to examine the effects of staff development on elementary teachers' ability and willingness to implement curriculum compacting (Reis, et al. 1992).

This study demonstrated the following:

- Curriculum compacting can be implemented in regular classrooms to provide more appropriate educational experiences for gifted and talented students.

- Staff development and peer coaching can improve teachers' use of the compacting process.

- Teachers will need additional training and help to be able to substitute appropriately challenging content and work to students whose curriculum has been modified.

- Curriculum compacting can have positive effects on students.

Recommendations

Several recommendations for teachers interested in the implementation of curriculum compacting have emerged from the findings of current research:

Start Small
Start with a small group of students for whom compacting seems especially appropriate.

Select One Area
Select one content area in which (1) the targeted student has demonstrated previous mastery or curriculum strengths and (2) you have the most resources available to pretest and to enrich and accelerate the content.

Experiment with Pretesting
Be flexible—try different methods of pretesting or assessment and experiment with different systems. Ask for assistance from faculty members, aides, or volunteers.

Compact by Topic
Compact by unit, chapter, or topic rather than by time (marking period or quarter).

Decide How To Document
Decide how to document compacted material and define proficiency based on staff consensus and district policy.

Find a Wide Variety of Alternatives
Request help from all available resources in order to create a wide range of opportunities and available alternatives to replace content that has been eliminated through compacting.

Keep Experimenting
Keep trying, reflecting on what has worked and field testing new ideas.

FREQUENTLY ASKED QUESTIONS ABOUT COMPACTING

During the last several years, we have conducted over four hundred staff development sessions that have included both awareness and follow-up training on curriculum compacting. Below is a sample of the questions most frequently asked and their answers, followed by a list of *all* the questions grouped by subject that are included in Chapter 4. **The number beside each question directs you to the page number on which the answer is provided.**

Q. *How much extra time does compacting take for an already busy classroom teacher?*

A. Compacting, we have found, actually saves teachers time after they have learned to effectively use it. Some front end analysis time often results in not having to correct many homework and test papers that youngsters would have done. Of course, additional effort is often required for teachers who need to substitute appropriately challenging material, but most teachers who have learned to compact effectively tell us that it takes no more time then their previous teaching practices. They also tell us that the rewards and benefits to *all* students make the process very worthwhile.

Q. *How should I grade when I compact curriculum?*

A. Students should be graded on the regular curriculum which has been compacted. Grades should reflect mastery of content *rather than time spent* in a subject. When you do substitute independent study, we don't think it should be graded. Our preference is to provide some qualitative, holistic evaluation of the work done.

Orienting parents and students to the process of compacting

Strategies to make compacting easier

4 CHALLENGES, RECOMMENDATIONS AND QUESTIONS

In this chapter, the challenges encountered by teachers when they implement the compacting process are discussed. Suggestions for the most effective ways to begin curriculum compacting are explained. Also included is a description of the most recent research on the effectiveness of compacting and the most frequently asked questions about compacting.

CHALLENGES AND PROBLEMS ASSOCIATED WITH COMPACTING

Teachers who are interested in providing a more appropriate content or skills curriculum for their above-average-ability students must realize that they will encounter several challenges when they initiate the compacting process. Although none are insurmountable, they must be recognized and a solution must be sought prior to the implementation of compacting.

PROBLEM 1: REPETITION IN THE GRADE LEVEL CURRICULUM

The first problem that teachers frequently encounter is caused by the previously discussed instructional technique called the "spiraled" approach to curriculum development (Tyson-Bernstein, 1988). Unlike objective-referenced instruction that introduces a small set of process or content objectives to a select group of students during a given school year, a spiraled curriculum repeats instruction in many objectives over several school years. This approach is advocated for the heterogeneous classroom because it allows students who are at various developmental levels to achieve mastery of these objectives over an extended period of time. The spiraled approach is used for large group, rather than small group, instruction and often results in many bright students repeatedly participating in instruction or guided practice of previously mastered skills or concepts.

A quick glance at the scope and sequence chart of a curriculum guide or the teacher's manual of a textbook series will reveal the extent of curriculum spiraling in your own curriculum. Most publishers list the learning objectives for each of several grade levels in this kind of chart, and by examining the changes between the grade levels, the extent of spiraling can be determined.

In what may be an extreme example of curriculum spiraling, Connie Muther (1987) reproduced the following Table of Contents from a language arts textbook series (see page 133). Imagine the frustration of a bright English student who must repeat the same instruction in how to write a character sketch for four consecutive high school years!

In order to deal with this problem, rather than assuming that every objective in a textbook's scope and sequence chart represents new or relevant learning, the teacher must decide which objectives are most appropriate for a given group of students. In

CHAPTER CONTENTS • GRADES 9–12

deciding this, the teacher must determine the grade level at which the skill or content objective is first introduced. Students can then be pretested on these objectives to determine to what extent they have already mastered them.

PROBLEM 2: POOR CURRICULAR ORGANIZATION

Although it is likely that many students will have above-average abilities in a number of academic areas, classroom teachers may not have the skills or tools to compact them all. The absence of district or state level curriculum guides often causes many teachers to question which content and skills they are expected to teach. In situations like this, the adopted textbook series usually becomes synonymous with the curriculum guide for the district and the teacher must use the teacher's guide that accompanies this series to identify the most relevant objectives for instruction. In other situations, an examination of the skills being tested at the end of a unit and the objectives listed for that unit in the teacher's guide often reveals gaps and inconsistencies. In some cases, it appears as if two different people wrote the objectives and the tests.

Additional problems occur when the objectives of the curriculum guide that is provided by the district do not align with the objectives in the textbook series nor the skills that are tested on the district's standardized achievement test series. The resulting dilemma must be remedied in a satisfactory manner if curriculum compacting is to proceed.

Other problems occur when courses of study are implemented without the use of curriculum guides. Without a clear knowledge of major goals and objectives, curriculum compacting becomes difficult at best. Yet, individual student's needs cannot be ignored until more detailed curriculum guides are created. The interested teacher can begin the curriculum compacting process with a content area that offers the most instructional support, such as the math and reading curriculum. An attempt should also be made later at the district level to identify curricular goals and objectives in every subject area. In the absence of a curriculum guide, this step can be a help in at least *beginning* the compacting process.

PROBLEM 3: ATTITUDES OF CO-WORKERS

Even though the arguments in favor of curriculum compacting are extremely compelling, the negative attitudes of co-workers can dampen the enthusiasm of teachers who support curriculum compacting. The reading supervisor who will not allow a classroom teacher to use out-of-level testing, the principal who evaluates teachers negatively if all students are not working on the same learning objective, or the fourth-grade teacher who objects when a third-grade teacher wants to accelerate bright students into fourth-grade math will all have a negative impact on a teacher who is trying to implement the curriculum compacting process.

In order to overcome the potential problems associated with negative staff attitudes, we strongly recommend that central office administrators, a task force of parents and teachers, and building level curriculum specialists be involved in the decision to adopt curriculum compacting as a school district policy. Formal adoption by the school board, information about compacting in the school newspaper, and parent workshops about the process can all help to create the impression among staff members that this innovation is *not* optional and is, indeed, here to stay!

PROBLEM 4: INSUFFICIENT ENRICHMENT RESOURCES

Another challenge that must be confronted is the need for the appropriate enrichment and acceleration materials or resources for the student who has a compacted curriculum. It is of little benefit to compact six months of grammar lessons for a child if the teacher has no enrichment or acceleration options to offer. If a gifted education specialist is available, this individual can certainly help the student pursue investigations or research during compacted time. Yet, if there is no gifted education program, this does not mean that compacting cannot be implemented as planned. A teacher in this situation can arrange for in-class enrichment or acceleration for the compacted student. The use of video or audio tapes, computer software, interest centers, classroom libraries, small group instruction, mentors and independent study can all provide enrichment and acceleration in the regular classroom. In order to provide these options, a classroom or building library of enrichment and acceleration materials can be organized to loan to classroom teachers who are implementing curriculum compacting. The resources of the library can be expanded annually as the budget permits. Our experience indicates that an initial budget of eight hundred dollars and an annual budget of two hundred dollars per building is usually sufficient to provide a beginning collection of enrichment and acceleration resources for a school building.

PROBLEM 5: THE NEED FOR FLEXIBLE CLASSROOM MANAGEMENT

The adoption of curriculum compacting is not a cure for all of the ills of our education system. Although compacting can alleviate student boredom, assure content mastery, and provide time for enrichment and acceleration, the procedure rarely works well in a classroom with a teacher who has management or organizational problems. The use of curriculum compacting requires that teachers use multiple teaching strategies and good classroom management techniques. The teacher with little knowledge of curricular objectives or a lack of experience balancing more than one student activity at the same time is apt to resist or have difficulty with the compacting process.

Similarly, the teacher who is using the same lesson plans year after year, the teacher who is accustomed to large group instruction, and the teacher who relies too heavily on seatwork or workbooks will need strong support in order to succeed with compacting. For these teachers, help must be provided on an individual basis, ideally by a peer coach or a gifted education teacher who can serve as a consultant or mentor.

PROBLEM 6: THE NEED FOR STAFF DEVELOPMENT

By reading this book, teachers will have learned most of what they need to know about the compacting process. They will then need to field test and practice adopting and modifying the examples and techniques discussed in this text to meet their own style and classroom management strategies. Teachers use various methods of recording achievement information, pretest results, and replacement strategies. If a teacher, enrichment coordinator or principal becomes committed to instituting curriculum compacting as a school or district policy, staff development becomes a necessity. Before teachers become interested enough to take the time to read a book like this on compacting, staff development should be provided to introduce them to the concept.

What types of staff development are necessary for teachers to implement a new strategy? Guskey (1986) defines staff development programs as "systematic attempts to bring about change - change in the classroom practices of teachers, change in their beliefs and attitudes, and change in the learning outcomes of students." Advances in recent research on effective schools and the variables that contribute to instructional effectiveness have increased attention on the need for quality staff development programs (Brophy, 1979; McDonald and Elias, 1976; Medley, 1977).

Showers, Joyce, and Bennett (1987) have provided a meta-analysis of nearly two hundred research studies, plus a review of the literature on staff development research. Following are several of the highlighted findings of the research:

1. What the teacher thinks about teaching determines what is done when teaching. In training teachers, therefore, we must provide more than "going through the motions" of teaching.

2. Almost all teachers can take useful information back to their classrooms when training consists of the following: (1) presentation of theory, (2) demonstration of the new strategy, (3) initial practice in the workshop, and (4) prompt feedback about their efforts.

3. Teachers are likely to keep and use new strategies and concepts if they receive coaching (either expert or peer) while they are trying these new ideas in their classrooms.

4. Competent teachers with high self-esteem usually benefit more from training than their less competent, less confident colleagues.

5. Flexibility in thinking helps teachers learn new skills which they can incorporate into their repertoires of tried and true methods.

6. Individual teaching styles and value orientations do not often affect teachers' abilities to learn from staff development.

7. A basic level of knowledge or skill in a new approach is necessary before teachers can "buy into" it (Showers, Joyce, & Bennett, 1987).

Guskey (1986) suggests that staff development efforts are not influenced by teachers' beliefs and attitudes but, rather, attitudes and beliefs are a result of teachers implementing new practices and observing changes in students' learning outcomes. This is in contrast to the popular belief that staff development programs influence teachers' attitudes and beliefs first, which in turn influence teacher's implementation of new teaching practices in order to observe the effects the new practice has on student learning outcomes. Guskey believes that the kind of teaching practices that are sustained are those which teachers find to be "useful in helping students attain desired learning outcomes" (1986). Therefore, a key factor in the endurance of any change in instructional practices is demonstrable results of the learning success of a teacher's students. Activities that are successful tend to be repeated while those that are not successful, or those for which there are not tangible evidences of success, are generally avoided (Guskey, 1986). Guskey states, "The point is that evidence of improvement (positive change) in the learning outcomes of students generally precedes and may be a prerequisite to significant change in their beliefs and attitudes of most teachers."

The support teachers receive following training of a new practice has been suggested as a critical component of the successful implementation of a new teaching practice

(Guskey, 1986; Hall & Hord, 1987; Joyce & Showers, 1982, 1983, 1987). What type of support is necessary and under what conditions? These questions were addressed in several research studies investigating the coaching of teachers who were trying to improve their teaching skills or implement new practices.

Baker and Showers (1984) have operationally defined coaching as the "provision of on-site, personal support and technical assistance for teachers." Joyce and Showers (1982) state that there are five major functions of coaching: (1) providing companionship, (2) giving technical feedback, (3) analyzing application; extending executive control, (4) adapting to the students, and (5) personal facilitation.

Joyce and Showers (1983) reviewed a number of research studies to determine the new elements of training needed to enable teachers to implement new teaching practices. Their suggestions (1982, 1983, 1987) involve detailed elements of training that must be present in order for teachers to successfully implement new strategies in their classrooms. These are the necessary components for training teachers:

1. The study of the theoretical basis or the rationale of the teaching method;

2. The opportunity to observe the model being demonstrated by persons who are relatively expert in the model;

3. Practice and feedback in relatively protected conditions (such as trying out the strategy on each other and then on children who are relatively easy to teach); and

4. Coaching one another as they work the new model into their repertoire, providing companionship, helping one another to learn to teach the appropriate responses to their students and to figure out the optimal uses of the model in their courses, and providing one another with ideas and feedback.

RECOMMENDATIONS FOR IMPLEMENTING CURRICULUM COMPACTING BASED ON CURRENT RESEARCH

During the 1990–1991 academic year, The University of Connecticut site of The National Research Center on the Gifted and Talented conducted a study to examine the effects of staff development on elementary teachers' ability and willingness to implement curriculum compacting (Reis, et al. 1992). This study addressed how much curriculum content could be eliminated for high-ability students by teachers who had received various levels of staff development, and investigated what would happen to students' achievement test scores, content area preference and attitude toward learning if curriculum compacting was implemented. Teachers from twenty school districts throughout the country were randomly assigned by district to three treatment groups that received three different levels of staff development (videotapes, books, peer coaching). After receiving staff development services, teachers implemented curriculum compacting for one or two students in their classroom who were selected for their advanced academic abilities. Seven districts were randomly assigned as control groups.

The control group teachers identified one or two high-ability students and continued normal teaching practices without implementing curriculum compacting. A battery of achievement tests (out-of-level Iowa Tests of Basic Skills - ITBS), content area preference scales, and a questionnaire regarding attitude toward learning were given to identified students in November, 1990, and at the completion of the school year.

The following represent some of the findings from the curriculum compacting study:

1. Ninety-five percent of the teachers were able to identify high-ability students in their classes and document students' strengths.

2. Approximately forty to fifty percent of traditional classroom material was compacted for selected students in one or more content areas in mathematics, language arts, science and social studies.

3. The most frequently compacted subject was mathematics, followed by language arts. Science and social studies were compacted when students demonstrated very high ability in those areas.

4. A majority of the teachers in all treatment groups said they would compact curriculum again; some said they would try again if they had additional information and assistance from a specialist.

5. A significant difference was found among treatment groups with respect to the overall quality of curriculum compacting, as documented on the Compactor. Treatment Group Three had significantly higher quality Compactors than Groups One or Two.

6. Eighty percent of the teachers were able to document the curriculum that high-ability students had yet to master, list appropriate instructional strategies for students to demonstrate mastery and document an appropriate mastery standard.

7. Replacement strategies consisted of three broad instructional activities: enrichment, acceleration and other (peer tutoring, cooperative learning, correcting class papers).

8. Teachers in Treatment Group Three used significantly more replacement strategies than did teachers in Groups One or Two.

9. While approximately ninety-five percent of teachers used enrichment as a replacement strategy, eighteen percent also used acceleration.

10. Replacement strategies did not often reflect the types of advanced content that would be appropriate for high-ability students, indicating that additional staff development and help from a specialist in the district would be beneficial.

11. Approximately sixty percent of the replacement strategies reflected students' interests, needs and preferences.

12. Anecdotal records indicated that three different types of requests were made by teachers as they compacted curriculum:

    • Additional time for students to work with the gifted specialist (if one was available)

- Assistance in locating additional appropriate materials
- Consultant assistance as teachers worked through the compacting process.

13. When teachers eliminated as much as fifty percent of the regular curriculum for gifted students, no differences in the out-of-level post achievement test (ITBS) results between treatment and control groups were found in Math Computation, Social Studies, Spelling and Reading.

14. In Science, Treatment Group One scored significantly higher on the out-of-level post test (ITBS) than did the control group whose curriculum was not compacted. Students whose curriculum was compacted in mathematics scored significantly higher on the math concepts post-test (ITBS) than those in the control group.

This study demonstrated the following:

- Curriculum compacting can be implemented in the regular classroom to provide more appropriate educational experiences for gifted and talented students.
- Staff development and peer coaching can improve teachers' use of the compacting process.
- Teachers will need additional training and help to be able to substitute appropriately challenging content and work to students whose curriculum has been modified.
- Curriculum compacting can have positive effects on students.

RECOMMENDATIONS FOR IMPLEMENTATION

Several recommendations for teachers interested in the implementation of curriculum compacting have emerged from the findings of the study:

Start Small

Start the compacting process by targeting a small group of students for whom compacting seems especially appropriate.

We have found that in the earliest stages of learning how to compact, it is better to try to implement the service for two or three students than it is to tackle a whole reading group or an entire classroom. Learning how to locate available pretests, identify strengths, modify curriculum, and replace with interesting and challenging alternatives takes time and effort. Therefore, starting with two or three students who obviously require the service makes the process easier.

Select One Area

Select one content area in which (1) the targeted student has demonstrated previous mastery or curriculum strengths and (2) teachers have the most resources available to pretest for prior mastery and to enrich and accelerate the content.

Research (Reis et al., 1992) on the compacting process indicates that the most frequently compacted content areas are mathematics, language arts, and spelling (which is often taught separately from language arts). The percentage of content eliminated in mathematics ranged from 39–49%; in language arts between 36–54%. Teachers preferred compacting in mathematics and language arts because it is easier to compact basic skills than content. Most teachers beginning the compacting process (approximately 70%) only compacted in one content area at first. Another 25% compacted in two content areas and the remaining 5% compacted in three or more.

Experiment with Pretesting

Try different methods of pretesting or assessment, and be flexible in accomplishing this by experimenting with different systems and asking for assistance from other faculty members, aides, or volunteers.

As stated, many different methods can be used to assess previous mastery of skills or the potential of students to move through content at a more rapid pace. Objective-referenced assessments can be used for all students in the class. A table can serve as a pretest center, and students can decide if they want to take the pretest. Reading or math consultants often help prepare or administer pretests, and other faculty members can be asked to help as well. Alternative assessment techniques (essays, portfolios, students' products) can also be used to demonstrate proficiency and content expertise.

Compact by Topic

Compact by unit, chapter, or topic rather than by time (marking period or quarter).

While teachers listed strength areas for selected students, they differed with regard to the method by which they organized the curriculum compacting process and in the degree of specificity with which they described content material identified for compacting. A small number of teachers compacted by time, indicating either weeks or a marking quarter. The vast majority of teachers compacted by units or chapters of materials and documented that they would compact, for example, parts of speech, two science chapters on matter, or a unit in social studies.

Decide How to Document

Decide how to document compacted material and define proficiency based on staff consensus and district policy.

Either the Compactor or a locally designed alternative form can be used to document the compacting process. In the research described, participating teachers varied in the degree of specificity with which they documented the material to be compacted. A small percentage of teachers did not list the subject(s) to be compacted. Approximately 15% of teachers listed just the subject area in the first column of the compactor, such as math or spelling. The majority of teachers listed specific units, such as the solar system, electricity and magnetism, plants, air and weather, and the human body.

Teachers used various strategies to measure and decide what constitutes proficiency in a content area. The most frequently mentioned strategy for measuring proficiency across all treatment groups was the use of units, chapters, and review tests. Other strategies included outlining, reading comprehension questions, reinforcement dittos, check-up pages, weekly tests with the class, teacher-selected problems, cooperative learning, and individual work at the board with the teacher.

The majority of teachers (80%) identified a specific proficiency standard by which to evaluate whether students had mastered the regular curriculum. The criteria for determining proficiency ranged from eighty to one-hundred percent, and the most frequently used standard was eighty-five percent.

Find a Variety of Alternatives

Request help from all available resources in order to create a wide range of opportunities and alternatives to replace content that has been eliminated through compacting.

The highest quality compactors were prepared by classroom teachers who had worked with a peer coach and who had other assistance available to them. This help was provided by teachers in the gifted or enrichment program or content area specialists who provided materials or help with pretesting.

In some cases, a librarian/media specialist also helped by working with targeted students on advanced research projects or study skills. It should be noted that the most difficult task of teachers in the study was replacing compacted content with appropriately challenging content and independent study options. Teachers primarily used two categories of instructional strategies: enrichment and acceleration. Twenty-four different strategies were used by teachers, as outlined below.

Enrichment Strategies Used in Column 3 of the Compactor

1. Math puzzles, word problems
2. Projects
3. Free reading
4. Computer time/games
5. Creative games
6. Critical thinking activities
7. Resource room time
8. Crossword puzzles
9. Individualized kits
10. Field trips
11. More challenging words
12. Research
13. Utilization of reference materials
14. Creative thinking activities
15. Practice in research skills
16. Reports
17. Game creation
18. Entering games/contests
19. Learning centers
20. Public speaking
21. Bulletin boards
22. Journal keeping
23. Science experiments
24. Mentor-guided investigation

Teachers indicated that their greatest challenge in the compacting process was finding a variety of appropriate replacement strategies to substitute for compacting material. As noted, many alternatives were used but advanced content was often difficult for teachers to locate. Those who did not use advanced alternatives were often able to get help from the persons or programs previously mentioned.

Only eighteen percent of teachers in the study used acceleration as a replacement strategy. In most cases, this low number is indicative of school districts in which a policy exists *not* to accelerate students beyond grade level textbooks so that students who are accelerated may simply cover material in October that they would not have done until May or June. This type of acceleration is often minimally challenging for very bright students and it often becomes necessary to locate other alternatives.

Experiment   *Keep trying, reflecting on what has worked and field testing new ideas.*

The compacting process becomes easier as it evolves into more than just a series of testing and record-keeping exercises. When teachers have used compacting for awhile, it becomes an acceptable alternative and a new way of thinking about learners and the grade-level curriculum. To achieve this kind of success with the process, organization, and task commitment become crucial.

FREQUENTLY ASKED QUESTIONS ABOUT COMPACTING

During the last several years, we have conducted over four hundred staff development sessions that have included both awareness and follow-up training on curriculum compacting. The following questions represent those that are often raised in both awareness and advanced sessions. Several categories of questions are included.

ORIENTING PARENTS AND STUDENTS TO THE PROCESS OF COMPACTING

Q. **Can I compact curriculum if my administrator doesn't know about or agree with the concept?**

A. Your school administrator should be informed about your plans to implement compacting because it is such a major innovation. Most administrators will be supportive of your attempts to provide individual attention to students with advanced learning capabilities. An administrator who does not understand this process, however, will not be able to support teachers in the process. Therefore, we believe that administrators should be consulted before the compacting process is started. Doing this may prompt your administrator to ask other teachers to join your efforts in curriculum compacting.

Q. **Should students be provided with an orientation to the compacting process?**

A. All students in a classroom should be introduced to the compacting process. It should be explained in very general and simple terms such as the following:

> Today you will take a pretest on material that will be covered in the next several weeks. The results will help me to see how much you already know so that I can determine if you can skip some of the material or if you will need extra time with me to be able to master it. Some students are good in some subjects and others are good in other subjects. You should all do your very best on this pretest. For those of you who already know some of the skills on this test, many options exist. In some cases you may have time to spend in the library pursuing independent reading. In other cases, some of you may be spending time in the enrichment center or you may be able to start an independent study project that you select yourself. Once the pretest results have been determined, I will be meeting with small groups of students to talk about the results and decide on alternate steps for this unit of study.

We also suggest that some time be given to all students to pursue various types of enrichment within the classroom. If only the students whose curriculum can be modified or compacted have the opportunity to work on interest centers or other types or enrichment experiences, students who need much more time to master basic skills will never be provided with that option.

Q. **Should I inform parents if their child's curriculum is compacted?**

A. Parents should be informed of the decision to compact their youngsters curriculum. We recommend that a parent letter similar to the one on page 143 be sent home. Parents should know that the compacting process has been started because it may change the amount of paperwork that their child brings home daily. For example, the number of

LETTER EXPLAINING CURRICULUM COMPACTING
ENRICHMENT PROGRAM

TO: Parents

FROM: Resource Room Teacher

RE: Your child's participation in the Resource Program

As you may know from previous correspondence and meetings, your child is involved in enrichment experiences in a resource room program. The time spent in the resource room will not result in your child missing essential work in the regular classroom. A careful assessment of your son's/daughter's strengths has resulted in an agreement with his/her classroom teacher to "compact" the curriculum in that strength area so that your child will not be repeating work. It is during time saved from curriculum compacting that your son/daughter will be in the resource room.

The form that accompanies this letter is the completed Compactor that has been agreed on for your son/daughter by your child's classroom teacher and me. You will notice your child's academic strengths are listed in the first column and in the second column are the activities that were used to document proficiency in the academic strength area. In the third column are listed some of the enrichment or acceleration activities that your child will be involved in during the time that he/she is working in the resource room.

Please call me if you have any questions. I will be glad to meet with you about your child's involvement in the resource program if you should wish.

Thank you for your continued interest in and support of our program.

Please sign this form to indicate that you have received this completed Compactor and return it to your child's school as soon as possible.

Student's name:_____

School:_____

Parent or Guardian's Signature:_____

Date:_____

"perfect" papers that were consistently being brought home may stop for a time and be replaced by other kinds of work or activities. Parents should be active partners with teachers in the compacting process.

Q. **What are parents' reactions to curriculum compacting?**

A. Parents in most cases have supported it enthusiastically. They are often appreciative and say that they wish that this had been done much earlier in their child's school career. The only concern of some of the parents is the lack of outstanding papers to place on their refrigerator doors. This is a legitimate concern for those who like to use this type of reinforcement. However, once they have been oriented to the process of compacting, parents often understand that this is a key feature of the practice and that their child will benefit from the elimination of work already mastered.

Q. **What rules should I give students in my class who are doing alternate work?**

A. Students whose curriculum has been compacted should receive an orientation to that process in which the rules are spelled out clearly. They may include the following: (1) During compacted time, if the teacher is with other students, appropriate levels of quiet should be maintained to enable the other youngsters to learn, and (2) students whose curriculum has been modified should not interrupt the teacher. (This often means that they will be involved in alternate work in a different space in the classroom and will not be able to interrupt.) Other rules that are helpful relate to students' movement around the classroom during compacted time and their daily or weekly activities during that time.

STRATEGIES TO MAKE COMPACTING EASIER

Q. **What is required *before* I can start compacting?**

A. It is helpful for teachers to have (1) a clear understanding of the curricular objectives; (2) the knowledge of which students have mastered those objectives or who can master them in less time; (3) background information about how to compact; (4) alternate activities and the assessment devices that will be necessary to document mastery.

Q. **How can compacting be adopted by a district in an organized *systematic* way?**

A. (1) Make it seem as though it is a regular part of teaching practices. (When administrators support the process it is much easier.) (2) Have teachers order enrichment materials, pretests and other instruments for determining proficiency. (3) Provide training, budget money for materials, and offer other support systems for teachers.

Q. **What subjects are the easiest to compact?**

A. Subject areas with a highly sequential curricular organization such as spelling, mathematics, and grammar are the easiest to compact.

Q. **Should I compact by time period (like every marking period) or by unit?**

A. Compacting is usually done by instructional unit. A "unit" generally refers to an instructional period that revolves around a theme, chronological time period, or instructional objective. Some primary level teachers prefer to compact by unit of curricular organization such as a level in the basic reading or math program. If an English teacher is teaching a unit on *David Copperfield*, the most efficient way to compact this unit is to modify the curriculum for students who have either read the novel or who could read and master the unit's objectives faster than it takes other students. Elementary teachers often compact for a basic skills unit such as long division.

Q. **How much extra time does compacting take for an already busy classroom teacher?**

A. Compacting, we have found, actually saves teachers time after they have learned to effectively use it. Some front end analysis time often results in not having to correct many homework and test papers that youngsters would have done. Of course, additional effort is often required for teachers who need to substitute appropriately challenging material, but most teachers who have learned to compact effectively tell us that it takes no more time then their previous teaching practices. They also tell us that the rewards and benefits to *all* students make the process very worthwhile.

Q. **Will I have more success if I start with *one* student or should I start with a *group* of high-ability students?**

A. Some teachers have had success compacting for one student, but many others are able to compact for an entire group without a great deal of effort. How one can be most successful at compacting depends on several factors: the amount of classroom space, the amount of available enrichment resources, the availability of a library, help from other faculty including the teacher of the gifted or media specialist, and the degree of administrative support. It may be easier to begin compacting with one extremely bright student, but it is often better for that student to be one of a small group. That way, the student does not feel uncomfortable being singled out.

Q. **Do you recommend compacting an entire semester, leaving the last two months free for student self-selected projects, *or* compacting 2½ days a week, and leaving the rest of the week open for alternate work?**

A. Most teachers prefer to compact two or three days a week, and set aside one or two days or short blocks of time for enrichment assignments. When you compact a semester, it demands tremendous time and energy to plan a full two months of enrichment options.

Q. **What type of staff development will help me and my colleagues begin to compact curriculum?**

A. The most effective staff development begins with a general overview of compacting. Three suggestions are offered:

- *It's About Time: Inservice Strategies for Curriculum Compacting* by Alane Starko (1986) provides a script, black-line masters which can be made into transparencies, and step-by-step guidelines for conducting inservice presentations on compacting. The book also includes suggested methods for compacting curriculum and simulation activities to provide practice.
- Two videotapes on compacting are included in the nine-part tape series *The Schoolwide Enrichment Model*. These tapes include an introductory and a slightly

more advanced overview of this process. The tapes and a manual are available from Creative Learning Press, P.O. Box 320, Mansfield Center, CT 06250.

- A staff development session can be prepared from the information presented in this book. A compacted overview of each chapter, annotated examples of compactors, and questions and answers can serve as handouts. After a general overview session, classroom teachers can meet and discuss how they will proceed with compacting. Major instructional objectives and necessary pretests need to be identified. Additionally, teachers can observe how other teachers effectively compact curriculum. Grade level meetings and the opportunity to work on a specific content area will be helpful for teachers who believe that compacting is important. .

Q. **You have said that students whose curriculum is compacted in language arts should use that time to participate in pull-out programs or resource rooms. What if the enrichment or gifted/talented teacher can't take the student during that time because he/she is in another school?**

A. If the enrichment or G/T teacher cannot take the student during compacted time, the classroom teacher must provide alternatives. Remember, curriculum compacting is *primarily* the responsibility of classroom teachers. Having someone to help with the replacement activities or alternate curriculum often makes the process much easier; however, if that person is not available, classroom teachers still have responsibility to modify curriculum for bright youngsters

Q. **Can compacting be considered a part of a gifted student's I.E.P. (Individual Education Plan) in states in which gifted education is considered a part of special education?**

A. Yes. In fact, many consultants for education of the gifted in state departments of education have indicated that the Compactor form provides a perfect rationale for an individual educational plan for a bright youngster.

FINDING CHALLENGING STUDENT WORK FOR TIME SAVED BY COMPACTING

Q. **How can I find *appropriately* challenging substitute materials? In other words, what if my students only want to read relatively unchallenging fiction?**

A. Finding appropriately challenging substitute materials is one of the biggest challenges in the compacting process. In compacting students in first and second grade, it is much easier to substitute challenging work because the youngsters have not yet learned to put out minimum effort. So the compacting process should be begun *early* with substituted work that will challenge youngsters in the areas that they seem to have both a strength and an interest. Interest is a key component of compacting. If what is substituted is only more teacher-selected harder work, many students will simply opt not to get involved in the compacting process. For example, if a third-grade student who is exceptional in mathematics is assigned harder math problems every time she finishes her math work early, she may learn quickly to slow down! Therefore, by first ascertaining a student's sincere interests and the kinds of activities the student might like to pursue, the challenge level of the material can be escalated within the student's interest area. This is the most difficult task for classroom teachers who are already very busy. It is easier in this process to get the assistance of a teacher of the gifted or a content area consultant or some other volunteer such as a community mentor who may work with the youngster. If those options are unavailable, the student should be given a variety of choices, all of which involve some degree of more challenging substitution work, and the opportunity to select work based on previous or emerging interests. Other options are also available to the classroom teacher such as developing curriculum units or tapping into some of the materials that are listed on pages 94–101.

Q. Do I have to substitute math work if I am compacting math or should I consider other content options?

A. Many teachers who compact in math believe that the time that is replaced should also be from math. Yet, it is our hope that students' interests would be considered when a teacher makes that decision. If the student is outstanding in mathematics, an alternative for math instruction that has been previously mastered may be acceleration to a higher level math class. If the student is comfortable with this option, and the parents agree that this provision would benefit the youngster, this is often a viable alternative. However, if the student would prefer to work on an alternate activity or a self-selected independent study, the teacher should make this option available.

Q. What if you are trying to replace what has been compacted with students' interests only to find your students have *no* interests?

A. Unfortunately, as students get older and reach adolescence, their academic interests often dissipate. We suggest that interests be assessed with the *Interest-A-Lyzer* to help focus or discover interests, or else various enrichment opportunities be provided to try to stimulate interests. If students absolutely indicate they have no academic interest, a variety of exciting, challenging classroom activities such as those listed in Chapter 3 may be substituted. Interest may develop at various times and we must keep trying!

COMPACTING IN SPECIFIC CONTENT OR SKILL AREAS

Q. Can we compact in other content areas such as art, home economics, industrial arts, or music?

A. We have seen outstanding examples of compacting in all content areas. Industrial arts and home economic teachers are often the first to offer examples of how they have been able to compact. An industrial arts teacher gave a marvelous example of compacting: A student entering his woodshop class had spent the summer building a case for a grandfather clock. He brought photographs of the clock case and proudly displayed them. At that time, the teacher decided to eliminate the first three simple assignments in woodshop from this youngster's curriculum, deciding that it would be inappropriate for him to have to make a simple bookshelf when his talents were obviously so much further developed. This is a perfect example about how work can be compacted or eliminated within a specific area and be replaced with independent project time.

Q. Am I correct in assuming that if I teach process writing, compacting is unnecessary?

A. No. If youngsters can demonstrate that they have mastered the major writing objectives for the curriculum in that grade level, they should be able to choose what they do during that writing time. Many teachers who use the process writing approach believe that youngsters should just move up another notch of difficulty in process writing. However, if the student has a burning desire to conduct research in a related area or spend additional time in the resource room, grade level competency in process writing should open up that opportunity.

Q. **Am I correct in assuming that if I teach the "whole language" approach, compacting is unnecessary?**

A. No. A whole language approach also works well with curriculum compacting. Quite often teachers who use a whole language approach have at their disposal mostly grade-level trade books or alternative reading assignments. For a youngster who is outstanding in reading or language arts, these books may not be appropriately challenging. Therefore, when whole language is used, objectives should still be clearly stated so that bright students can demonstrate mastery. Simply replacing time with grade-level trade books or with options that are available to less able members of the class may not be appropriate. Remember, materials that replace the regular curriculum should always be appropriately challenging.

GROUPING AND CLASSROOM MANAGEMENT STRATEGIES

Q. **Is compacting harder to do in a heterogeneous class than it is in a homogeneous class?**

A. Compacting is easier to accomplish with a group of youngsters who have similar abilities. It isn't always accurate to say that compacting is more difficult in a heterogeneous class because a wide range of abilities, interests, and motivation often exist even within a homogeneous class. For example, students in an accelerated homogeneous English class may have very different backgrounds and interests in the subject area. Some students may be exceptional in interpreting literature, while others are there simply because they have high scores but don't care for the subject area. We have found in our field tests, however, that compacting is easier to accomplish when flexible grouping can be used.

Q. **Can I compact curriculum for my bright students without the help of a teacher of the gifted?**

A. Yes! While having a teacher of the gifted can make the job a little easier by procuring additional resources or enrichment materials or even upgrading the challenge level of regular curricular materials, the classroom teacher is still the person who is primarily responsible for modifying the regular curriculum. We have found that classroom teachers must take the major responsibility for implementing columns one and two in the Compactor, and many classroom teachers *want* to participate in helping to determine which activities and opportunities students should select for the third column of the Compactor.

Q. **How do you manage the rest of your classroom when the kids who have had their curriculum compacted start to "act up"?**

A. Students whose curriculum has been compacted should receive an orientation to that process in which the rules are spelled out clearly. They should understand their responsibilities, including using the time that has been provided for alternate activities appropriately. If they are not, the teacher should work with the student and his or her parents to determine the reason for their behavior. It is extremely important that classroom teachers be firm in their expectations of how students use their time.

Q. **How can I organize classroom space to make compacting easier?**

A. Many teachers who use compacting extensively have provided space for individual student stations in some part of their classrooms with a desk or a table and two or three chairs for independent study or free reading. A small library corner with some pillows or alternate seating arrangements can be extremely helpful for all youngsters. Some space for the learning centers or interest centers described in Chapter 3 is also helpful.

Q. **At what grade level should compacting begin?**

A. Curriculum should be compacted as soon as youngsters enter school. We have conducted inservice sessions with Montessori pre-schools in which curriculum is modified beginning at age three or four. When the compacting process begins in kindergarten, students learn to use independent time more easily and their freedom of choice more appropriately.

Q. **If I compact for my advanced students and let them leave for alternate activities, won't the quality of classroom discussions suffer? What if I really believe that students who are compacted would benefit from a particular discussion or special lesson?**

A. Many teachers have expressed this concern, which is merited to some degree. However, remember that less able students are sometimes intimidated by the presence of brighter students, and, consequently, won't contribute to the discussions. Students who may not test as well often feel inferior or threatened by the precocious verbal ability and intelligence of the higher ability youngsters. To resolve the problem, teachers might try some classroom sessions with the gifted students and some without them; if the discussions succeed with the advanced students, then it makes sense to include them.

Q. **What type of flexible grouping allows compacting to be done most easily?**

A. The type of flexible grouping that works best for compacting is certainly not a tracking system in which grades or test scores determine which track students are placed into early in the year. Ideally, students whose curriculum is being compacted will be in and out of various lessons in the classroom (depending on their needs and mastery of objectives), and this is easily accomplished in a heterogeneous classroom at the elementary level. However, in a curriculum such as math, science or basic skills in language arts, having a homogeneously grouped class or a cluster group of high-ability students within a class makes curriculum compacting much easier to facilitate. This is because teachers then know that the youngsters who are in this group are above average in the subject and should be compacted because they do not need the review.

Q. **If we use ability grouping in math and reading, do we still need to compact the curriculum?**

A. Yes. Even with high-ability grouping and specific subjects, students have differences in rates, paces, and interests. Compacting their curriculum can meet these needs.

COMPACTING IN ADVANCED CLASSES

Q. **What is the difference between compacting curriculum in an elementary classroom and in a secondary content class? Is it harder for secondary teachers?**

A. Compacting in an elementary classroom is often easier than it is in a secondary content class. Generally, elementary teachers have students for a longer block of time and are able to see particular students display competence within several different content areas. Elementary teachers can usually get a clearer picture of student ability earlier than secondary teachers. Secondary teachers often have to base decisions about compacting on a fifty-minute class a day. Because they have more students who are in and out of their classrooms and less time to consider individual differences, they often need to place youngsters in groups to be able to compact effectively. Our field tests (Reis & Renzulli, 1985) indicate that compacting at the secondary level is much easier once students are grouped so that those who like the subject, are fairly good at it, and want their curriculum modified to allow for various options are grouped together.

Q. **What is the difference between *basic skills* compacting and *content* compacting?**

A. This is explained in Chapter 2. Briefly, basic skills compacting involves testing youngsters on skills that they may have already learned, and proficiency can be easily documented. Content compacting involves allowing youngsters to move at their own pace through material that they have not yet mastered but can master in a fraction of the time that it would take their less able peers.

Q. **What about compacting an honors class? Can it be done?**

A. Yes. Even though this is a "so-called" homogeneous group, anyone who has taught in that situation realizes that there is really no such thing. Some students are more interested in the subject, some are more motivated, and some have a better background in one particular component of the subject than others. Therefore, compacting is completely appropriate and has been very effective in many honors classes.

Q. **What's the difference between compacting curriculum in an honors class and a talent pool class like those suggested in the Secondary Triad Model?**

A. The difference between compacting curriculum in a honors class and a talent pool class depends on the type of regular curriculum presented in those classes. An honors class generally deals with a more advanced curriculum. A talent pool class such as those advocated in the Secondary Triad Model, presents the regular curriculum with options for student initiative instead of a more advanced, teacher-presented curriculum.

DETERMINING MASTERY

Q. **How can I guarantee that a student has mastered objectives if I hadn't planned to use the textbook for that student?**

A. Remember that a textbook is not the tool that is necessary to guarantee mastery of objectives. The major learning objectives that are being covered by the textbook have to be identified, and if the student has already mastered them, it is probably inappropriate to use the textbook with that student. So we would strongly suggest that mastery of objectives exists before the textbook is used for pretesting.

Q. **Who is responsible for the pretesting?**

A. The person responsible for pretesting students is usually the person who teaches the regular curriculum. In many cases, classroom teachers who have implemented curriculum compacting seek and receive help from a reading or math consultant, or the teacher of the gifted if one is available.

Q. **Define mastery. How do I know if my students *really* know the work they are testing out of?**

A. It is difficult to define mastery. Most educators agree that mastery indicates knowledge of the learning objectives which guide any lesson. Benjamin Bloom defines mastery as knowledge of at least 80% of the major objectives in any unit of learning. We believe that a faculty should discuss the extent of mastery before the compacting process is started at the school and that teachers should be allowed to use their own professional judgement concerning individual students. Sometimes a short conversation or an essay question helps to define mastery better than a multiple choice or matching test.

Q. **What other ways can I guarantee mastery if no pretests or post tests are included with the textbook?**

A. We have made several suggestions (in Chapter 3) about the guarantee of mastery if pretests or post tests are not included with the regular curricular materials. Teachers can, for example, give an essay or have a discussion with students or use questions in content area textbooks that would reflect advanced level mastery. Mastery can be assessed in many ways that are even more effective than a twenty-item pretest or post test provided by a publisher, and this is an area that teachers can use their creativity to help determine.

GRADES AND COMPACTING

Q. **How should I grade when I compact curriculum?**

A. Students should be graded on the regular curriculum which has been compacted. Grades should reflect mastery of content *rather than time spent* in a subject. When you do substitute independent study, we don't think it should be graded. Our preference is to provide some qualitative, holistic evaluation of the work done.

Q. **What if a group of students who have their curriculum compacted do not want to do any other work? Can their grades reflect this?**

A. No. There are other ways to handle this. If you find that students are not using their time for alternative study wisely, you should talk over the problem with them. You might reiterate the concept of compacting, and explain what the next step would be if behavior doesn't change (such as a parent meeting). Compacting represents a radical educational departure for most students. Some students have never been given any options or had the responsibility for planning their own learning, or they have not learned how to work independently, and it takes time for them to adjust.

COMPACTING FOR NON-IDENTIFIED STUDENTS

Q. **Should curriculum be compacted for underachievers?**

A. Underachievers must be considered for compacting. Youngsters who underachieve are often bright students who have simply given up on trying to do all the work that is required of them because they know that they already mastered it many years earlier. Some students learn to underachieve because they are bored with the regular curriculum, and we have found, in many case studies, that compacting has an impact on the underachievement problem facing so many bright youngsters in our schools today.

In many instances, these students have also discovered that finishing their lessons before their classmates only means that they will be assigned more of the same work. By orienting them to the compacting process, we can give them an incentive to do better in their classwork. For example, if a youngster can demonstrate proficiency in grammar, he or she may then earn the opportunity to select a novel to read, view filmstrips about famous authors, write original short stories, compose poetry or select an area of interest in language arts. Being allowed to select what may be done during time in which the student demonstrates curriculum mastery often encourages an underachieving student to demonstrate mastery.

Q. **Do *average* students ever benefit from curriculum compacting?**

A. Yes, most definitely. According to our field tests, many average students get great value from curriculum compacting in one or more content areas. We believe that the compacting process actually helps reverse the "dumbing down" of the curriculum and that benefits all students, as do the enrichment materials brought into the classroom for use during compacted time.

Q. **What about my lower ability students? Can they participate in enrichment opportunities?**

A. All students, regardless of ability, should be given time to enjoy enrichment opportunities. While it is true that many students will not be eligible for curriculum compacting, every student should learn the problem solving, creative thinking skills and other facets of process training that alternative activities provide. Teachers could schedule a special time for these activities, such as Friday afternoons from 2-3 P.M.

APPENDICES

ELIMINATING TRACKING WILL HARM STUDENTS

By Joan Beck

Is it unfair to group public school children by ability? To allow some youngsters to move ahead faster, to learn more than others? What if the children in the faster classes are more likely to be white and middle-class and most of those learning less are minorities and poor? Is tracking by ability then unacceptable racial segregation? When the goal of providing all children equality of education conflicts with the goal of helping all children learn up to the level of their abilities, which should take precedence? Support for ability grouping—by first-grade reading sections, by subject matter, by across-the-board tracking, even by special schools for the gifted and talented—rises and falls as much in response to political pressures as academic rationales.

Now, opposition to grouping is growing, largely reflecting the desperate concern for helping poor, minority youngsters at risk of academic failure. Some school systems are dismantling existing track systems. Other educators are even talking about phasing out the popular Magnet schools so their resources can be diverted to struggling neighborhood schools.

Opponents of ability grouping make several strong arguments. It can be difficult, for example, to identify all the "gifted," "talented" and "bright." Formal tests are often inadequate. Teacher judgments can be biased by family background, behavior and appearance. Some bright children will be missed because they don't fit compliant, middle-class stereotypes or have difficulty speaking English.

Further, children left behind in slower tracks or groups suffer a serious loss of self-esteem and from a lack of brighter classmates and role models from whom to learn. Because the "bright" groups move ahead faster, slower youngsters can't ever catch up and are stuck forever in the academic pits. Bright kids draw the best teachers and the most resources, opponents charge. Slower youngsters get dull drill, plodding lessons, inexperienced teachers.

Some of the school systems backing away from ability grouping have found an ally and an excuse in the Carnegie Foundation. Last year, a report by its Council on Adolescent Development strongly condemned tracking as "one of the most divisive and damaging school practices in existence."

The Carnegie report cited "the psychic numbing" children in the lower tracks experience from a "dumbed-down" curriculum, the widening gap in achievement between faster and slower groups and the increased racial isolation of ability groupings.

Instead, it proposed that schools deal with students of widely diverse academic abilities by teaming them together in cooperative learning projects in which brighter students help slower classmates and "students receive group rewards." The report also advocates using capable students to tutor others.

Such proposals do irreparable injustice and harm to bright children, who are just as entitled as other youngsters to an education appropriate to their abilities. Yet the smarter children are, the more likely their classes will leave them bored and unchallenged, with their great potential unfulfilled.

Bright children already know most of what they are expected to learn during an average school year, studies show. To expect them, as Carnegie does, to spend much of their class time helping slower learners is an inexcusable waste of their irreplaceable learning time. They need the challenge of new ideas and new material and opportunities to learn at the accelerated speed most comfortable for them. To expect them to sustain a love of learning while marking time waiting for slower students to catch up is like asking Michael Jordan to be challenged by playing basketball indefinitely at a local "Y."

Bright children are much more likely to be middle class than minority poor. (Some incalculable part of intelligence is assumed to be inherited and fostering their children's learning is one mark of successful middle-class families, white or minority.)

But the remedies lie in protecting all children's developing brains through good prenatal care and using proven early learning techniques to increase intelligence long before first grade—not in holding smart youngsters back. Instead of treating high intelligence and talent as a sort of shameful secret, schools should be doing everything they can to find giftedness and learning potential in all children, to nourish it, cherish it and encourage it—especially in youngsters from families that lack the resources to do so themselves. Bright children aren't entitled to more resources or better teachers than other youngsters. But they are due an equal share—and an education that is a good match for their abilities.

Educators who refuse to acknowledge the special needs of high-ability children—because of a preoccupation with at-risk youngsters, a misreading of research on gifted or a lopsided focus on equality instead of excellence—need to look ahead to the nation's next century.

The new drugs, genetic therapies, inventions, energy solutions, transportation and housing systems, economic improvements, foreign policy strategies, government and business expertise, environmental leadership and human rights advocacy will have to come from today's children. We can't afford to make their schooling a holding-back operation—whatever the motivation.

'EXCEPTIONAL' RULING PITS SCHOOL DISTRICTS
AGAINST PARENTS OF GIFTED

By Julia M. Klein

On his first day at kindergarten, Terry Auspitz read a poem out loud—and was sent to the back of the room for talking. For this reprimand, the five-year-old drew a logical conclusion: "I didn't know you weren't allowed to read in school" he told his mother.

Other frustrations followed for Terry and his parents, Judith and Richard Auspitz of Warminster, Bucks County, as they fought to obtain what they believed was an appropriate education for their highly gifted child, now a sixth grader who celebrated his twelfth birthday this month. They faced teachers who said their hands were tied by the administration and administrators who said their programs were adequate for Terry's needs. In all, the Auspitzes have spent seven years asking the Centennial School district to give their son advanced instruction in both reading and math—the two academic areas in which he excels.

The district has replied that its 150-minute weekly enrichment program for the gifted— a program approved by the state—is all it is legally required to provide. The state Department of Education and the Commonwealth Court have disagreed. They have ordered the district to offer advanced instruction to Terry within his regular classroom. The court held that having an approved special-education program is not sufficient. It ruled that a district also must attend to the individual needs of each gifted student. Its decision, if it is upheld, could have far-reaching implications for the education of the gifted throughout Pennsylvania.

"As I understand it, (the decision means) a gifted student is entitled to individualized programming every day, all day long," said N. Robert Laws, director of pupil personnel services for the neighboring Central Bucks School District. That is the message advocates for the gifted have been promoting for years, and "many districts are out of compliance on this issue," said Barbara S. Labowitz, president of the Delaware County/ Main Line chapter of the Pennsylvania Association for Gifted Education. She said that if the decision, which Centennial has asked the court to reconsider, is affirmed, PAGE will instruct its members on how to use the ruling to get a better education for their gifted children. Said Laws, anticipating trouble to come: "If every parent believes that their (gifted) child is entitled to an individualized and differentiated program, the cost implications could be astronomical." And, if districts pour money into programs for the gifted, "it will reduce the amount of funds available to all other segments" of the student population, said Michael I. Levin, an attorney for the Pennsylvania School Boards Association, which filed a brief in support of Centennial.

Education for the gifted in Pennsylvania is a relatively new phenomenon, the outgrowth of a 1977 state law that includes gifted children—generally those with I.Q. scores of 130 or above—among those deemed "exceptional" enough to require specialized programs. From that state mandate have flowed a wealth of paperwork and a hodge- podge of programs that vary widely from district to district.

In the Centennial School District, the Auspitzes encountered a standard response to the state's requirements: 150 minutes a week of enrichment activities that stress such abilities as critical thinking and creativity. For the rest of the week, Terry, like most gifted elementary school children, sat in a regular classroom where only sporadic accommodation was made for his special talents. What the Auspitzes were requesting was another kind of gifted programming: acceleration, or the teaching of advanced subject matter.

A few school districts embrace acceleration as their main vehicle for gifted education—Marple Newtown, for example, has self-contained, accelerated classes for its gifted children from first grade on. And administrators in some other districts say they will make individual adjustments—including acceleration—for their most-gifted youngsters. All these accommodations are supposed to be recorded on a document called an Individualized Education Program, or IEP, which describes a child's achievement levels, goals and objectives for his education, and the programs being offered to meet them. Some districts, however, concede that they write IEPs to match their special-education programs and not for the individuals in them.

Darlene Mammucari, supervisor of gifted programs for the Rose Tree Media School District, said that filling out IEPs separately for each child could be "very cumbersome" and "could take away from instructional time." Instead, the district meets with parents collectively to "go over group goals for all students." Parents who complain get individual conferences and individualized IEPs, Mammucari added. If parents and a district do not see eye to eye on an IEP, parents may withhold their signature—as the Auspitzes did—and then take the district to a state Department of Education hearing.

If Centennial had accepted the decision of the secretary of education and *given* Terry advanced reading and math instruction, the matter would have ended there. But by pursuing the case through the courts, Centennial, if it loses its eventual appeal to the state Supreme Court, has opened the way to statewide changes in gifted education. How profound those changes would be—and how much they would cost—remains a matter of debate. Levin, the attorney for the state school boards' group, said he expected the decision to reduce the discretion of school districts "to shape and mold the types and quality of programs they provide." In addition, if a district is obliged to spend more money educating its gifted students, he said, it will have less to finance programs for other students. Finally, Levin said, the decision "eliminates any objective way of determining what a gifted child is entitled to" and allows parents to claim that whatever a gifted child needs, he is entitled to receive.

John Philip Diefenderfer, solicitor for the Centennial School District, said that, if the decision is upheld, the result may be a bureaucratic nightmare. "We're not against quality education. We're not against gifted education or even quality gifted education," he said. "We do have to have a consistent framework within which to operate, or we'll get so caught up in our own paperwork that every kid will have a file a foot thick, and we'll be too busy shuffling papers to educate kids."

Advocates for the gifted, on the other hand, say that the Commonwealth Court decision makes no new law, but merely clarifies what the state and other courts have said in the past. Tim Potts, a spokesman for the state Department of Education, said that the court decision offers "court approval for what our policy has been all along."

"The question is not that this decision is going to change the law," said Thomas E. Coval, attorney for the Auspitzes and an expert on school law. "The question is, are parents who have a gifted child who they believe is not getting an appropriate education ... going to ask that the program be tailored to meet the needs of the individual child? I think that in the past they have not."

PAGE leaders have hailed the decision as a landmark. Chapter president Labowitz said many districts have been "very resistant to accelerating kids at the elementary level in reading and math," just a Centennial was. "This provides a great deal of support for parents," she said. And Theodore H. Davis, a former PAGE board member and an expert on Individualized Education Programs, said the decision will force districts to pay more attention to the components of the IEP, including evaluation procedures.

Labowitz and Coval say districts can meet the needs of their gifted students without spending vast sums of money. And Davis said that some additional state funds are available to districts that write grant proposals. But, he added, "I'm not suggesting that it (the level of funding) is appropriate and adequate."

At the district level, the Centennial case appears to have occasioned mostly confusion and uncertainty. Some school district officials say the case may push them faster in directions they were heading anyway—toward greater individualization and programs that combine both enrichment and acceleration. Other districts, many of which offer programs similar to Centennial's say they are adopting a wait-and-see attitude while the case winds its way through courts.

In Marple Newtown, for example, Ed Eppley, director of special education, said plans already were underway to individualize IEPs and supplement the district's accelerated program with enrichment activities. And Abington, which now provides only an enrichment program to its gifted elementary students, is considering "offering more of an accelerated program," said Teresa Montanaro, supervisor of special education. But Montanaro said she wondered whether children not labeled "exceptional" will end up getting short-changed. "We're already getting to the point where if you're a parent of a run-of-the-mill, average child, you don't seem to have many rights at all," she said

ABILITY GROUPING

RESEARCH-BASED DECISION MAKING SERIES

GUIDELINES BY
JAMES K. KULIK

1 Although some school programs that group children by ability have only small effects, other grouping programs help children a great deal. Schools should therefore resist calls for the wholesale elimination of ability grouping.

2 Highly talented youngsters profit greatly form work in accelerated classes. Schools should therefore try to maintain programs of accelerated work.

3 Highly talented youngsters also profit form an enriched curriculum designed to broaden and deepen their learning. Schools should therefore try to maintain programs of enrichment.

4 Bright, average, and slow youngsters profit form grouping programs that adjust the curriculum to the aptitude levels of the groups. Schools should try to use ability grouping in this way.

5 Benefits are slight from programs that group children by ability but prescribe common curricular experiences for all ability groups. Schools should not expect student achievement to change dramatically with either establishment or elimination of such programs.

THE NATIONAL RESEARCH CENTER
ON THE
GIFTED AND TALENTED

The University of Connecticut
362 Fairfield Road, U-7 • Storrs, CT 06269-2007

NRC G/T

L Cooperative Learning

RESEARCH-BASED DECISION MAKING SERIES

RECOMMENDATIONS BY
ANN ROBINSON

1 Cooperative learning in the heterogenous classroom should not be substituted for specialized programs and services for academically talented students.

2 If a school is committed to cooperative learning, models which encourage access to materials beyond grade level are preferable for academically talented students,

3 If a school is committed to cooperative learning, models which permit flexible pacing are preferable for academically talented students.

4 If a school is committed to cooperative learning, student achievement disparities within the group should not be too severe.

5 Academically talented students should be provided with opportunities for autonomy and individual pursuits during the school day.

**THE NATIONAL RESEARCH CENTER
ON THE
GIFTED AND TALENTED**

The University of Connecticut
362 Fairfield Road, U-7 • Storrs, CT 06269-2007

This abbreviated explanation of Compacting can be used with the Parent Letter on page 142 to inform parents of the process their child is entering.

OVERVIEW OF CURRICULUM COMPACTING

Curriculum compacting has three major objectives: to create a more challenging learning environment, to guarantee proficiency in the basic curriculum, and to "buy time" for more appropriate enrichment and acceleration activities. Curriculum compacting is a procedure used by classroom teachers that adapts the regular curriculum to meet the needs of above-average students. Work that students have previously mastered is eliminated, and work that they can master at a faster pace than their classmates is streamlined or *compacted*. The time gained through this system is then used to provide students with appropriate enrichment or acceleration activities.

CREATING A MORE CHALLENGING LEARNING ENVIRONMENT

Many above-average students spend a great deal of time doing work they already know. A recent study of fifth- and sixth-grade average readers found that 78% to 88% of them could pass pretests on the basal readers before they were covered in class. Better readers were performing at 93% accuracy on the comprehension skills pretests. One reason so many students know the curriculum before it is taught is that contemporary textbooks have been "dumbed down." This phrase, used in 1984 by Terrel Bell, former secretary of education, was used to sum up the trend of decreasing difficulty from year to year in the most widely used textbooks: as much as two grade levels in difficulty over the last ten to fifteen years.

Textbooks also repeat material to reinforce learning. Only 25% of the pages in typical seventh- and eighth-grade mathematics texts contain new content. Students in grades two to five encounter only 40–65% new content in their math books over the course of the school year. By eighth grade, the amount of *new* content drops to 30%, and these estimates are conservative.

As a result, our above-average students may not be appropriately challenged. Imagine what it must be like to spend hour after hour completing exercises and activities that you have known for years! Adults would never tolerate the type of repetitiveness that many of our brightest students face daily. Often, these youngsters find everything they encounter in school so easy that they never really learn how to work; they learn to expend *minimum* effort. In 1992, in a national study, three-hundred elementary classroom teachers were asked to implement curriculum compacting for high-ability students they selected in their classrooms. These teachers were able to eliminate an average of 34–50% of the curriculum in five content areas.

If students are consistently bringing home papers with perfect scores, the assignments may be too easy. We can remedy this by initiating the curriculum compacting process, increasing the challenge level of the work students are expected to complete, and providing enrichment experiences commensurate with their abilities.

GUARANTEEING PROFICIENCY IN THE REGULAR CURRICULUM

We live in a "credentialing" society; mastery of skills is considered by many to be indicators of progress in the traditional curriculum. So if we can clearly demonstrate that a bright student has already mastered a great deal of the regular curriculum with the results of pretests, unit tests, level tests and final yearly assessments, we can *document* their proficiency and provide them with a different curricular experience.

FINDING TIME FOR ENRICHMENT AND ACCELERATION ACTIVITIES

Students who complete their work quickly are often "rewarded" with more work. Inevitably, many students learn to slow down. High-ability, secondary-level students who had not registered for honors classes, when asked why, said, "Why should we? We'll do twice as much work, write two term papers instead of one and probably earn a lower grade!"

If, however, students' curriculum is compacted, they will realize that demonstrating proficiency in basic curriculum can earn them the opportunity to become involved in some alternative type of work in which they have a high interest. This also eliminates the problem of students having to make up hours of work that their peers have completed during a time that they were involved in the resource program. Compacting their curriculum allows students to participate in enrichment programs *during* their curricular strength time.

Many good classroom teachers already compact the curriculum as part of their daily tasks. For a skill which most students require one or more review worksheets to understand, a teacher in many instances will substitute more challenging work for a student who has mastered the skill. This is "compacting" in its simplest form. As another example, on the days that grammar is taught in an upper-elementary-grade classroom, students are divided into two or three groups. Some of the bright students have previously mastered all of the grammar that is to be covered as a part of the regular curriculum for the entire year and are provided with advanced reading materials and challenging language arts enrichment activities; some become involved in creative or expository writing in one section of the room. Others receive a library pass on the days that grammar is taught to work on an advanced, independent study project. Those students who know very little of the grammar and need the review work with the teacher in another section of the classroom.

Spelling is easily compacted. Many above-average children consistently achieve top scores on spelling tests, yet are expected to do the same routine review tasks assigned to poorer spellers. If they are allowed to take a pre-test on Monday, and do well on it, they can work in other areas during the spelling time: perhaps research a topic or begin reading a challenging fiction or non-fiction book. Thus, curriculum compacting can be accomplished with students with various strengths and abilities.

THE COMPACTOR

A form entitled the *Compactor* is used by teachers to document the compacting process. It is divided into three columns arranged sequentially to represent the stages of curriculum compacting (see attached copy of the form). In the first column, the teacher identifies a content area in which the student has strengths or has demonstrated proficiency and cites evidence of that ability (this might include achievement scores, prior grades, or informal discussions with a previous teacher). In the second column, the teacher lists materials that the student needs to master to meet curricular objectives and indicates the procedures that can be used to achieve mastery at a faster pace (for example, independent or small group work with students of similar ability), how mastery will be assessed, and the standard (for example, 80%, 90%, 100%).

The time saved through compacting the curriculum is then used to provide a variety of enrichment or acceleration opportunities for the student, and these are listed in the third column of the Compactor. Enrichment might include student-selected independent investigations based on interests, mini-courses, and alternative reading assignments. Acceleration might include material from the text unit or chapter, the next chronological grade level textbook or completion of advanced work with a tutor or mentor. Alternate activities listed in the third column reflect a challenge and rigor commensurate with the student's abilities and interests.

IDENTIFYING CURRICULUM AREAS TO BE CONSIDERED FOR COMPACTING

The two essential requirements for successful compacting are (1) careful diagnosis and (2) a thorough knowledge of the content and objectives of a unit of instruction. Once these requirements have been met, the actual procedures for carrying out the process are quite simple. Teachers must first identify the content areas in which students display above-average ability or have demonstrated mastery. Column one of the Compactor, Curriculum Areas To Be Considered for Compacting, is used to record general and specific indications of students' strengths.

General indications of strength are found in students' records, standardized tests, classwork or teacher observations. Classroom teachers can spot students who finish tasks quickly and well, or the ones who finish reading assignments first or who appear bored during instruction time and who consistently daydream in class. These students are then considered for curriculum compacting in those areas. Some students will tell their teachers that the assigned work is too easy or that they are bored in class. Others will ask for extra reading assignments or suggestions for independent study. Other students will carry extra reading material to help them productively use the spare minutes they have saved from finishing assigned work earlier than the rest of the class.

CONCLUSION

Curriculum compacting can be considered an integral part of any school program of above-average students. It can be used regardless of program design or model and has far-reaching implications for students who achieve at above-average levels in most areas. If curriculum compacting is widely implemented, a more appropriate match could be achieved between the needs of our most able students and the textbooks and curricular materials they use on a daily basis.

REFERENCES

Abruscato, J. (1978). *Earthpeople*. Santa Monica, CA: Goodyear/Scott Foresman.

Abruscato, J. (1977). *Whole cosmos*. Santa Monica, CA: Goodyear/Scott Foresman.

AGRI (American Genealogical Research Institute) Staff. (1975). *How to trace your family tree: A complete and easy-to-understand guide for the beginner*. Garden City, NY: Doubleday.

Archambault, F.X., Westberg, K.L., Brown, S., Hallmark, B. W.,Zhang, W., & Emmons, C. (in press). "Regular classroom practices with gifted students: Findings from the Classroom Practices Survey." *Journal for the Education of the Gifted.*

Armbruster, B.B., Osborn, J. and Davison, A.L. (1985). "Readability formulas may be dangerous to your textbooks." *Educational Leadership.* 47(2),18–20.

Armbruster, B.B. & Anderson, T.H. (1984). "Structures of explanation in history textbooks, or so what if governor Stanford missed the spike and hit the rail?" *Journal of Curriculum Studies.* 16, 181–194.

Baker and Showers (1984). "The effects of a coaching strategy on teachers' transfer of training to classroom practice: A six-month follow-up study."Paper presented at the Annual Meeting of the American Educational Research Association, New Orleans.

Baum, S. (1988). "An enrichment program for the gifted learning disabled students." *Gifted Child Quarterly*, 32(1), 226–230.

Bee, C. P. (1980). *Secondary learning centers*. Santa Monica, CA: Goodyear/Scott Foresman.

Berk, R. A. (Ed.). (1986). *Performance assessment:* Methods and applications. Baltimore, MD: Johns Hopkins University Press.

Betts, G. T. (1986). "The autonomous learner model." In J.S. Renzulli (Ed.), *System and models for developing programs for the gifted and talented* (pp. 27–56). Mansfield Center, CT: Creative Learning Press, Inc.

Birdwell, R. (1974). *Hydroponic gardening*. Santa Clara, CA: Woodbridge Publishing Co.

Blackburn, J. E. (1976). *One at a time all at once*. Santa Monica, CA: Goodyear Publishing Company, Inc.

Blake, J., & Ernst, B. (1976). *The great perpetual learning machine*. Boston, MA: Little Brown and Company.

Brophy, J.E. (1979). "Teacher behavior and student learning." *Educational Leadership.* 37, 33–38.

Brown, W., & Rogan, J. (1983). "Reading and young gifted children." *Roeper Review*, 5(3) 6–9.

Carey, S. (1978). *Kid's America*. New York, NY: Workman Publishing.

Carnegie Council on Adolescent Development. (1989). *Turning points: Preparing American youth for the 21st century*. Washington, DC: Carnegie Council on Adolescent Development.

Chall, J. S. & Conrad, S. C. (1991). *Should textbooks challenge students?: The case for easier or harder textbooks*. New York: Teachers College Press.

Chall, J. (1967). *Learning to read: The geat debate*. New York: McGraw-Hill.

Clark, S. (1978). *Kid's America*. New York, NY: Workman Publishing.

Clifford, J. A., Runions, T., & Smythe, E. (1986). "The learning enrichment service (LES): A participatory model for the gifted adolescents." In J.S. Renzulli (Ed.), *Systems and models for developing programs for the gifted and talented* (pp. 27–56). Mansfield Center, CT: Creative Learning Press, Inc.

Commission on Excellence in Education. (1983, May 4). "A nation at risk: The imperative for educational reform." *The Chronicle of Higher Education*, 11–15.

Dallas Independent School District. (1977). *Aaahs*. Dallas, TX: Services Center.

Educational Products Information Exchange Institute. (1980–81). *Educational Research and Development Report*, 3 (4).

Elliott, D. & Woodward, A. (1990). "Textbooks and schooling in the United States." *Eighty-ninth yearbook of the national society for the study of education*. Chicago, IL: The Univerity of Chicago Press.

Farr, R., & Tulley, M. (1985). "Do adoption committees perpetuate mediocre textbooks?" *Phi Delta Kappan*, 66(7), 467–471.

Feldhusen, J. F. (1989a). Synthesis of research on gifted youth. *Educational Leadership*, 47(1), 6–11.

Feldhusen, J. F. (1989b). "Why the public schools will continue to neglect the gifted." *Gifted Child Today*, 12(2), 55–59.

Feldhusen, J. F., & Kolloff, M. B. (1986). "The Purdue three-stage enrichment model for gifted education at the elementary level." In J.S. Renzulli (Ed.), *Systems and models for developing programs for the gifted and talented* (pp. 126–152). Mansfield Center, CT: Creative Learning Press, Inc.

Feldhusen, J.F. & Moon, S.M. (1992). "Grouping gifted students: Issues and concerns." *Gifted Child Quarterly*. 36 (2), 63–67.

Flanders, J.R. (1987). "How much of the content in mathematics textbooks is new?" *Arithmatic Teacher*. 35,18–23.

Gagnon, P. (1988). "Why study history?" *Atlantic Monthly*. 262, 43–66.

Gates, A.I. (1961). "Vocabulary control in basal reading material." *Reading Teacher*.15, 81–85.

Gibbs, J. (1987). "Tribes, a process for peer involvement." Santa Rosa, CA: Center Source Publications.

Glassock, P., & Weber, S. (1980). *Castles, pirates, knights and other learning delights*. Carthage, IL: Good Apple.

Goldberg, M. M. (1958). "Recent research on the talented." *Teacher's College Record*, 60, 150–163.

Gold, M. J. (1965). *Education of the intellectually gifted*. Columbus, OH: Charles E. Merrill.

Gowan, J. C., & Demos, G. D. (1984). *The education and guidance of the ablest*. Springfield, IL: Charles C. Thomas.

Guskey, T. R. (1986). "Staff development and the process of teacher change." *Educational Researcher*. Volume, No. (May) 5–12.

Hall, G.E. & Hord, S.M. (1987). *Change in schools: Facilitating the process*. Albany, NY: State University of New York Press.

Heuer, J., Koprowicz, A., & Harris, R. (1980). *M.A.G.I.C. K.I.T.S*. Mansfield Center, CT: Creative Learning Press, Inc.

Ho, K. (1990). "Parents must act to change schools." *Education Week*. 9(35), 20.

Hockett, J.A. (1938). "The vocabularies of recent primers and first readers." *Elementary School Journal* 39, 112–115.

Holmes, D., & Christie, T. (1978). *Thumbs up*. Carthage, IL: Good Apple.

Horn, E. (1937). *Methods of Instruction in the Social Studies*. New York: Charles Scribner's Sons.

Johnson, M. (1981). *Bright ideas*. Buffalo, NY: D.O.K. Publishers.

Joyce, R.B. & Showers, B. (1982). "The coaching of teaching." *Educational Leadership*. 40, 4–10.

Joyce, R.B. & Showers, B. (1983). *Power in staff development through research in training*. Alexandria, VA: ASCD.

Joyce, R.B. & Showers, B. (1987). "Student achievement through staff development." New York: Longman, Inc.

Judy, T. A., & Steeley, D. D. (1978). *Using learning centers with not-yet readers*. Santa Monica, CA: Goodyear/Scott Foresman.

Kaplan, S. N., Kaplan, J. A., Madsen, S., & Taylor, B. K. (1973). *Change for children*. Santa Monica, CA: Goodyear Publishing Company, Inc.

Kirst, M. W. (1982). "How to improve schools without spending more money." *Phi Delta Kappan*, 64(1), 6–8.

Klare, G.R. (1976). "A second look at the validity of readability formulas." *Journal of Reading Behavior*, 8. 129–152.

Klein, J. (1986, March 16). "'Exceptional' ruling pits school districts against parents of gifted." *Philadelphia Inquirer*.

Komoski, P. K. (1990). "Needed: A whole-curriculum approach." *Educational Leadership*, 47(5), 72–78.

Kulik, C. C., & Kulik, J. A. (1982). "Effects of ability grouping on secondary school students: A meta-analysis of evaluation findings." *American Educational Research Journal*, 19(3), 415–428.

Kulik, C. C., & Kulik, J. A. (1984, August). "Effects of ability grouping on elementary school pupils: A meta-analysis." Paper presented at the annual meeting of the American Psychological Association. Ontario, Canada. (ERIC No. ED 255329).

Kulik, J.A. & Kulik, C.C. (1992). "Meta-analytic findings on grouping programs." *Gifted Child Quarterly*, 73–77.

Labuda, M. (Ed.). (1985). *Creative reading for the gifted: A design for excellence* (2nd Ed.). Newark, DE: International Reading Association.

McDonald, F.J. and Elias, P. (1976). *The effects of teaching performance on pupil learning* (Vol. 1, Final Report). Beginning Teacher Evaluation Study, Phase 2, 1974–1976). Princeton, New Jersey: Educational Testing Service.

McGreevy, A. (1982) *My book of things and stuff: An interest questionaire for young children.* Mansfield Center, CT: Creative Learning Press, Inc.

McKnight, C.C., Crosswhite, F.J., Dossey, J.A., Kifer, E., Swafford, J.O., Travers, K.J. and Cooney, T.J. (1987). *The underachieving curriculum: Assessing the U.S. mathematics from an international perspective.* Champaign, IL: Stipes.

Medley, D. M. (1977). *Teacher Competence and Teacher Effectiveness: A research Review of Process-Product Research.* Washington D.C.: American Association of Colleges for Teacher Education.

Mehlinger, H. (1989). "American textbook reform: What can we learn from the soviet experience?" *Phi Delta Kappan.* 71, 29–35.

Muther, C. (1987). "What do we teach, and when do we teach it?" *Educational Leadership*, 44, 77–80.

Ohanian, S. (1987). "Ruffles and flourishes." *Atlantic Monthly.* 260(3), 20–22.

Pilon, G. (1988). *Workshop way.* New Orleans, LA: The Workshop Way, Inc.

Porter, A. (1989). "A curriculum out of balance: The case of elementary school mathematics." *Educational Researcher*, 18(5), 9–15.

Reis, S. M., Westberg, K.L., Kulikowich, J., Calliard, F., Hébert, T., Purcell, J., Rogers, J., Smist, J., Plucker, J. (1992). *An analysis of the impact of curriculum compacting on classroom practices:* Technical Report. Storrs, CT: The National Research Center on the Gifted and Talented.

Reis, S. M., & Renzulli, J. S. (1985). *The secondary triad model: A practical plan for implementing gifted programs at the junior and senior high school levels.* Mansfield Center, CT: Creative Learning Press, Inc.

Renzulli, J. S. (1977). *The enrichment triad model: A guide for developing defensible programs for the gifted.* Mansfield Center, CT: Creative Learning Press, Inc.

Renzulli, J.S., & Smith, L.H. (1978a). *The compactor.* Mansfield Center, CT: Creative Learning Press, Inc.

Renzulli, J.S. & Smith, L.H. (1978 b). *The learning styles inventory: A measure of student preference for instructional techniques.* Mansfield Center, CT: Creative Learning Press

Renzulli, J. S., & Reis, S. M. (1985). *The schoolwide enrichment model: A comprehensive plan for educational excellence.* Mansfield Center, CT: Creative Learning Press, Inc.

Renzulli, J. S., Reis, S. M., & Smith, L. H. (1981). *The revolving door identification model.* Mansfield Center, CT: Creative Learning Press, Inc.

Ringer, R. J. (1973). *Winning through intimidation.* Los Angeles, CA: Los Angeles Book Publishers Co.

Robinson, A. (1992) *Cooperative Learning and the academically talented student.* Storrs, CT: National Research Center on the Gifted and Talented.

Rogers, K.B. (1991). *The relationship of grouping practices to the education of the gifted and talented learner.* Storrs, CT: National Research Center on the gifted and Talented.

Rogers, K. B. (1989). *A research synthesis on the effects of ability grouping.* Presentation at the National Association for Gifted Children, Cincinnati, OH.

Savage, J. F. (1983). "Reading guides: Effective tools for teaching the gifted." *Roeper Review*, 5(3), 9–11.

Sewall, G. T. (1988). "American history textbooks: Where do we go from here?" *Phi Delta Kappan*, 69(8), 554–558.

Showers, B., Joyce, B. and Bennett, B. (1987). "Synthesis of research on staff development: A framework for future study and a state-of-the-art analysis." *Educational Leadership.* November 1987.

Slavin, R. E. (1987). "Ability grouping and students achievement in elementary schools: A best evidence synthesis." *Review of Educational Research*, 57(3), 293–336.

Starko, A.J. (1986). *It's about time: Inservice strategies for curriculum compacting.* Mansfield Center, CT: Creative Learning Press, Inc.

Steen, L. A. (1989). *Everybody counts: A report to the nation on the future of mathematics education.* Washington, D.C.: National Research Council of the National Academy of Sciences.

Stiggins, R. (1987). "Design and development of performance assessments." *Educational Measurement:* Issues and Practices, 6(3), 33–42.

Tannenbaum, A. J. (1986). "The enrichment matrix model." In J.S. Renzulli (Ed.), *Systems and models for developing programs for the gifted and talented* (pp. 126–152). Mansfield Center, CT: Creative Learning Press, Inc.

Tannenbaum, A. J. (1983). *Gifted children: Psychological and educational perspectives.* New York, NY: Macmillan Publishing Co., Inc.

Taylor, B. M., & Frye, B. J. (1988). "Pretesting: Minimize time spent on skill work for intermediate readers." *The Reading Teacher*, 42(2), 100–103.

Toovey, I., & Nitzgorski, B. (1982). *Mission: Possible.* Mansfield Center, CT: Creative Learning Press, Inc.

Treffinger, D. J. (1986). "Fostering effective, independent learning through individualized programming." In J.S. Renzulli (Ed.), *Systems and models for developing programs for the gifted and talented* (pp. 126–152). Mansfield Center, CT: Creative Learning Press, Inc.

Tyson-Bernstein, H. (1985). "The new politics of textbook adoption." *Phi Delta Kappan*, 66 (7), 463–466.

Tyson-Bernstein, H. (1988). *A conspiracy of good intentions: America's textbook fiasco.* Washington, D.C.: Council for Basic Education.

Tyson-Bernstein, H. & Woodward, A. (1989). "Nineteenth century policies for 21st century pactice: The textbook reform dilemma." *Educational Policy.* 3(2), 95–106.

Usiskin, Z. (1987). "Why elementary algebra can, should, and must be an eighth-grade course for average students." *Mathematics Teacher.* 80, 428–438.

Westberg, K.L, Archambault, F.X., Dobyns, S. M., & Salvin, T.J. (in press). "The classroom practices observational study." *Journal for the Education of the Gifted.*

Willows, D.M., Borwick, D. and Hayvren, M. (1981). "The content of school readers." In G. E. MacKinnon, and T. Gary Waller (Eds). *Reading Research: Advances in Theory and Practice.* New York: Academic Press, 100–175.

Much concentration
satisfying yet painful
I think I did well
(working for vision